Object-Oriented Databases

Dimitris N. Chorafas / Heinrich Steinmann

PTR Prentice Hall, Englewood Cliffs, New Jersey 07632

Library of Congress Cataloging-in-Publication Data
Chorafas, Dimitris N.
    Object-oriented databases / Dimitris N. Chorafas and Heinrich
  Steinmann
    p. cm.
    Includes bibliographical references and index.
    ISBN 0-13-491804-5
    1. Object-oriented data bases. I. Steinmann, Heinrich, 1931
  II.Title.
  QA76.9.D3C476 1993
  005.75-dc20   92-27384
                                                      CIP

Acquisitions editor: Paul Becker
Editorial assistant: Noreen Regina
Cover design: Wanda Lubelska
Cover design director: Eloise Starkweather
Copyeditor: Lynne Lackenbach
Art production manager: Gail Cocker-Bogusz
Manufacturing buyer: Mary E. McCartney
Illustrations by Eva-Maria Binder and Patricia Guttierrez

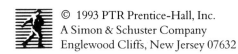

© 1993 PTR Prentice-Hall, Inc.
A Simon & Schuster Company
Englewood Cliffs, New Jersey 07632

The publisher offers discounts on this book when ordered in bulk quantities. For more information, contact Corporate Sales Department, PTR Prentice Hall, 113 Sylvan Avenue, Englewood Cliffs, NJ 07632. Phone: 201-592-2863; FAX: 201- 592-2249.

Printed in the United States of America

10   9   8   7   6   5   4   3

ISBN 0-13-491804-5

Prentice-Hall International (UK) Limited, *London*
Prentice-Hall of Australia Pty. Limited, *Sydney*
Prentice-Hall Canada Inc., *Toronto*
Prentice-Hall Hispanoamericana, S.A., *Mexico*
Prentice-Hall of India Private Limited, *New Delhi*
Prentice-Hall of Japan, Inc., *Tokyo*
Simon & Schuster Asia Pte. Ltd., *Singapore*
Editora Prentice-Hall do Brasil, Ltda., *Rio de Janeiro*

Contents

CHAPTER *1*

WHAT IS MEANT BY OBJECTS?   1

CHAPTER 2

THE CONCEPT OF INHERITANCE: A CORNERSTONE IN OBJECT SOLUTIONS   24

CHAPTER 3

CONSTRUCTING THE OBJECT-ORIENTED ENVIRONMENT   38

CHAPTER 4

CHALLENGES WITH OBJECT-ORIENTED DATABASES   52

CHAPTER *5*

WHY AN OBJECT DATABASE?   66

CHAPTER *6*

OBJECT-ORIENTED PARADIGMS AND LONG
TRANSACTIONS   80

CHAPTER *7*

APPROACHES TO OBJECT-ORIENTED
PROGRAMMING   92

CHAPTER *8*

META-PROGRAMMING IN AN OBJECT
ENVIRONMENT   104

CHAPTER *9*

OBJECTS AND THE PROCESS OF PROTOTYPING   119

CHAPTER *10*

PROTOTYPING THE DISTRIBUTED SOLUTION   132

CHAPTER *14*

BEYOND RELATIONAL DATABASE MANAGEMENT SYSTEMS   181

CHAPTER *15*

LIMITATIONS IN RELATIONAL DATABASES   194

CHAPTER *16*

DBMS FOR OBJECT-ORIENTED DATABASES   210

CHAPTER *17*

CHAPTER *18*

CHAPTER *19*

CHAPTER *20*

OBJECT-ORIENTED DBMS MADE IN JAPAN   264

CHAPTER *21*

OBJECTS AND DATA LEVEL PARALLELISM   280

CHAPTER *22*

THE CHALLENGE OF HIGH PERFORMANCE COMPUTING   294

Foreword
An Introduction
to Object-Oriented Databases

John Pfaltz, PH.D.

In the information sciences there has been a traditional separation between data and the algorithms that process such data. Over the years there have been efforts to unify this duality, as in intelligent systems written in LISP, which can execute their own data; but for the most part this duality is as firmly rooted in computer science as is the mind-body duality of Descartes in philosophy. It is firmly rooted in the architectures that we use: A memory register is not an arithmetic register.

In many applications, such as computation and traditional bookkeeping, this duality is of little consequence. The separation of the mathematical domain from the theorems and procedures that are valid over the domain, or of the corporate books and ledgers from the accountants and management who use them, have their counterparts in the computational model itself. But in newly emerging applications and disciplines, such as more general information processing or knowledge databases, the duality can have unfortunate consequences. We can begin to appreciate these consequences by asking ourselves, "What is information?" or "What is knowledge?."

This is not an easy question to answer. However, it is clear that pure data—that is, some sequence of bits stored on a disk—is neither information nor knowledge. Some might assert that information is data that generates, or modifies, an action in the external world; that is, it is "useful data" in the sense that it is actually used. For example, in a knowledge base, data must actually constrain or modify the behavior of the system in order to be considered "knowledge." In this view, obvious tautologies or irrelevant axioms are not knowledge, because they are never used. This kind of functional definition of information actively involves an external context and an understanding of its actual use in that context.

Alternatively, one can, as a more narrowly conceived database technician, attempt to divorce oneself from the actual use of the data and assert that data becomes information when it is made available, and presented to, a decision maker in a form that *could* be used in a decision process. But either view assumes that information involves both data and a user, and that the transfer between them is essential. This approach significantly extends the role of information management from just storing and retrieving data to processing it appropriately and engaging in at least half of the vital supplier/user interface.

In the authors' view, the fundamental issues facing information management in the 1990s are much broader than just storing bytes on gigabyte disks and retrieving them rapidly with well-specified query procedures. Such manipulation of passive data is just one end of a data processing spectrum. The center of this spectrum includes forms of *active* data that can modify the presentation of passive data and can help to shape and formulate appropriate queries from incompletely specified requests, and at its other extreme can be part of the decision-making process itself. Consequently, the reader should not expect to find just a manual of state-of-the-art object-oriented database techniques; this is not such a book. Instead, this book is more visionary. It explores and brings together in a single volume many of the new ideas regarding how we may expect information to be managed in the next decade. Some of the information management approaches covered are relatively well developed, with practical versions emerging, and about to emerge, in the commercial marketplace. Others are only in prototype form, and some are purely experimental. A few, we can expect, will turn out to be impractical or just downright "wrong." Nevertheless, given the current ferment in database management arising from new storage technologies, inexpensive distributed-processor workstations, and techniques of massively parallel processing, serious database professionals must become aware of these new concepts in order to evaluate their applicability in their own domain of application.

The authors have chosen the object-oriented approach to database management as their vehicle of development. This is a natural choice because in object-oriented programming one also seeks to blur the duality between data and process. Objects have state, that is, associated passive data values; but they also have behaviors, which are active. The object-oriented approach is not the only database model that attempts to fuse passive data with active processing to generate data. The reader should also be aware of a novel approach that David Gelernter has developed in his "Linda" system, and the approach to data parallel algorithms that Daniel Hillis has embodied in the "connection machine," in which each data element is a complete but tiny processor. Nevertheless, the authors' choice to focus on object-oriented methods is a wise one. The object-oriented approach has already shown itself to be extremely valuable in the development of human/machine interfaces in distributed networks. Thus it is a proven tool for implementing the most basic data transfer step that underlies all conceptions of information, and that we know will be fundamental in all future database applications. Moreover, there have been successful object-oriented implementations of CAD/CAM systems and of knowledge-based systems to which many database applications will have to interface. Finally, object-oriented programming is a relatively mature approach for which stable software has, and is being generated.

However, object orientation is not a single unified approach either to computing or to data representation. It is a general way of thinking that both colors, and is colored by, one's application area. For example, in expert and knowledge-based systems the concept of meta-objects is crucial; in operating and pure database systems they are irrelevant. How does one therefore present the object-oriented approach to database representation? One can elect to present in an all-inclusive manner the myriad developments that are emerging under the object-oriented database banner, or one can choose to filter the presentation so as to concentrate on those that are "most promising." The authors have chosen the former path, which, I believe, is the correct one; because the latter would have them imposing their personal view of the object-oriented database field. Still, by presenting the broad panorama of object orientation with all its possible interpretations, the authors are certain to upset virtually every reader who already has some familiarity with the field. For example, I find myself taking violent exception to a number of their assertions, but in every case, the assertion is one that is accepted by some subset of the computer science and data modeling communities, and which, for that reason should not be ignored.

Consequently, the reader is warned that he, or she, cannot approach this provocative book with a passive mind. Not all of its ideas can be accepted at face value, as the authors themselves acknowledge in their discussion of object-oriented SQL in Chapter 8. The reader must actively test each idea, each concept, and each data management approach against their understanding of what is computationally practical and their experience with a particular field of application. One result of this critical approach will be a filter that dismisses some sections, even some chapters, as impractical or irrelevant for their purposes. But another result of such an active involvement will be a much better understanding of what individuals and companies can expect to be the information requirements of the future, what methodologies may be available, and which paths should be aggressively followed and developed.

On many fronts, new information management applications have pushed the relational database mode, and its associated implementations, to their limits. New database technologies based on the object-oriented model are coming to the fore. This book presents the best overview of ways to think about, and use, these object-oriented databases that is available today. Awareness of its contents is of vital importance to anyone who claims to be a database professional.

> John Pfaltz, PH.D.
> Professor of Information Science
> and Director, Institute for Parallel Computation,
> School of Engineering and Applied Science
> University of Virginia

Preface

A popular illusion holds that books are inanimate objects belonging to clois-tered shades and academic quiet, away from the world of action. According to this misconception, books are full of impractical theory therefore of little significance to business people.

Yet, throughout industry there is plenty of evidence that far from being of only theoretical potential books are frequently dynamic, capable of changing the direction of events. This is the case with the description of new scientific and technological developments which have the power to overtake the processes and concepts with which we have been dealing for years, and hence have become a second nature to us.

The advent of object-oriented solutions in information technology fits this description of a new wave of change. One of the critical advantages of object orientation is the simplification achieved through semantics, the abil-ity to give meaning to our queries when communicating with the sprawling distributed databases which we have constructed and we use daily. The fol-lowing domains offer the best opportunities for the implementation of this approach:

- Computer aided design (CAD)
- Computer aided manufacturing (CAM)
- Computer integrated manufacturing (CIM)
- Complex market-oriented operations (Forex, securities)
- Cross-functional projects (risk management)
- Cross-departmental projects (cost control)
- Cartographical implementations

- Computer assisted software engineering (CASE)
- Office automation (OA)

Object-oriented database systems, their representation, control, and consistency is the subject of the present book. Object representation is the basis of a new concept: The trend to intelligent distributed databases which will dominate the 1990s.

This reference under no condition means that all database management systems (DBMS), which so far have provided good services, will be scrapped. Companies are not going to discard over a couple of years their millions, often hundreds of millions, of dollars in programming and DBMS investments to join a revolution—even if object solutions were a revolution, which they are not.

Object-oriented approaches are an evolution, not a revolution, and clear-eyed companies are actively looking for better solutions to their problems. This is particularly true of operations in the nine domains just outlined—but the serious reader should be warned that object representation is no cure for all illnesses. It is just a step forward that is worth trying.

This book starts with the fundamentals. In a comprehensive manner requiring no prerequisite knowledge, Chapter 1 explains what is meant by objects, elaborating on the concepts of type and class. Chapter 2 focuses on inheritance, as well as the meaning of data abstraction, encapsulation, polymorphism, metarules, constraints, concurrency, and dynamic binding.

Chapter 3 builds upon the background provided by the first two chapters, explaining how to architecture an object-oriented environment. Its topics include the handling of object-based messages, referential integrity, versioning, and ad hoc queries. Chapter 4 presents the crucial issues associated with semantic modeling and conveys the role of object solutions on software reusability.

A pillar on which this whole approach rests is the difference between the record-based database management that we have had so far—whether on relational, network, or hierarchical principles—and object orientation. This change alone would justify an object database; the facts behind this statement are the subject of Chapter 5.

A great deal of work can be successfully done through object solutions that cannot be satisfactorily accomplished otherwise. Long transactions is a good example, and it is the theme of Chapter 6. This, however, brings under perspective the need to handle programming concepts.

Software engineering and database management have traditionally been separate disciplines. Classically, file management technology has concentrated on static issues of information storage; programming handled the dynamic software aspects.

However, since the development of relational database models and the evolution of fourth generation languages, the two disciplines have been combining towards systems that model both processes and data. This has been further underlined with object-oriented solutions.

Chapter 7 introduces the main approaches to object-oriented programming, including the new discipline characterizing software engineering. Metaprogramming in an object environment is the subject of Chapter 8, which also presents the Object SQL (OSQL) shell.

Since experimentation is key to successful implementation, the theme of Chapter 9 is that of prototyping by using objects, including graphical solutions, to aid in man-machine communication. In an implementation sense, Chapter 10 carries this concept further by discussing how prototyping can help distributed database solutions.

Given the fact that able approaches to the management of databases and object programming are interwoven, Chapter 11 devotes itself to the nuts and bolts of object software. Particular attention is being paid to C++ as an assembler level language.

The focal point of Chapter 12 is spatial and temporal semantics. This is by no means a theoretical issue. It involves the concept of computer-generated space as well as the modeling of temporal data and the patterns which exist in semantic representation. Chapter 13 presents practical examples on this very subject.

Chapter 14 discusses the limits of relational DBMS. First, the notion of a multidatabase is defined, then capitalizing on the background already built regarding long transactions, Chapter 15 demonstrates why object solutions perform better than relational ones.

Thereafter, interest is shifted to the notion of an object database management system—and why its functionality goes well beyond the relational capabilities which are dominant today. Chapter 16 presents the reasons for this new departure in database management—and the goals we are after.

The characteristics of specific object-oriented DBMS are explained in Chapters 17 to 20. Choosing among available commodity software is not easy; there are more than a dozen alternatives to select from:

- Chapter 17 discusses Ontos and Gemstone
- Chapter 18, Versant and Object Store
- Chapter 19, Iris and Pegasus

Chapter 20 presents the main object DBMS made in Japan: Mandrill by Hitachi, Odin by NEC, MIB by Mitsubishi. Also, the fundamental work on practical applications done by the Electrotechnical Laboratory.

The book concludes with the treatment of objects in connection to data level parallelism. Chapter 21 demonstrates that an object orientation is not just the better approach for the new generation of computers—it is the only one which can be effective. Parallelism is vital, and this should not be surprising. Nature itself is massively parallel.

Subsequently, Chapter 22 introduces the challenge of high performance computing and communications (HPCC). Taking a hypercube architecture as an example, it explains how Input/Output intensive applications can be handled in an able manner through object orientation—which amounts to new perspectives in computation.

The main emphasis of this book is practical: How can object-oriented concepts be put to fruitful use? At the same time, to enhance the reader's background, some of the presentation is directed at the ongoing research on object-oriented solutions and the results which have been obtained so far.

The book is addressed to information technology practitioners who want to upgrade their knowhow—as well as researchers who wish to understand the issues, tools, and architecture of the coming wave in database management. In addition, this book can be used by students who are taking courses in object-oriented systems, DBMS, or programming languages.

The authors feel indebted to a number of information technology scientists and to corporate and university researchers who contributed facts and ideas during the extensive research which has taken place throughout 1991 in the United States, Japan, and Europe. The companies which made a contribution and the participants to this research are identified in the Acknowledgments.

Particular indebtedness is felt by the authors to the object-oriented database and programming specialists who reviewed and commented on parts of this work. Dr. Dennis McLeod and Dr. John Pfaltz have been most helpful in this regard. To Eva-Maria Binder goes the credit for the artwork, typing and index.

Dimitris N. Chorafas
Heinrich Steinmann
January, 1993

Chapter 1

What Is an Object?

1-1 INTRODUCTION

The word *object* is often used to describe an entity that encapsulates an *information element* (IE)★ as well as *operations* on it. The objects that we will treat in this text are comparable but not identical to Smalltalk objects, abstract data types, actors, agents, monitors, and other terms that are used practically synonymously, and that we will examine together with their definitions and their differences.

In section 5 we will define an object as being an instance of a *class.* But careful readers will wait until the concept of a class is first defined, trying to create their own idea of an object from the examples in the first four sections of this chapter.

The objects operating in an environment are often *active,* but in a more traditional, object-oriented view they can be *passive* (such as abstract data types), responding to direct requests. Active objects are capable of initiating independent actions, as they include (1) operations, (2) rules, and (3) instance variables.

An example will make this important concept of passive and active objects more clear. Let us imagine an interactive screen with text captions and display fields pertinent to a general ledger master file, as shown in Fig. 1.1†

★The term *information element* (IE) is preferred to *data* because we increasingly focus on *multimedia:* text, graphics, voice, moving image, and data.

†An interesting insight into the development of interactive screens comes from a recent project. Each screen required half a day of work with the Oracle DBMS and three to five days with DB2. Benchmarked against Oracle, an object DBMS performed significantly better: productivity of more than 1000 percent compared to DB2.

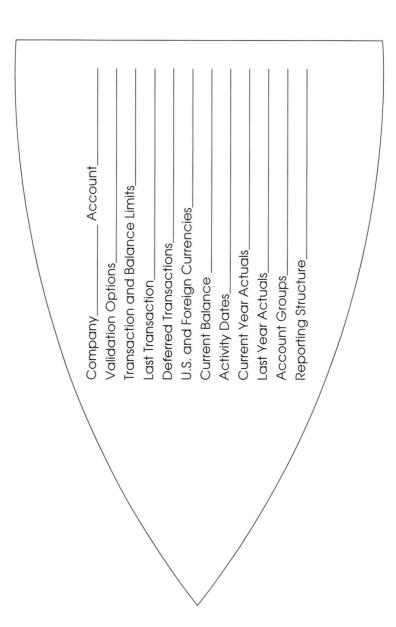

Company _____ Account _____
Validation Options _____
Transaction and Balance Limits _____
Last Transaction _____
Deferred Transactions _____
U.S. and Foreign Currencies _____
Current Balance _____
Activity Dates _____
Current Year Actuals _____
Last Year Actuals _____
Account Groups _____
Reporting Structure _____

Figure 1.1 Interactive presentation of a general ledger master file.

Regarded simply as a display format, this is a purely passive object of text and positions. Into this, however, active processes pour the values to be displayed. Alternatively, as in Smalltalk, the screen display can be regarded as an active object, obtaining the values that it needs and even possibly changing its configuration depending on early values.

While this example helps clarify the important distinction between active and passive objects, providing a basis for later concepts, it is wise to keep in mind that

> There is no agreement in the object-oriented community on the different definitions and the paradigms that help in documenting them.

As we have seen, two different interpretations can be given to a paradigm as simple as a screen display. At the same time, however, as this example helped to demonstrate,

> There is a parallelism between real-world objects and computing objects: Transactions and accounts are business operations; their mapping, calculation, and interactive presentation lie in the computing domain.

As specified by its operations and rules, the behavior of an active object is shared by the instances of the same class.* The contents, however, are *private,* and each object has its own collection of instance variables capable of taking action on its own behalf.

Associated with every active object is a set of procedures and functions that define meaningful operations on that object. In this sense, an active or dynamic object *encapsulates*† both state and behavior within the same computational unit. Whether they are passive or active,

> Objects are callable *runtime* entities,‡ an example being an active screen.
> Objects take up space in memory and have an associated *address.*
> From a design perspective, objects *model* the application domain.

These particular references characterize all object-oriented systems and distinguish them from other, earlier solutions. More than that, they constitute the enabling mechanism for more efficient software development.

---

*As stated, definitions of "class" and "object" are forthcoming, but a text becomes unreadable if it is replete with definitions at the very start.

†The act of enclosing in a capsule that is system-addressable.

‡Some people prefer to talk of activating objects or of performing requests via message passing.

1-2 INFORMATION ELEMENTS IN AN OBJECT LANDSCAPE

We shall begin with a simple record-based file and illustrate how individual *records* (tuples) can be regarded as objects, each with its own storage address. Later in this chapter we will say that an object orientation can be instrumental in liberating programmers and users from the inflexible record structure, but because records are what most people today know and understand, there are good reasons to start with such an example.

Along the lines of this paradigm, a *file* (relation) can be regarded as a sort of nameable and callable object, which is comprised of subobjects or records. In Chapter 2 we will say more about such a hierarchy of entities and the inheritance mechanism that characterizes them.

Following the strategy of going from more familiar concepts to those less familiar to the reader, Fig. 1.2 presents a logical system flow that can be served through an object-oriented solution, though for nearly 40 years it has been characterized through file and record approaches.

One simple processing stream is utilized in this paradigm, with all journals entering the system through a single point regardless of their source. Once they are submitted, journals are completely controlled within the system. This enhances the integrity of general ledger accounting, which is taken as an example. It also provides an excellent ground for the use of classes and objects.

Any accounting subsystem must be able to interface to the general ledger database without major modifications. This is difficult to accomplish with files that are incompatible among themselves because of their diverse origins. Heterogeneous databases today are the rule rather than the exception.★

A better opportunity comes from the fact that, contrary to the often monolithic file and record structures, objects represent a fine-grain mechanism. Such a mechanism is more flexible to view, organize, and manipulate. Objects are also more amenable to translation in terms of data structure and reformatting.

The aforementioned object characteristics can be of help to enduser-defined editing. In turn, this assures that, in our example, the accounting information entering the general ledger is valid and meets the unique requirements of the company.

An object orientation is also useful in error recycling or suspense posting. It sees to it that user efforts are captured and controlled by the system. For instance, object-oriented erroneous journals are more easily stored to prevent loss of data and to eliminate the need for total reinput, and simple

---

★See also D. N. Chorafas and H. Steinmann, *Networked Databases,* Academic Press, New York and San Diego, 1993.

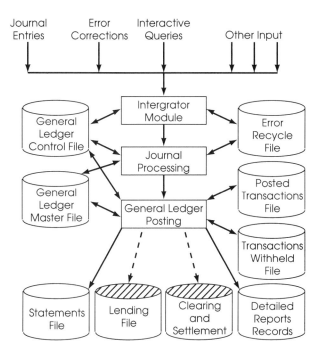

Figure 1.2 A logical system flow that can be served through object orientation.

turnaround procedures are generated by the system and the user, correcting errors with minimum input but better control.

All this should by no means be interpreted to mean that objects are absolutely superior to any other system solution to database management.

What these statements aim to bring to the reader's attention is the fact that an object-based mechanism can be more responsive to all types of journal entries coming from any automated subsystem. In the example we are considering, this might include standard period-end journals (such as labor distribution), warehousing and inventory control entries, or accrual entries with system-generated reversals.

Purists bent on the supremacy of "this" over "that" approach, for instance, of object over relational, Codasyl, or hierarchical models, might say that all good things flow from the object orientation. Once again, this is not strictly true. What is true is that we are now confronted with the need to handle more complex transactions and queries—hence we must have and share better tools.

In earlier times, the processing graph in Fig. 1.2 might well have been served through relational, Codasyl, or even hierarchical models. But as transactions become increasingly complex, this is less and less true—hence our interest in the benefits an object orientation can provide.

One of the leading money-center banks, for instance, developed a complex client portfolio program for asset management. Extrapolating from their previous experience with database management systems (DBMS), where eight to ten database accesses per transaction were sufficient, the analysts failed to see that something had radically changed.

Long, complex transactions like those involved in asset management pose totally different database requirements than simple transactions of the debit/credit type. Only after the programs were ready and operating did the analysts find out that they were faced with 1000 database accesses per transaction, which is two orders of magnitude more than the usual case, resulting in huge delays in response time. It is precisely these vastly different requirements that press for the adoption of new technology.

In a similar manner, the relatively simple general ledger transactions to be executed in the main body of Fig. 1.2 can become a complex transaction if a lending file as well as clearing and settlement files are brought into the picture. The transaction becomes a long one, with client files and settlement files operating on-line. Object orientation may not be ideal for doing this job, but relational, Codasyl, and hierarchical approaches are part of the problem rather than of the solution.

Figure 1.3 helps in comprehending the possible role of object-oriented approaches in a variety of crucial fields—or at least what we hope eventually to get out of them. This figure shows a data communications and database environment that has been largely served so far through hierarchical and relational models. At the heart of the diagram are the simple solutions that we have used for a couple of decades:

Simple queries of SQL type—as opposed to the complex analytical queries users today require, particularly in connection with decision-support systems.

Simple transactions of current accounts—as opposed to the long transactions needed today in a growing number of applications

Bisynchronous (BSC) communications protocols—rather than frame relay and asynchronous transmission modes.

Simple media, essentially data, rather than digital streams of text, data, graphics, moving image, voice—the multimedia trend.

Servicing complex computing and communications environments is a process that seems to become more difficult every year, with new problems arising from applications perspectives that underpin all computing:

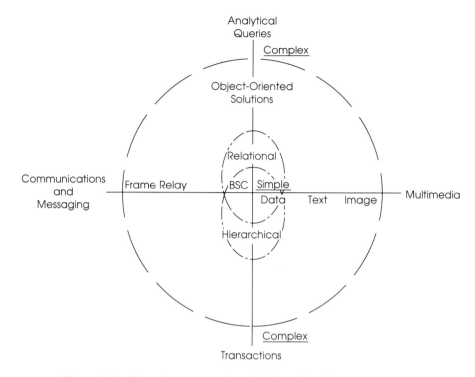

Figure 1.3   Changing patterns in a distributed database environment.

1. Queries become increasingly more ad hoc and more analytical.
2. Multimedia approaches call for changes in basic technology.★
3. The volume and frequency of transactions increases.
4. Long transactions multiply with respect to short transactions.
5. Messaging and communications move toward frame relay solutions.

    Years of experience have taught us that, to be carried out successfully, the creation and maintenance of a comprehensive business model requires both discipline and a comprehensive set of tools. Object orientation provides the discipline; the tools are still being developed.

    This domain of discipline design and its associated structure of software tools has achieved its original research goals and is now entering the applications domain, focusing on the sharing of programming products and information elements by diverse groups of developers and end users. To achieve practical goals, we need not only objects and object-oriented tools,

---

★Some systems experts think that multimedia and reusable software are basically hype. They are wrong on both counts.

but also efficient methods able to filter, select, combine, store, retrieve, and discriminate among objects. We need to *manage* the objects in a network-wide sense. This is the kernel of the work that has to be done during the 1990s.

1-3 OBJECTS IN A DYNAMIC OPERATING ENVIRONMENT

We have said that objects are entities that encapsulate information elements and operations into a single computational unit. Object models can differ, however, in terms of their internal behavior. Hence, for computational reasons, it is necessary to specify how the different objects act, and how they interact with one another.

A similar statement can be made regarding the goals we try to reach by using objects. An object is something in the world we try to model: a computer system, a physical entity such as a car or a table, as well as logical entities mapped through information elements and commands. For this reason, it was stated in the introduction that some objects are (passive) information elements, other objects are rules and commands, and still others combine both references into an active setting.

The distinction between real-world objects and computational objects can be further explained by taking a Boeing jumbo plane as an example. A computational 747 object does not weigh many tons and does not usually get to 40,000 ft. Yet conceptually there is a close connection between a real aircraft and an object in a database that represents it.

Since active objects react to their environment according to their internal rules, they might be examined in isolation. Basically, however, objects are *cooperative structures,* and their strength comes from the fact that concepts which have so far been elaborated permit them to act and interact in a network-wide manner.

The concept of objects and of their usage did not arise overnight, but has developed through theory and practice over a number of years. We can find in its origins the notions of *conceptual schemata,* dating to about 1965; *linguistic constructs*, such as Simula, of the late 1960s; *semantical representation* of the mid-1970s, and *entity-relationship* (E-R) models of the early 1980s.★

Figure 1.4 shows a chronological representation of the developing notion of objects, classifying the different concepts that converge into the object definition, by order of increasing sophistication. This accounts for 30 years of research leading to semantic and object-oriented database solutions.

Every time a new step is reached, more insight and foresight is being

---

★Some purists believe that E-R is a fad, but they are wrong. Science progresses through small successive steps—not by long leaps.

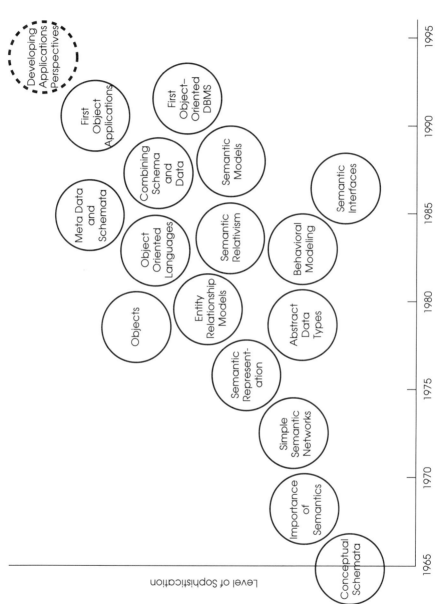

Figure 1.4 The steady evolution in semantics and object orientation.

9

gained. Semantic representation is much more rich than flat tables; entity-relationship models are very near the object representation.

Considered from a database management system perspective, the entities in a database system are typically accessed by reference to particular attributes. For instance:

> The department entity whose name is *Securities*
> The account entity whose name is *George Brown*

However, identification only by way of properties presents numerous problems: An attribute value can change, and consistency relationships are difficult to maintain. *Securities* is too broad a term; *George Brown* may have many different accounts.

Even when it is feasible, maintaining consistency relationships between objects has a significant overhead, particularly when the value of the attribute identifying an object is changed. This led to the need to distinguish an object's identity from its current value.

The current value can change, but the identity is unique. Theoretically, such identity should be generated by the system. Also, theoretically, the current value should be created by the system and never reused.

The distinction between *object identity* and *object value* is important. If we return to the preceding file/record or relation/tuple example, the observation can be made that files and records have implicit identity: the file name, or the record sequence number.

As a result, the step needed to give them explicit symbolic identifiers is a small one. The fields of a record do not have independent identity; they are not addressable without the record number. But objects do not benefit from such structured approach.

This is precisely why objects are so much more flexible than records. With long, complex transactions and queries we do not need all of a record's contents as in old data processing. We only need one or two fields (or objects) from each record—but we must also access a large number of records per transaction, as the example with 1000 database accesses documented.

Coordination is achievable because of the meaning embedded in a complex transaction. This leads to the concept of *surrogates* associated with semantic data models. It is also the background of the entity-relationship approach to the representation of

> Information elements,
> Programs,
> Modules,
> Dictionaries, and
> Libraries.

There are, however, problems associated with this approach, one of them being the manipulation of represented objects. In a relational implementation, for example, operations relating to complex objects will require bringing together explicitly all of the components of that object prior to performing an operation.*

Neither is E-R a unique solution. There exist different approaches to it, such as RM/T by Codd, E-ER by Elmarsi and Navathe, as well as the original E-R by Chen. There is as well a bridge between functional data models and the object-oriented model known as Taxis, by Mylopoulos and Wong.

Other researchers have tried to address one of the approaches around the problems connected to complex objects, the so-called *predefined general operators,* which can be seen in the boundary between record-and object-oriented models. In this case, E-R aims to provide data structuring mechanisms that move toward object models.

1-4 UNDERSTANDING THE WAY OBJECTS WORK

Understanding objects and the way they work is synonymous with comprehending how they cooperate. Such comprehension, however, is not necessarily universal, since object orientation remains a term that is interpreted differently by different people. This point has to be kept in mind as we establish the basic characteristics that constitute an object-based solution. Furthermore, as will be explained in the introduction to Chapter 3, this text will not discriminate between *object-oriented* and *object-based* solutions, considering that with both the key element is inheritance.

Objects can be *ephemeral* (short-lived) or *persistent.* Normally, as discussed in Section 2, the values of transient variables remain intact until the process terminates—at which point they are lost. By contrast, persistent objects outlive the process that created them.

A question that originally came up in object research is: "Why not to produce persistent object characteristics determined on a per-object basis?" This could be done fairly smoothly by simply adding a keyword to a programming language, selecting our objects on the basis of what we try to achieve with them. This can enable a variable to outlive the execution of the process in which it was created.

Some object DBMS add a persistent storage class declarator to the supported language, for instance, C++. This keyword may be applied to the declaration of any object, which then lives essentially for the life of the database.

The objects of a dynamic operating environment consist of *private* data

*The software shell enforces object orientation and manages what is retrieved.

structures that can operate with or without associated commands but with networking interfaces. Such interfaces are often known as *public* or external, having the goal of interconnecting the object to the outside world, and vice versa.

The set of services that an object provides may be described in the form of an *interface to requests,*★ which may be generic or parochial. The user may issue the same request to different kinds of objects that provide similar services. Performing a request may involve the execution of a class of operations. Hence objects may be classified in terms of the services they provide, while interfaces are classified in terms of the requests they handle. A *request* is a statement defining a service to be carried out by objects. It has a name, identifies the object providers, can take arguments and produce results.

A generic request may be issued to different objects that assure similar services but involve different implementations or behaviors. The request itself does not determine how the services will be performed, but rather identifies what must be executed to perform the service. Several objects may participate in providing a service in response to such a request.

The concept of requests is most important for real-time interactivity, underpinning the fact that an object is part of a network. There are various degrees of interaction between objects, resulting from the need for one activity to know of actions performed by another. Depending on the degree of interaction, different forms of information sharing are required, with a high degree of sharing needed for cooperating activities.

Within the networking environment in which it operates, an active object may execute in parallel with other objects within a *domain*. Webster's defines *domain* as territory under one government or ruler, dominion, ownership, possession, estate, the sphere or field of activity or influence. In mathematics, the term is used in the latter sense. Objects are active within a domain. New domains can be created dynamically and identified by their objects, the latter being passed from one domain to another. The domain may be

Idle, when no processing is taking place,

Active, when processing goes on, or

Blocked, when waiting for the response to a call message it has send to another domain or to an object.

Objects operating within this domain-oriented perspective embody *abstractions* and provide *services*. In other terms, they are not just a collection

★See also X3/SPARC/DBSSG/OODBTG Final Report by ANSI. New York, September 17, 1991.

of information elements and commands. Typically, the abstraction they embody is meaningful to the users:

> People,
> Programs,
> Other objects,
> Machines, and
> The network as a whole.

Such abstractions are mapped into the object's memory which is structured as a list of variables, each with specific information.

$1-5$ THE CONCEPT OF A CLASS AND ITS IMPLICATIONS

Within an object-oriented environment, objects are organized into *classes,* which can contain values, methods, and programs. An easy way to introduce classes is as *file formats* or *relational schemata.* This approach permits one to expand a bit and illustrate *methods.*

1. The *file formats* in the transactional database we saw in Section 2, for example, may be standard journal entries, accrual journals, repeating journals, translated journals, but also accounts payable and accounts receivable.

Each file format contains the lowest level of detail and is typically used for account analysis. Each can be instantiated, correspondingly creating objects.

Normal object-oriented design practice is to model a collection of related real-life objects in the application domain with one class or a lattice of related classes that are homogeneous. This too is an example of the freedom this approach provides in the restructuring of database contents, regrouping file objects with the same file format (or record objects with the same layout) through a *class membership.*

2. If we associate a class to a *schema,* then we adopt the alternative paradigm of an object pattern.

A schema is the framework that defines the components of a database and their relationships. The concept behind this approach is valuable in many cases. One of them is the need to convert information elements from one DBMS to another in a heterogeneous environment.

3. Used in reference to active objects, *methods* are the code that determines an object's behavior, such as the calculation of an object's cost or price.

Except for class objects modified during a dynamic schema evolution, no objects in a system will contain data or methods about classes. But methods are a powerful tool with significant potential in future implementations.

With reference to Fig. 1.1, shown earlier, methods can be introduced as the way that an active screen display obtains the data it needs. This requires interactions between objects, as objects in the screen display have to be extracted from file formats.

The concept of *classification* is also a cornerstone of object-oriented solutions, as it is to the broader subject of rational database organization as well as to a knowledge engineering implementation.

A class is the *abstraction* of shared characteristics,

An object is an *instance* of a class and therefore a basic runtime entity.

This duality, *class-object,* underlines all applications.

Each class in a *schema* has basic features. First and foremost, a *class name* identifies the class, though synonyms can also be permitted. Second, each class name must be unique with respect to all class names used in a schema. For notational convenience, class names may be strings of uppercase letters and special characters, or other symbols.

Third, the class has a collection of *members;* these are the entities that constitute it. The phrases "the entities in a class" and "the members of a class" are practically synonymous. Fourth, each class in a schema is a homogeneous collection of one type of entity, at an appropriate level of abstraction.

A class construct supports information hiding through the separation of the class interface and class implementation. Such separation permits the class interface to be mapped into several different implementations, and at the same time sees to it that the operators in the external interface represent the possible behaviors of that object. One of the responsibilities of such operators is to provide for controlled access to the attributes of the object, which would be hidden from users of the class.

One of the less clear concepts found in the literature, and in practice, concerns the difference between *class* and *type.* There is a certain amount of confusion between the two concepts,* but there is as well an essential distinction in that

---

*Indeed, the distinction between type and class is not at all clear in the mind of most object-oriented experts, the two terms being used practically interchangeably in much of the literature.

A *type* specification refers to the conceptual, logical issues. Data values have type.

A *class,* on the other hand, refers to the implementation template of a specific abstract data type. Objects have a class.

The type is a *predicate* Boolean function defined over values than can be used in signature to restrict a possible parameter or characterize a certain result. Types classify objects according to a common interface.

If a type defines how objects are implemented and used, then applications are implemented by defining new types. A type consists of

A set of operation interfaces,

Code for the operations, and

Data structures that define the representation of objects.

Defined objects are organized into a hierarchy, allowing operations implemented by a parent type to be inherited and reused by a child type. Type *inheritance*★ promotes uniformity among types; we will discuss inheritance in the next section.

A class is part of the design that can be instantiated to create multiple objects with the same behavior, an object being an instance of a class. As contrasted to types, classes classify (which means distinguish) objects according to a common implementation.

The careful reader of these definitions will appreciate that *class* and *type* are closely related and therefore that they tend to be used interchangeably. They often become an author's or user's preferred terminology. Still other specialists employ the terms class and type as if they were very different. Both tend to be wrong:

- *Class* has an *extentional* meaning, denoting the set of objects which conform to the type,[†] whereas
- *Type* is an *intentional* definition of the characteristics of a set of objects.

Hence, in a deductive database sense,[‡] the concept of class belongs to the distributed databases in a network. Type will dominate the deductive, hence intentional layer structure.

The databases we deal with in our applications environment are typically subject to a number of *integrity constraints.* These are mapped into

---

★See also Section 6.

[†]A. Brown, *Object-Oriented Databases,* McGraw-Hill, London, 1991.

[‡]Read: in an intelligent database.

An *intentional database* (IDB) layer, which is rich in knowledge, able to interpret data values, provide remote data access (RDA) primitives, and manage the database as a whole.

The classical database and its contents, as we have known it over 30 years (since the invention of mass storage media), is the lower layer of the overall structure:

The *extensional database* (EDB) essentially consists of a set of facts and their values, stored and retrieved as requested by users—people, software modules, terminals.

This two-layered approach can be nicely served by entity-relationship and object approaches. It will be administered by the knowledgebank management system (KBMS) rather than the database management system (DBMS).

$1-6$ SEMANTICS AND THE PROCESS OF INSTANTIATION

An object is a resource. Objects are being defined to implement interactive user sessions as well as to encapsulate processes and information elements. We have also stated that objects are grouped into classes for specification purposes. Relations between and within classes help to express specialization and generalization of the issues represented by the class(es) themselves.

The paradigm underlying this last point is *inheritance.* We will return to the concept of inheritance,★ which, next to that of a class, is a pillar of object orientation. However, before continuing the discussion of class, it is wise to consider the notion of *instantaneity,* which is mapped in Fig. 1.5.

At any given moment, as a result of stimuli that it receives, a class existing in an initial state may generate state 1 and state 2. Subsequently, state 1 may generate state 11 and state 12. Each state contains a different hierarchical layout of *object instantiation,* which can be represented by a constraint graph with different status assignments.

Superficially, this looks like a rather inflexible hierarchical representation. In reality, it is the opposite. All these states are instantaneous and short-lived, hence *ephemeral.* They are generated to satisfy a specific requirement implied by the stimulus (which may be a message), but also contain "sunset" clauses that will phase them out as soon as the requested service has been rendered (with the exception of persistent objects).

★Discussed and explained in Chapter 2. Too many definitions are counterproductive, but inheritance is too important a concept to be ignored at this point.

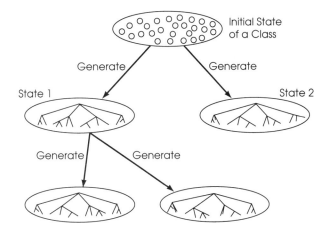

Figure 1.5   A class and its inheritance.

Something similar happens in a Unix implementation with the creation of forks, except that forks deal only with operations while the instantiation of a class involves information elements and rules. This concept allows significant adaptation to ongoing requirements but, at the same time, it uses the computationally efficient hierarchical structures—doing so for only as long as the services are required.

Semantic notions are in the background of this procedure. There is inheritance-type semantic connotation in a hierarchical tree, less so in a network (owner-member) approach, even less with the relational model.

Semantics play a major role in our life and in our business. In Switzerland, the value of the William Tell legend, for example, lies in its semantic significance. It has therefore continually inspired the creative talents of writers, opera composers, visual artists, and craftspeople throughout the centuries. The French Revolution glorified William Tell as the epitome of freedom, and even today his crossbow serves as a mark of origin for Swiss products.

Using semantically rich objects in a computational environment, we enhance the semantics through the instantiation of an ephemeral hierarchical representation, while retaining the flexibility of entity-relationship solutions, which are richer than flat files.

Classes hold information on their shared instances and objects. For example, the class "computer" can represent hundreds of objects such as different types of computers found in a given installation. This class-object paradigm provides support for system modularization. This is one of the jobs that classes do well: Modules represent procedural thinking, where programs act on data; objects encapsulate the data and the operations together. Class design is clearly no traditional code modularization, which does not imply the existence of abstract data types.

A different way of looking at the same subject is to visualize a class design as *wrapped inside* an application design, including the identification of the objects pertinent to a problem domain. Within such an applications environment, each kind of entity leads to a class description, which should be a comprehensive and complete model in itself. The class defines a set of possible objects, thus becoming the construct for a given implementation. It is precisely in this sense that a class is seen as an abstract data type, (as defined in Chapter 2), with implementation details being private to that class.

Such definition helps in terms of better comprehension of the reference made in Section 2 about public interfaces. Having a public interface to an object allows sharing of implementations, creation of object instances, and operations in a dynamic context.

A uniform public interface extends and generalizes the idea of an abstract data type. Hence it can be seen as the "soldering iron" of a class, itself composed of two types of class methods:

1. *Accessor functions,* which return meaningful abstractions about an instance's state
2. *Transformation procedures,* used to move an instance from one state to another

Through this mechanism, objects can effectively share implementations, permitting the creation and manipulation of *object instances.* This is essentially what makes the power of a class and permits operations within a dynamic context.

1–7 OBJECT-ORIENTED VERSUS RECORD-BASED MODELS

The fine-tuning of the class mechanism should see to it that the implementation of one object may not only share the implementation of another object, but also refine it or extend it. This further underlines the object-class duality and what we just said—that an object is an instance of a class.

Having a modifiable state consisting of a set of references to other objects or classes and communicating with them by call-reply exchanges, the object both receives and sends stimuli. The particular characteristic of this model is that objects can communicate only if they have agreed upon a particular protocol. For one object to influence another, there must be a user who knows what requests are supported by the target, as well as a *meta*★ level that defines the sort of requests that can be answered.

★The concept of meta is treated in Chapter 2.

Class is a meta-idea with respect to a common object. It is advisable not to become confused by the trick of some purists or object language vendors of having an object point to a class object to get class variables. This is a hidden implementation detail that has no place in a discussion at the concept level of object databases.

Many of the foregoing notions underpin all database management systems that have been developed since the 1960s, and they are valid to some extent even with simple file structures—though at the time we did not think of them in that way. But while there is similitude between the established concepts of a DBMS operation (hierarchical, network, and relational) and those of an object orientation, there are also significant differences.

If iteration aids comprehension, let us repeat that object-oriented solutions are *not* presented as worthy of unconditional praise, with all good things flowing from them: The knowledgeable reader can find various counterexamples where, for instance, relational models are able to respond to heavy-duty database requirements. But the knowledgeable reader will also appreciate that there is a growing list of transactions and queries where hierarchical models are impotent and relational ones are reaching the limits of what they can do.

Just as it is unwise to convert old serial programs to parallel supercomputers, it does not help much to go wholesale from old database models to new ones. Transition has to be selective.

Those fields are best for object-oriented applications that today are suffering under the old, established database models. Complex transactions of the type we saw at the beginning of this chapter are an example. Applications where the record structure becomes a limiting factor are another case.

It is also well to keep in mind that differences can be found within the object orientation itself. One of the most fundamental is best exemplified by bringing into perspective the distinction between

Record-based database models characterizing the hierarchical, network, and relational approaches of the past decades, and

An episodic memory organization.★ Over the years, implementation started at the relational level, proceeded beyond relational solutions, and today is object-based.

Figure 1.6 makes this distinction and also demonstrates what it takes in terms of conceptual evolution in order to support increasing flexibility. Today, memory-based objects in a distributed database context is a valid and helpful metaphor.

Record-based database models dominate the database systems in practical use today. They include relational models as well as partially relational

★Made by Prof. Dennis McLeod, University of Southern California.

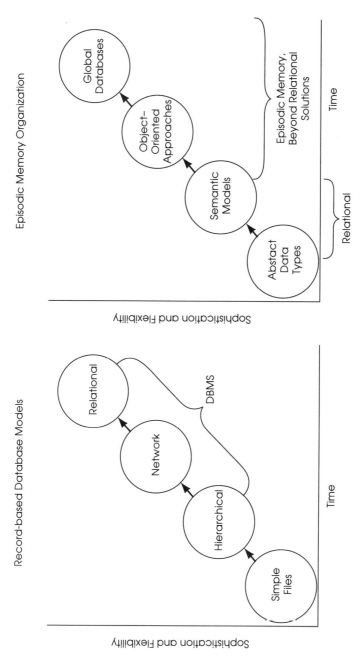

Record-based Database Models

Episodic Memory Organization

Figure 1.6 The transition from record-base models to episodic memory.

(pseudo-relational) ones, not just the hierarchical and network types. While there is considerable variation among the versions of these models embodied in a particular DBMS, their common ground is the use of the *record construct,* and the fact that they employ *interrecord* links.

When enriched with abstract data types and semantic modeling beyond the flat file concept, relational DBMS help provide linkage between record-based approaches and an episodic memory organization. They do so with simplicity by capturing interrecord relationships in a uniform manner, as well as by using common data values, but there are also limits.

Continuing simplicity and uniformity is the fundamental characteristic of an *episodic memory* organization, which goes beyond relational reference and at the same time uses the notion of object types rather than records. In this case, each information element is stored *as is;* as a callable entity, it does not need to be incorporated into arbitrary groupings of the record type.

Episodic memory-oriented solutions must be comprehensive, and this is facilitated by the fact that a class is the object paradigm that serves as a conceptual modeling tool. Such solutions offer the needed protocols, as well as tighter coupling of data and functionality, than abstract data types alone can provide. In this sense, classification can be seen as an artifact of the application design process. Classification within an episodic memory landscape is used in conjunction with a model-based approach, and models can be constructed and reconstructed according to runtime demands, yielding a technique that is very flexible.

Through classification, which underpins many artificial intelligence constructs, design chunks are closely identified with the real-world concepts they model. Such an approach is quick to adapt to changes in problem specifications as they arise in a dynamic operating environment.

1-8 FINE-TUNING THE CLASS CHARACTERISTICS

We have said that object-oriented solutions describe encapsulated data structures and operations. Each object's behavior is defined by the operations written for that object. While in many situations this approach is quite appropriate, it also presents limitations in terms of describing dynamic processes at large, where an object's behavior changes in an active manner through time.

There has also been a tendency to overemphasize what can be achieved with objects. Values, for instance, are not necessarily expressed through object-oriented paradigms.

The still-thin experience in object applications also means that some of the available capabilities are underutilized. An example is the use of *agents,* to which reference will be made in Chapter 22 as the coming wave in computing.

An agent is an entity capable of communicating with other agents as well as with human users. Through knowledge engineering, the agent is proactive rather than reactive to user requests.

Agents may change state as a result of an external communication or other event, or as a result of an internal event. A communication takes place if two agents make matching output and input offers. Each expresses its desire to change through messages. The behavior of the agent itself may change due to this new state—the terms agent, state and behavior being, up to a point, interchangeable.

With either more sophisticated agent applications or the state of the art today, there are administrative requirements to be observed, and this underlines the need for *class management*. Administrative duties must handle a number of issues known from database management systems, such as data modeling, access methods, and authorizations.

Examples of new requirements are class evolution and class packaging for reuse reasons. Inherent to class packaging is the problem of representing an object class so that the needed information can be easily located and incorporated within an application.

This helps explain why the class concept is used both to determine a collection of objects and as a *template* by which objects can be created. Class characteristics can be employed to check the consistency of expressions. Furthermore, while the notions of *class* and *type* differ considerably, a class declaration can act as a type declaration.

There are other advantages from fine-tuning the class concept. Seeing the class of objects as the abstraction of shared characteristics helps in defining:

A static specification of behavior

A flexible runtime entity

Authorized responses to incoming messages

Responsibilities for generating new instances

The last item brings to the foreground the concept of *inverse inheritance,* which can be viewed as delegation to another, higher-level class (superclass, meta-level). In reality, however, we are talking about an association of different concepts. Inverse inheritance is sometimes called *generalization* in the semantic database literature.

Distinct issues may be involved within a comprehensive object-oriented environment, each with its own definition, but many of their underlying characteristics are interconnecetd. Still, it is wise to classify them into a dozen categories, keeping in mind that these support one another and benefit from one another's attributes:

1. Class and inheritance
2. Metarules, constraints, equilibration★
3. Data abstraction and procedural abstraction
4. Encapsulation and signatures
5. Polymorphism and distributed concurrency
6. Dynamic binding and integrative ability
7. Message passing and behavior monitoring
8. Extensibility and interoperability
9. Referential integrity and garbage collection
10. Multimedia and versioning
11. Query relevance, hypermedia, and semantic modeling
12. Reusability and architecturing

Class, inheritance, meta-rules, and constraints are high-level design and analysis characteristics. Equilibration is necessary to assure that the system we are building is complete and that there are no contradictions in its rules.

Polymorphism, (defined in Chapter 2), distributed concurrency, message passing, and dynamic binding are lower-level design references, but definitely necessary in any implementation sense. Reusability is a steady goal, and in the longer term it cannot be achieved without architecturing. We will examine each of these terms individually.

★The assurance that there are no contradictions in the system. The term has been advanced by the ICOT Project in Japan.

$\mathcal{Chapter}$ 2

The Concept of Inheritance, A Cornerstone of Object Solutions

$2-1$ INTRODUCTION

The concepts of class and inheritance are inseparable, as discussed in Chapter 1. An example of inheritance is the class of PERSON with attributes NAME, AGE, GENDER, ADDRESS. We can have subclasses of DOCTOR, with additional attributes SPECIALITY and OFFICE; and PATIENT, with attributes COMPLAINT and OUTSTANDING BILL.

PATIENT, in turn, could have a subclass SENIOR CITIZEN, which is characterized by AGE >65. Each of these inherit the PERSON attributes. Moreover, we can have objects denoting patients who are themselves doctors; hence *multiple inheritance.*

Together the concepts of class and inheritance form a combination that is useful in many ways. This is a nice symbiosis, with plenty of semantics and synergy.

Any given class may inherit from one or several classes. When, whether directly or indirectly, class X inherits from class Y, then class Y is a *superclass* of X and X is a *subclass* of Y.

Both inheritance and *meta*—the concept of a higher level in a layered structure—underlie an object orientation. Being intentional, as explained in Chapter 1, they do so by means of types rather than of classes. Since, however, class and type are related, we tend to think that meta and inheritance are connected to the notion of class.

A class that inherits operations from a superclass can *redefine* or *override* them, thus providing itself with considerable flexibility. There is a difference between redefinition and overriding: In redefinition, both the body and the signature* of the operation are changed; in overriding, only the body is changed—the signature remains *as is.*

A number of rules have to be obeyed to redefine an operation, but within the perspective of inheritance we typically focus on what should remain the same: the name, the number of parameters, the class of each parameter, and the class of the result value in the redefined operation.

Redefinition may be necessary for a number of reasons. One of the most frequent is that operation B may be a redefinition of operation A, by becoming a specialization of A at a given instance. The flexibility of this *given instance,* which may follow a class-defined inheritance or override it, means that we can associate objects to operations, and imply constraints permitting that aspects of the database can be represented *declaratively.*

Underlying class and superclass methods is the realization that objects have components that can themselves be objects inheriting basic characteristics from their parents.

$2-2$ INHERITANCE, SPECIALIZATION, AND GENERALIZATION

Abstract data types (ADTs) come from operational aspects of a system, not from a particular design mechanism, though the ADT concept is more or less associated with relational and object constructs. ADTs occur due to the fact that encapsulation is enforced, not because methods and data designs are inherited from superclasses.

In a similar manner, inheritance does not imply much about constraints, which are associated with a class instance generator. Possibly and usually, this takes place with the update methods of a class.

Transformation procedures incorporate the concept of generalization when we go from class to superclass; and of specialization when we move the other way. Both are done through *property inheritance,* keeping in mind that:

Objects exist in the real world.

Actions can also be regarded as objects.

Objects have various attributes, some of them inherited.

Values can be associated with an object by means of a property list.[†]

---

*Which for some specialists means codes attached to an object. But ANSI's OODBTG Final Report (pages 4–19) refers to signatures as to the number (arity) and types of arguments to a method, and the type of the result.

[†]For instance, in a LISP environment. The concept of a property list is not universal across object implementation.

The concept of inheritance is indivisible from that of *specialization,* and its inverse, *generalization.* Both are important kinds of relationships supported by a class/subclass construct. Figure 2.1 illustrates this relationship between a type and its subtypes.

In this example, the type MOTOR VEHICLES has three subclasses: TRUCKS, BUSSES, and PERSONAL CARS. Each has further subclasses. Attributes are inherited by a subclass from its superclass, but the subclass may have additional attributes not necessarily possessed by the superclass—hence the specialization.

The high-level motor vehicle model provides a simple semantic notion through which are supported the modeling constructs:

Class
Subclass/superclass
Attribute
Instance

Conceptually, the database is modeled as a collection of objects, each object being an instance of a class or classes. In this connection, inheritance is defined by the superclass and subclass properties of type objects.

In the high level motor vehicle model, every instance of a subclass inherits the attributes from its superclass. A subclass can be defined by restricting the class characteristics by means of a selection predicate. This

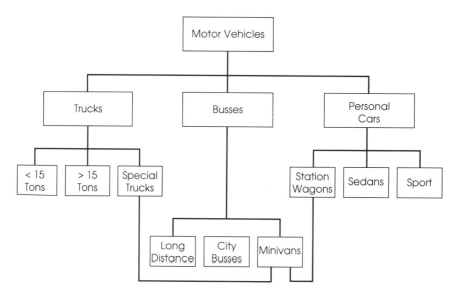

Figure 2.1   Supertypes, subtypes, and attribute inheritance.

helps establish the values of one or more attributes of instances in the super-class.

Both the concept of class and that of inheritance have a great deal to do with the fact that objects are abstract data types associated with something specific. They are both facilitated and affected by the object structure, which includes both information elements and operations on them.

The inheritance mechanism supports extending object-oriented designs by facilitating the reuse of existing definitions. This eases the development of new definitions while the amount of specification and implementation inherited by a new class grows, as the inheritance structure becomes progressively deeper.

In the sense of this discussion, inheritance is primarily a mechanism by which object implementations can be organized to share descriptions. This is achieved through a *classification* of objects based on common behavior and/or common external interfaces. Thus we can distinguish between implementation inheritance and interface hierarchy.

More to the point, the concept of inheritance provides the relation between classes that permits the definition and implementation of one class based on characteristics of other existing classes. In this sense, inheritance is a promising concept, allowing software artifacts to be developed from reusable parts, rather than writing every routine from scratch.

Originally, the concept of inheritance in computer programming was introduced in Simula (the simulation language of the late 1960s) as an organizational tool for classification. It capitalized on the fact that objects can be defined as members of a class, sharing procedures of that class.

This approach becomes much more powerful when we consider that members of a class may themselves be classes. Classification promotes modularity by putting all entities with common characteristics in one place in a given matrix.

The organization of objects using classification provides knowledge in terms of *representation.* This concept essentially makes the characteristics of one class visible to its members (the objects). By the same token, inheritance minimizes the incremental effort of adding new primitives while at the same time it facilitates *rapid prototyping.*

In conclusion, with object-oriented approaches, dependencies are expressed by the notion of inheritance, which leads to the feasibility of *instance variables.* For example, a new class can refer to previously existing classes by inheriting from them: A whole environment of attributes and methods can be inherited and made directly available to a new class.

There are, as well, *dependency* relationships, which we will discuss after introducing the concepts of meta-data, meta-rules and data abstraction.

Inheritance is not the only way to express dependencies. Real-world structures can also be modeled by object reference and by object acquaintances. Some languages capture these dependencies without pure inheritance.

Instance variables of a new subclass reside in the objects of that new class. They can make use of all the inherited methods and class variables along their individual inheritance path(s). But they cannot directly make use of instance variables in other objects, because this would violate encapsulation.

$2-3$ META-RULES, CONSTRAINTS, AND EQUILIBRATION

Any system worth its salt is *constrained*. Constraints act as the guidance and control on any given situation; they are based on knowledge and rules derived from a layer of meta-knowledge. Meta-knowledge is knowledge about knowledge, just as meta-objects are objects about objects, meta-rules are rules about rules, and meta-data are data about data. Meta-knowledge provides a system with an understanding of knowledge as well as the ability to fill in missing rules or information.

One of the earliest examples of meta-knowledge implementation in connection with database management is the notion of the *schema*.

- A schema represents a list of constraints.
- Internal schemata reflect constraints internal to the system.
- External schemata map constraints connected to enduser viewpoints.
- Meta-data is synonymous with the schema concept, and a crucial element in the formalization of relationships.

Meta-knowledge guides an artifact in supplying default values. It helps it acquire further procedural knowledge and assures that it can control the lower layers of its structure. Thus, the concept of *meta* is very important in object-oriented solutions.

Meta is the key to a *causal* connection. It can serve as a command language providing controls as well as linkages—a whole infrastructure for the development of a layered architecture. Such a layered architecture is fundamental in object orientation, as we have seen when we examined

- Superclasses, classes, subclasses,
- Superobjects, objects, and subobjects.

In essence, we have spoken of classes, objects, and inheritance in a unified way—as any class can be part of another class, as any system can be the subsystem of another system. The role of the higher level is that of meta on the lower one(s), which not only inherit(s) the characteristics of the higher, but is (are) also subject to its constraints.

This is not written in a superclass/class/subclass sense, but in a way reflecting the layered *open system interconnection* (OSI) architecture. It is, however, proper to add that the notions of meta-data, meta-classes, and meta-knowledge are extremely confused in the literature.

If we assert that for all objects of type PERSON we must have AGE > 0, we do not have meta-data but an enforcible constraint which, however, will be inherited by all subclasses. If, in the subclass JUVENILE, we have AGE < 18, then we are refining the constraint.

The *meta* concept can be better explained by a certified check that has imprinted on it "Not valid for more than $10,000."

- The lower layer has the date of issuance and the amount in dollars, say, $5000.
- An upper, invisible meta-layer tells that the bank which issued it will debit the issuer's account two working days earlier, and the beneficiary's bank will credit his or her account three working days later.*
- The $10, 000 limit is a constraint. If a gifted crook adds a leading "1" to the check, making it worth $15,000, he invalidates the check through this act.
- Finally, the fact that it is a certified check assures that it cannot bounce. It has been debited to the client's account at issuance.

Constraints are something beyond the structure that controls the data to be stored in the slots built to the schema's specification. This is a reflection of the philosophy of information science, and it should not make it harder to understand this book's concepts.

The existence of constraints, and software to track them, assures that they are observed at all times. Appropriate software *traces* for discrepencies such as errors or other events that deviate from the established procedures. Tracing is typically actuated through a meta-level, but the language of the meta-level cannot be the language of the system. It has to be a meta-language.

All these are fundamental notions behind the act of *architecturing* in a flexible, layered manner. Any layer may have one or more modules that can themselves be objects or contain objects. But without a higher level, a meta-level, there can be no coordination between these objects. They will never perform as a system.

In contrast to *superobjects,* which may contain many other objects, meta-objects are the *interpreters* of objects. This higher-level layer permits a logical and physical split between meta-object and object. It creates an excellent form of self-representation, as objects can access and modify their meta-objects through *tracing* involving inheritance and equilibration. A

---

*This is one way in which banks make money, through a difference in interest days.

meta-object assists the user in understanding the object(s) beneath it, including functionality, limits, and constraints.

In other terms, the meta-level is in complete control of the object level. Most often, the linkage is *heuristic,* but this does not exclude an *algorithmic* implementation.

Not everyone agrees with this broader view of meta-objects. Some people consider them as basically pieces of code sitting in slots as attributes of, say, frames. Still others see them as closely related to meta-data and meta-rules—through them influencing the behavior of a domain-specific database and rule base.

2-4 THE CONCEPT OF MAPPING

Mapping is a concatenation of attribute names that allows a user directly to reference the value of an attribute of an object. In general, a mapping is written as a sequence of attribute names and functions. The meta-level implies much more than that, as it constitutes a higher commanding authority. This higher-level authority has knowledge engineering characteristics.

While the field is still under development, and therefore some definitions—particularly the limits of definitions—can vary among researchers, there is agreement on the need for meta-levels. Gödel said: "We cannot have a system unless we step out of this system and explain it." This is the essense of the meta-level.

Some information technologists, including the authors, think that Gödel's dictum is appropriate for all systems. Others believe that Gödel's statement describes the essence of a passive, descriptive meta-level. The distinction is only half valid, because in object solutions the meta-level is typically active: It does not just describe or explain, it controls and constrains.

The utility of the meta concept is easily shown through implementation examples. Runtime class objects are meta-class objects. For each class in the system, there is a corresponding object that stores information about the class as a whole. This object helps in implementing class-level operations by acting as class constructor and destructor.

Within this operational landscape, the meta can also act as the conceptual interface between a computer artifact and a subject in the real world. Such a process facilitates conceptual modeling by providing a two-way approach between the generalization and the specialization that is a way of producing instances.

As a conceptual interface between an artificial system (therefore an artifact) and a real subject, meta is helpful in mapping acting as the commanding instance of conceptual modeling. Meta-objects describe or help to interpret other objects within the perspective of this artifact.

Meta-data is a good example along this line of reasoning. All DBMS store and manipulate several kinds of meta-data. For instance, a relational DBMS must know:

The name of each relation
The number of attributes
The name and type of each attribute
The storage representation
The access paths for each relation

The creation of a meta-layer above these attributes is critical for the effective management of resources as well as in defining the best structures for logical and physical databases.

The meta concept is particularly powerful because the taxonomic relationships that it provides enable descriptive information to be shared among multiple objects through inheritance. In addition, the internal structure of a layered solution makes feasible automatic maintenance of semantic integrity constraints.

The statements that we make are valid all the way from meta-objects, meta-data, and meta-rules to meta-languages. As a facilitator, the language we employ influences the results obtained. But few of us think of the constraints the linguistic mechanism implies—hence its structure of meta-layers.

Since they are languages about languages, meta-languages act as abstractions and controls of lower-level linguistic constructs. Therefore the concepts just described are even more significant at a meta-linguistic level.

Application-specific aspects of the problem can be formulated in a very-high-level production-rule language. Meta-rules influence the inference system. Meta-variables can range over any language construct expressed at the object level.

A meta-language can be used as the foundation of a *versioning* mechanism, which we will discuss in subsequent chapters. A version or viewpoint is the user's own, resulting from interrogating the system about the objects as well as the concepts that are present, and also generating an explanation of the conclusion.

Equilibration makes use of meta-knowledge to assure that at all times the object-oriented system is consistent. The concept of equilibration is very important, not only because our artifacts must be complete, consistent, and noncontradictory, but also because they have to emphasize an organized behavior that can be assured through supervisory processes. We have more to say about this when we discuss *demons*.

2–5 DATA ABSTRACTION AND PROCEDURAL ABSTRACTION

One of the most important concepts in object-oriented approaches is *abstraction*. By this we mean that are interested in the behavior of an object rather than in its representation; in other words, we will ignore representation details connected to usage until such usage becomes well specified in a runtime environment.

Abstraction is a way of doing higher-level design without being affected by implementation details. This permits treating design problems in a manner that allows certain critical issues to be considered early and throughout the design process. Abstract solutions are descriptions that stand for an equivalence class of detailed solutions. As such, they are represented by description levels.

Data abstraction can thus be seen as a central reference which, in a vertical sense, benefits from the meta concept and an object-oriented methodology. Subsequently, as shown in Fig. 2.2, in a horizontal sense it contributes to the structure of an object-oriented language and the resulting applications.

Data abstraction can be done by *specification* and *parameterization*. To various degrees, both methods are supported by object-oriented languages.

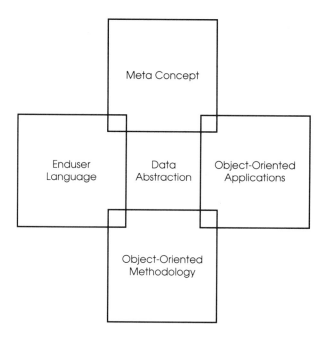

Figure 2.2 Quarterspaces impacting on data abstraction.

Abstraction by specification of the macroconcept (macroscopic view) leads to a grand design without reference to details, assuming such details will be developed later in conformance to a system view and its implementation.

This approach is effectively applied by assuring that the external (public) interface of a class constitutes the specification of that class. It helps define the legitimate operators of the data contained in instances of the class, and constitutes a rather standard feature of object-oriented languages.

Abstraction by parameterization concerns the type of data to be manipulated, abstracting it from the specification of how it is to be handled. Parameterization is key to software reusability. However, in its current status it is applicable only with some artifacts and is not as generic as inheritance. While many people talk of parameterization, both theoretical background and implementation paradigms leave much to be desired.

Abstraction based on parameterization is handled by most object-oriented languages at the operator level, but not necessarily at the class and superclass levels. As a result, the meta concept is not properly supported.

This duality of specification and parameterization leads to *procedural abstraction,* which has worked well for some selected domains. An example is mathematical and statistical libraries, which are today offered by most computer manufacturers and software vendors.

Whether through specification or parameterization, data abstraction and procedural abstraction embedded in an object-oriented environment should make it possible for users to ignore the details of object implementation, and for implementors to be able to provide new solutions without affecting the users. When this happens, we will be well placed to take advantage of abstract features regarding extensibility, homogeneity, code reuse, and other object-oriented benefits.

The concepts of data abstraction and procedural abstraction can also be helpful in many domains beyond what is perceived as the more limited domain of system design. For instance:

Reusability and portability as a function of general-purpose object types, and through the mechanism of inheritance

Maintainability, through the separation of interfaces and implementation

Reliability, by means of strong-type checking and rigorous quality control

Concurrency and network-wide distribution, using object independence and the message-passing communications model

In conclusion, by being applications-independent, abstract data types become object-based paradigms for capturing conceptual information.

They also transform themselves into the building block of more complex systems, which can be designed not only for assembly but also, and quite importantly, for disassembly and reuse.

2-6 OBJECT ENCAPSULATION AND POLYMORPHISM

An object must be able to identify itself and its characteristics. Ease of handling is assured through *encapsulation.* Concurrent object environments should be designed in such a way that encapsulation contributes to the integrity of the internal state of objects when they are called to perform their part.

Are objects callable entities? One of the computer manufacturers says that they are and tends to equate its mammoth relational database system with abstract data types—which, this same computer vendor suggests, are the essence of object orientation.

However, the preceding paragraph is an anathema to many American computer scientists, who think and feel in precisely the opposite way. Said one of them as a response:

- This is violation of metaphor! Who says that objects are callable?★
- Objects are autonomous. They cooperate with other objects, processes, and users by agreeing to respond to proper messages.
- Objects are not slaves! They have integrity.
- If objects were merely procedures or even just abstract data types, they would be "callable." Show some proper respect!

Encapsulation is a foundation of object orientation. It is not necessarily made for ease of handling, but it helps. Encapsulation assures the integrity of data and the uniform, proper access through, and only through, the object's methods.

This is a fundamental notion, but from an implementation viewpoint some users think that indeed the facilities provided by encapsulation and inheritance increase the efficiency with which endusers and programmers can work in building large, complex systems. Nevertheless, the way it is practiced today in object-oriented environments, *encapsulation* has three possible meanings:

1. The act of integrating components into a class system
2. The mechanism for controlling access to services by different users
3. Protection afforded through the enforcement of abstraction limits.

★Objects don't need to be callable by Peter, Paul, and Mary. They can be so through messages passing from other objects. As for autonomy, it is always constrained.

The fact that objects are encapsulated means that users are prevented from direct access to the information elements associated with an object. Instead, they employ a *request for services,* which are performed by objects.

- A *request* involves a method executing some code on object contents.
- Such a request identifies the service being asked, hence the operation, as well as the objects that are to perform it.

Most relevant is the possibility that objects can be identified unambiguously and reliably, a process known as *object reference.* Requests may also include other parameters and return results.

This brings into perspective the concept of *signatures,* that is, codes attached to an object. They give information about one or more aspects of that object, such as its level of security, but can be extended to carry other information as well:

A node signature reflects the number, direction, and possibly the type of links that are attached to that node.
The links themselves can carry signatures describing their pointers or anchors.

Strong typing done on the basis of signatures—such as operation names and arguments—tells us little or nothing about the behavior of concurrent and mutable objects. What strong typing does, however, is guarantee that all expressions are type-consistent, though runtime checking may be required.

In this sense, signatures and strong typing help in equilibration. They provide reference points for the establishment of necessary procedures to assure that the systems we build are complete and consistent—as well as that they include no contradictions in their signs and rules.

Encapsulated objects can be *polymorphic,* with one component having different properties in several new locations. A practical example is filial (child) objects.

This principle contributes to the object model and is assisted by the process of communicating by messages. Each dynamic object may share properties according to a classification hierarchy—but also specifies both information elements and activities.

In an implementation sense, polymorphism means the ability to take more than one form. In an object-oriented domain, a polymorphic reference associates itself to instances of more than one class. There is, however, a contrary approach to the issue of polymorphism. While it admits that many members of the object-oriented community are proud of this process, it also suggests that polymorphism is one of the worst aspects of the object orientation.

This argument stands on the premise that to have operators and operator symbols with completely different semantics, depending on their context, is to invite disaster. If one uses polymorphism, it suggests, one should also be warned against its misuse. This is indeed a fair warning.

Polymorphism can also be seen as the property that objects of different forms respond appropriately to the same message. In Chapter 11 we will see that this can be very important in object programming approaches.

Over time, the dynamic type of a polymorphic reference may change. This happens, for instance, during program execution. By contrast, a static type is determined from the declaration of the entity in the program.

- The *dynamic type* makes itself evident at runtime, and the interpreter must keep all polymorphic references automatically tagged.
- A *static type* typically occurs during computation and determines the set of valid characteristics the object can accept at runtime.

All objects, and most particularly those of a dynamic nature, are subject to concurrency in execution. Concurrency artefacts should be compatible with a user-server structure of object-oriented programs. They should facilitate the development of applications by reusing and adapting existing objects.

$2-7$ CONCURRENCY AND DYNAMIC BINDING

Etymologically, *concurrency* refers to the potentially parallel execution of parts of a computation. In a concurrent environment, program chunks may be handled in parallel, providing the flexibility to interleave the execution of components of a program on a single processor through decomposition, or distribute such execution among several processors operating in tandem. Concurrency abstracts away some of the details in an execution, permitting one to concentrate on conceptual issues without having to be concerned with a particular order of execution. The latter will be taken care of by the decomposition algorithm and the programmatic interfaces.

Concurrency leads to cooperative problem solving, which rests on an interconnection network in terms of execution. As most objects carry their own computational process, they may communicate with other objects to share the intermediate results being computed.

Cooperative problem solving, however, requires a form of *dynamic binding*. This is assisted through process declarations able to introduce the objects that will be used in a given configuration. Newly declared objects and processes do not necessarily start immediately; they can be suspended until the whole configuration has been set up or there is some other trigger to execution.

Binding instructions generate links between newly created processes and their objects. *Port binding instructions* transmit multimedia streams, *signal binding instructions* transmit high-priority events and exceptions.

An example of port binding is a simple conference system for multi-user communications in a networking environment. Commands create windows, write incoming messages, incorporate objects, and let users talk with each other.

As an example of signal binding, consider the case where a given process tries to locate an object among different databases, processors, and software modules attached to the network. Such search can be performed in parallel by different processes. As the object is located by one process, all others must be informed so that they can stop searching.

This example introduces the need for command variables and monitoring variables. Command variables are visible within the process but can be changed at any time by the environment. The process may use these variables either by reading their content explicitly or by associating handlers to them.

Monitoring variables play a different role. They are visible by the environment and can be altered by the process. In this sense, they perform the reverse function of command variables.

As we have emphasized from the start, polymorphism and dynamic binding are low-level design constructs, oriented to a particulr implementation. The above discussion explains why. It also helps in understanding the difference that exists between lower-level and higher-level design constructs. The latter, as we have said, are class, inheritance, and the meta concept.

Chapter 3

Constructing the Object-Oriented Environment

3-1 INTRODUCTION

A system architecture presents us with the need for fundamental choices. These determine what we will do well and what not, but the art of architecturing large artifacts is only now being developed. There are no a priori criteria for choices; only a basic system study can define fundamental requirements and how to characterize the products we want.

Conceptually, as well as in the way it has been practiced in other domains, an architecture refers to a set of *design principles* that define relationships, interactions among elements, and ways and means for integration.

In an object-oriented implementation, such design principles characterize various parts of a network of objects. They also refer to decisions leading to the establishment of an infrastructure and the definitions necessary to support artifacts and new developments that concern them. In this text, we will make no distinction between object-oriented and object-based architectures. The two terms will, more or less, be used interchangeably because among researchers, as well as writers, there is no general agreement on a rigorous way of looking at their differences—if any. One way of distinguishing between the two notions is outlined in Figure 3.1.

According to some practitioners, the difference between the object-based and object-oriented approaches lies in the fact that in an *object-based* system, objects encapsulate a collection of services accessible by a message-passing interface. Typically, objects have an identity and a mutable state. By contrast, the same definition suggests that, in an *object-oriented* environment, objects can be instantiated from classes with subclasses defined by inheri-

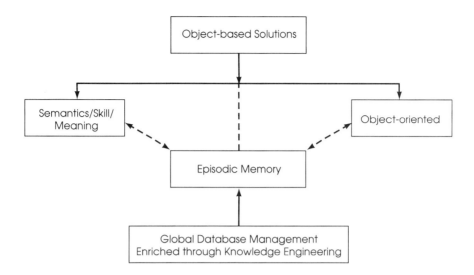

Figure 3.1   Object-based versus object-oriented solutions

tance. As we have seen, classes are also objects, with new classes possibly created at runtime.

These differences are not quite satisfactory; therefore, should a distinction be made between object-oriented and object-based solutions, then the latter should constitute the more general term. It could act as a metalayer to

1. *Semantic database* models, which are embedded in an applications environment and define a given database schema, and
2. *Object-oriented* approaches with primitives provided to support object classification and structuring, as well as semantic integrity constraints.

The reason many researchers make no clear-cut distinction between these two concepts is that to a significant extent they overlap. They both lead toward *episodic memory* solutions, which, as we have seen in preceding chapters, place themselves in contradiction to *record-based* database approaches and help to modernize them.

In other terms, the real difference is between episodic memory and record-based constructs, not between object-oriented and object-based. Another key difference exists between the absence and the existence of a methodology that spells out the tasks to be accomplished and the means by which to accomplish them—as well as the tools to facilitate the documentation and validation of the model, including the generation of designs. This is the sense of architecturing.

The services to be offered through architecturing an episodic memory artifact should always be kept in perspective. We have to plan both for current requirements and for future needs, but we should *act only after study:* employing design principles, defining relationships between components, and assuring the interaction of attached devices.

We should also recall that in its higher layers a system architecture permits a stable basis for planning and gives a common direction. At its mid-level it defines formats compatible among dissimilar systems; and at its lower level it occupies itself with protocols and the handling of messages. All three levels are important in an object-oriented sense.

3–2 HANDLING OBJECT-ORIENTED MESSAGES

The *messages* that particularly interest us in an object environment are of a very specific type. Objects have associated messages, which are sometimes referred to as *methods.* By representing design components as objects capable of sending and receiving messages, the responsibility for assimilating run-time changes becomes distributed.

The object-oriented representation supported by a message-passing model is the dominant scheme. This is evidenced in the support for it to be found in a large number of recently announced knowledge engineering tools and other artifacts for object-oriented programming.

Messages can be received by a class of objects or a single object only when the domain defined by them is idle. Messages sent to a domain that is active or blocked are queued up and wait to be delivered, which typically happens on a first-come, first-served basis.

This notion is important since, in object-oriented applications, messages are the only form of interobject communication. Through this mechanism we help define a call-reply exchange as a protocol composed of a call message from a user to an object, followed eventually by a reply message from the object back to the user.

Reflexes initiate a new activity by sending a start message to an object. No reply is expected from such a start message, and the sender executes immediately after invocation of the operation.

In their fundamentals, message-passing paradigms can be seen as exercises in self-reflection. Reflection is a relatively new area of research, particularly in projects where the issue of a machine's self-consciousness is being studied. *Meta-reasoning*—that is, reasoning about the process of reasoning using meta-knowledge—is a form of self-reflection.

Reflexes are special operations. Their existence sees to it that requirements for future execution range from the support for an object-oriented approach all the way to programming and the appropriate linguistic interfaces, including reusable software characteristics.★

★As we will see in Chapter 4.

In all instances of operating on objects, activities (and therefore roles) generate or accept mail by exporting and importing contents from objects of message type. As an object, each message is independent from its originating or receiving role instance. Further, the message itself can have rules of behavior that are inherited from its type and not necessarily from the originating role.

For example, a given message may not be initiated if the originating role is not of higher authority than the receiving role. Other objects can take part in the communication as routing objects, still others retain their independence of control. The originating activity may enforce its protocol rules and user interface(s), or the message might imply its own rules and influence its routing. The receiving activity could also enforce its protocol rules and user interface(s).

This, however, is not the general case. In many object-oriented environments there is only one type of message with only one user interface and one communication protocol. But at times there is the need for many different types of message objects, hence the polyvalence requirements.

3–3 MESSAGE PASSING AND LINGUISTIC REQUIREMENTS

For object-oriented applications development, several types of links are appropriate, such as control, data flow, and composition. The latter tells which components represent parts of objects, which scripts combine to generate new kinds of objects, and so on. Other crucial links regard inheritance and instantiation, and the mechanics of message passing.

The concept behind the message-passing approach is akin to that of pipes in UNIX implementation. The *pipe* is an input/output buffer that accepts one input and gives one output. In such an environment, programs are connected with pipe files that have the ability to pass data from a writer to a reader.

All input and output are done by reading or writing files, because all peripherals, including the user's terminal, are files to the file system. This has the advantage that a single, homogeneous interface handles all communications between a program and peripheral devices using it.

In this process, the pipe is the communications link, created either by the program itself or interactively by the programmer. Processes, and therefore programs, can thus pass information elements to each other in a convenient manner.★

By analogy, we can think of a roughly similar process with objects. For

---

★See also D. N. Chorafas, *Fourth and Fifth Generation Programming Languages,* Volume 2, *Which Unix?, McGraw-Hill, New York, 1986.*

reasons of clarity, it is always rewarding to be able to refer to a better-known process such as UNIX, where all input and output is done by reading or writing files, and all peripherals (including the user's terminal) are files in the file system. This has the advantage that a single homogeneous interface handles all communications between a program, the files it accesses, and the devices using it.

The ideas we discuss have to be well understood because messaging is a standard feature with objects. As we have seen in Chapter 1, object-oriented languages execute both standard features—other examples being encapsulation and inheritance—and lower programmatic details such as polymorphism, concurrency, and distribution.

In the general case, as Chapter 11 will explain, object-oriented programming builds on the concepts of objects by supporting patterns of classification, decomposition, and software reuse. Network-wide, this can be nicely achieved, for example, through the inheritance that allows all instances of a particular class to share the same method. In this sense, we can divide linguistic supports into two main categories:

1. Operation-oriented languages, which are based on remote procedure call primitives. They are best suited for computations where processes interact as users and servers.
2. Message-oriented languages supporting one-way message passing, best applied with pipelined computations.

Each class imposes specific requirements on the features of linguistic design and its primitives. At the same time, while various approaches have been followed for the design of concurrent object-oriented languages, not all of them are suitable for programming.

Some of the linguistic requirements for interactive, message-passing solutions arise from planning problems: The user has to predict the consequences of an event. However, progress in modeling techniques and the fast accumulation of information elements do mean that more powerful supports have to be made available.

Integrative approaches are important, as current problems involve numerous models, each dealing with a different aspect of the total problem and thus calling for some overall problem-solving strategy. We must focus on the detailed interactions that would arise in the use of a particular object approach, including behavioral patterns pertaining to the problem.

Other requirements also must be observed. Alert users play an important role in the inference process. Also a significant part of the solution is the means of interaction in the visualization domain.

Quite often, one of the requirements is to enter and display problem elements in a detailed context. The user should be able to establish a suitable map from reference databases. Objects associated with a specific problem should be introduced by interactive definition, through message-exchange capabilities, or imported from other sources.

Browsing should be available at the meta-level as well as over the objects used, for instance, in a visualization. The interface to the inferencing module must have the capability to establish instantiations in mapped contexts as a part of an inferencing step.

There is also a need for a programmable interface that supports integration of the object domain, the symbolic problem domain, and the visualization requirements. All this tends to suggest that object-oriented programming presents significant challenges.

One of the issues to be carefully assessed is the concurrency features of the language, which must be compatible with the notions underlying object-oriented solutions. Examples on the latter reference are encapsulation, data abstraction, inheritance, and meta-linguistic concepts.

3–4 REFERENTIAL INTEGRITY AND GARBAGE COLLECTION

According to the ANSI OODBTG Final Report, *referential integrity* is a kind of constraint that guarantees that all referenced objects exist. This is not a messaging issue, and it has little or nothing to do with design constraints limiting to whom an object may legally send a message. Referential integrity is a database issue.

- *If* the design of a class involves an instance variable—in other words, a reference to another object that is a reference variable—not an included or owned object that is part of aggregation,
- *Then,* to have full referential integrity the object database management system must assure the existence of the referred-to object.

In this sense, referential integrity assures the integrity of an object's *context,* defined as the set of acquaintances of that object. For networked environments, this reference is valid through the network wherever the object exists, including its images and clones.

An object's images and clones make particularly difficult the support of referential integrity, which has been addressed in various ways, including the use of equilibration and demons. A *demon* is a supervisory process. Demon predicates make object-oriented programming easier and more effective.

Suppose that a demon predicate is defined in the components a certain class inherits. When an operation on an object of this class is invoked, the demon will be called implicitly. Two types of demon calls typically need to be supported:

1. Before demons
2. After demons

A *before demon* is called prior to the primary predicate of the class. An *after demon* is called after the primery predicate. This methodology has been established by Simpos, the UNIX-based operating system of the new-generation computer technology built by ICOT.★

In a fairly similar manner, it is helpful to distinguish between object-oriented environments with and without garbage collection.

- If there is no garbage collection, any object referenced in the context of a sensor can be freed at any time, which automatically invalidates the sensor's action.
- In systems with garbage collection, a reverse problem occurs. No object can be destroyed as long as there is a single reference to it.

In other terms, as long as there are sensors referencing an object in their context, this object cannot be set free or, for that matter, eliminated.

Garbage collection is important because some of the facilities supported by object-oriented approaches tend to increase the amount of unwanted and unnecessary information elements, hence of garbage. For instance, this is the case with versioning. Unlike ordinary, nonversioned storage systems, with versioning a large proportion of the garbage results by maintaining many versions of an IE that are no longer explicitly needed.

Even when a user deletes a node, the system will not necessarily save the space, though the node will no longer be visible to the user. The solution is in the institution of an *extruder* function, as shown in Fig. 3.2, which may take either of two forms:

1. The definition of *sunset* actions to be performed at the moment an object is created, thus pruning memory contents automatically
2. The utilization of a garbage collection mechanism to do the cleaning job postmortem

Some specialists on object databases argue that there is little significance to sunset clauses for object-based DBMS operations. They add that these are concepts for managing main storage as well as auxiliary memory.

★See also D. N. Chorafas and H. Steinmann, *Supercomputers*, McGraw-Hill, New York, 1990.

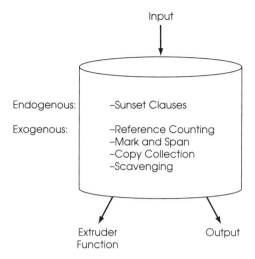

Figure 3.2   Input/output and extruder functions.

But there are practical reasons for this approach, some of them relating to persistent objects and others to daily database operations.

Let us begin with the fact that garbage collection is more difficult in an object database system than in certain language artifacts. Then, let us consider the problems of referential integrity in this manner:

1. Let object A have a variable referring to object B.
2. Imagine that object A is a computational object representing an order for 100 tons of steel and B is the object describing USX, the steel manufacturer.
3. When object A is deleted, what happens if object A is the last once in the system with a pointer to B?

In a programming language, B would be subject to garbage collection. But in an object-oriented database, autonomous objects must be explicitly deleted, which makes the job that much more challenging. Hence the wisdom of sunset clauses supervised by demons.

In other words, as in the case with knowledge engineering constructs, object-oriented programming can generate a large number of objects that remain in memory after the end of their useful lives. As long as they are needed, these objects will be allocated dynamically—but in reality they will be used for a limited period of time, thus creating a garbage collection problem.

Ideally, an automatic garbage collection scheme should be incorporated into the execution environment, thus easing programming effort and avoiding possible coding or memory swapping errors. The provision of such a scheme, however, should account for the overhead that it causes and therefore the burden it brings to system performance as a whole.

$3-5$ OBJECTS AND THE TREND TOWARD PARALLISM*

To avoid interrupting the running jobs, parallel garbage collection mechanisms run best on parallel computers. This further supports the premise that object-oriented solutions do best within the realm of parallelism, which is the developing trend in computation.

The larger and more parallel-oriented a system is, the more likely it is to be limited by conventional software programming techniques. Object approaches can solve these problems and make higher-speed computation possible, by exploiting parallel processing.

Object solutions contribute to the trend toward parallel processing by assisting both with performance-related and functional problems helping to create engines that can be operated at any time, from anywhere, by anybody. Scalability is a common objective in the design of multiprocessors—yet scalability has no commonly accepted, precise definition—other than the flexibility that it makes feasible.

Many specialists believe that object orientation underlies scalability inasmuch as the increase in performance that it makes feasible is related to communication patterns in applications programs, and the communication infrastructure provided by machines and their software.

The implementation of object solutions has other advantages as well. For instance, we can use objects to aid in experimental scalability and employ the latter to study larger machines. For designers of new architectures:

- Small but powerful experimental prototypes can demonstrate the viability of ideas in much larger engines; and
- If a system can be shown to scale well for a certain class of algorithms, then it is meaningful to write simulators.

As one of the reviewers of the original manuscript remarked, an architecture is either scalable or it is not. Many architectures offer only limited or no scalability—the most evident example being those based on mainframes.

Bus-based parallelism can scale only within the limits created by the bandwidth of a bus. More complex interconnection schemes for multiple-

---

*Chapter 21 addresses the issue of data-level parallelism, and Chapter 22 treats the challenge of high-performance computing. This is only an introductory discussion.

instruction, multiple-data-stream (MIMD) machines are limited by the cost of synchronization, network hardware costs, and pin-outs on chips.

There may be fewer limits on single-instruction, multiple-data-stream (SIMD) machines, but general-purpose commercial ones, such as the CM-2 and MasPar MP-1, have limits in the construction of their backplanes. Objects make these machines easier to use.

Measurements done on simulators concerning certain algorithms can be used to predict the behavior of larger aggregates. The best way to optimize is through prestudies. Simulation and experimentation are helped by object orientation. However, as the preceding section suggests, there are prerequisites associated to an object approach within a large and complex system.

Reference has been made to garbage collection, and to a considerable degree, garbage collection is a performance issue. Like with LISP programs, for instance, object manipulation tends to create intermediate data structures (the garbage), which can proliferate rapidly and take over all available memory unless a mechanism is devised to take care of them.

Garbage collection problems also arise with magnetic disk storage (secondary storage). In this case, copying is a suitable mechanism, since it compacts and increases locality of reference. This is helpful with segmented and multilevel address spaces, reducing the amount of paging and swapping.

All these are examples of periodic garbage collection mechanisms whose goal is to detect objects that have become unnecessary and eliminate them. This contrasts to proactive sunset clauses that create an aging scheme able to identify frequently accessed objects. Those that are not used very frequently are delegated to slower storage or better deleted outright.

3–6 MULTIMEDIA, VERSIONING, AND AD-HOC QUERIES

Software artifacts can contain complex structures, consisting of a network of components. Such components may be *multimedia:* data, voice, image, text, and graphics—used throughout the software development cycle and throughout the lifecycle of implementation.

Multimedia solutions are increasingly in demand, but finding them is a challenging, often taxing business. Classical data processing cannot respond to the integration of different media into one bit stream, to be manipulated in a comprehensive and efficient manner. Object-oriented approaches might provide the answer.

Multimedia information may include a complex web of relationships, involving interobject links. They may also encompass a substantial number of individual people and project teams whose activities can be described in terms of roles. *Versioning* is required precisely because of these various roles.

Versioning is essential in all modern software projects. There is an increasing need for:

Configuring a software system to a particular environment

Introducing slight changes to code and documentation as required by each enduser

Keeping track of such changes within the perspective of configuration management

Such a mission can be accomplished through a versioning mechanism. Versioning is also necessary for relating the different releases of a software system, introducing modifications for better adaptation, finer detail, or experimental purposes. In this sense, we can view a software project as a collection of activities that can be manipulated by versioning the various artifacts being produced.

A versioning system can support a comprehensive business modeling methodology, including information elements, functions, and rules of logic. It typically features an efficient interface with its users, permitting them to operate in forms mode, graphics mode, and in a description language that applies over defined segments of the business.

A complete model for describing objects should include mechanisms for viewing them at different levels of detail, for instance, using roles to describe the communication with lower-level objects as well as with higher-level objects (meta-object level). Through proper software, we can decompose the object descriptions, showing them graphically, and represent complex behaviors, role-state transitions, dependencies, and constraints between roles.

Such facilities are essential to the support of ad-hoc queries and for visualization of the answer to these queries, whether we deal with simple cases or with complex ones to be decomposed into subqueries. There are also other characteristics that should be accounted for. For instance:

- Historically, queries have been *"crisp,"* addressing an equally crisp database and giving a crisp response.

A crisp query asks for a yes/no answer; it is typically cast in a black-or-white form, accepting no grays—such as are implied by "fuzzy" queries.

- Increasingly, however, queries are *not crisp.* They are *fuzzy,* and the databases they address contain equally fuzzy information elements.

Classical, record-based data processing chores cannot handle queries involving vagueness and uncertainty. Object-oriented approaches are much better suited for this task.

Furthermore, as the user can only employ a computer and communications aggregate by interacting through its interface(s), the interface(s) has (have) to allow the whole network to be usable, not just the local workstation. We therefore need simple and practical methods for evaluating how good an interface is as well as promote the interactivity with information elements in distributed databases.

3-7 SERVING THE ENDUSER THROUGH VISUALIZATION

The design of an agile interface—more precisely, a *human window,* goes beyond versioning to include the whole issue of *visualization,* the conversion of data into graphics and images. From a purely hardware perspective, visualization involves the use of graphical computation aids with sufficient power and functionality to do calculations on three-dimensional multimedia information elements, and to interactively manipulate three-dimensional surfaces as well as shaded displays.

From a software viewpoint, not only object manipulation but also knowledge engineering-enriched facilities are necessary to create, display and operate a database that fully describes the three-dimensional geometry of an object. This is as true of a manufacturing environment connected to computer-aided design and layout studies as it is to financial operations.

Mapping the foreign exchange market into the computer and visualizing by currency, exchange rates, interest rates, country risk, and currency risk is an example of financial operations. All information elements and commands pertinent to this application may be objects. The presentation may take the form of a radar chart.*

A similar point can be made in connection to experimentation. For instance, knowledgeable users will want to watch the results of a simulation unfold visually. To this end, they:

Monitor and control the computation, much as one would interact with a flight simulator

Access both private and public databases in real time

Determine also in real time, through visualization, what the results from the computational phase mean

---

*For visualization through radar charts see also D. N. Chorafas and H. Steinmann *Implementing Networks in Banking and Financial Services,* Macmillan, London, 1988.

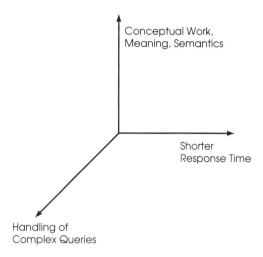

Figure 3.3   Axes of reference in an object orientation enriched through knowledge engineering.

Versioning and visualization play significant roles in all these tasks. In a fully interactive environment, intelligent tools can be instrumental in analysis and in presentation of the final results, provided they can capitalize on fast and effective networked database accesses, hence on object-oriented solutions. In other words, object-oriented solutions are not developed just for the pleasure of doing something different but for specific implementation purposes.

Another example of an application that cannot be handled effectively without object orientation is *concurrent engineering.* The Defense Advance Research Projects Agency (DARPA) Initiative in Concurrent Engineering (DICE) has selected the combination of *Ptech* object methodology modeling and the *Ontos* object database management system,* as part of its $100 million research and development program in this domain.

Assisted by knowledge engineering, object-oriented approaches and computer graphics permit managers and professionals to see shapes and predict forces previously hidden to human senses. As Fig. 3.3 suggests, this puts emphasis on *conceptual* work, which is the true professional job; reduces the time spent in data analysis; and permits more complex, analytical queries than have been possible so far.

Enriched through object-oriented approaches and artificial intelligence, agile software breaks up the original ad hoc query into an internal representation that can be described by fuzzy sets, neural nets, or rule notation. It coordinates the search for information in the object database, in

---

*The Ontos DBMS is discussed in Chapter 17.

tables, or in other file references, and returns a response in natural language.

Performance characteristics are commensurate with the fact that during the 1990s users will exercise much greater influence over the design of the systems they have to work with. In some cases, this will be achieved through sheer force of will within the corporate political environment, but in other cases it may be achieved through technology in terms of an *a priori* satisfaction of user needs.

Also, human–machine dialogue will be much more open ended and easily modifiable by the users themselves to deal with changing operational circumstances and individual needs. Object solutions will be key in obtaining commentable results, improving the performance of all systems elements to such a degree that response times will no longer be a discernable problem except in specific and acceptable circumstances such as very complex file searches.

Chapter 4

Challenges Connected with Object-Oriented Databases

4-1 INTRODUCTION

Chapters 1 through 3 focused on the definitions that underpin and characterize an object-oriented solution. They did so by providing specific implementation examples, all the way to the final goal of user interactivity with the information resources. Computers of any type, and the logical solutions that go with them, are there to serve the organization employing them—not vice versa. It is therefore very important to remember that object applications should be made with useful paradigms, or they will not last long.

Typically, interactivity between a computing and a communications system will be very important in supporting users in their daily tasks:

1. Reaching information elements in distributed intelligent databases
2. Employing programmatic interfaces to retrieve, communicate with, and manipulate the stored information elements

In this chapter we will look closely at both these topics emphasizing the notion of reusable software and its importance in computing. Subsequently, based on this background, Chapters 5 and 6 will consider why we need an object database. Chapters 7, 8, and 9 will take a look at object-oriented programming, though without attempting to provide a programming manual.

We do know, of course, why we need databases at large. Their main goal is to provide facility in storing, retrieving, and manipulating information elements. The advantage of using an object-oriented approach is information elements and operations on database contents can be linked to-

52

gether. The object-oriented design is useful because of its dynamic aspects, given the complexity of working through more traditional approaches.

As discussed at the end of Chapter 3, object databases are not searched in sequential fashion but in parallel, with particular emphasis on query relevance and flexible interlinking. If a flat file structure prevails, for instance, there will be a separate processor for each tuple whose task is to store the information in that row and to wait for a query. If a query requires some part or all of the information that is stored on a processor, the latter will respond; otherwise it will do nothing.

In an object-oriented database organization, on the other hand, a more elegant solution is possible. In terms of search time, it no longer matters where in a database an object is located. A system optimizer sees to it that databases, or sections thereof, that are accessed frequently are searched first. This reduces response time and increases flexibility for the enduser.

4-2 DATABASE ACCESS AND QUERY RELEVANCE

The database models we develop in the future must consider object behavior requirements when classes have already been defined and composed. Such models will increasingly be tailored for reusability of object class specifications, the basic mechanism providing a description of the behavior of objects of a given class in a specific application. Thus:

> Computational requirements can specify implementation of each object in a given object-oriented language.
>
> Operations and properties associated with an object can be partitioned according to the different roles played by that object.
>
> For each role, state transition graphs can be associated with incoming and outgoing messages, per the instantiated role and at each state.

Database designers should keep in mind that both endusers and software developers are likely to pose imprecise or vague queries. Hence there is a need for *query relevance* feedback in order to deal with fuzzy queries.

In this connection, some people working on object-oriented approaches advance the notion of *fuzzy objects*. They see them as a natural extension of artificial intelligence (AI) and fuzzy sets.★

Fuzzy objects are not, at least at this time, a central component of object-oriented solutions. The focal theme is different, centering on the ability to architecture a distributed database in an able manner and to partition an encapsulated object's operations and properties.

★I. Graham, *Object Oriented Methods,* Addison-Wesley, Boston, 1991.

During the 1990s and beyond, the main problem of information technology implementation will be efficient, network-wide database access. This is true not just in terms of accessing files and making table lookups, but also, if not primarily, in a multidatabase sense.

- The more we integrate the applications we already have and those we develop, the more we will need database-wide access and client-server models to support it.

This drive toward integrated networked solutions raises the important question of how an object database system can be best built. Must it depend on an object programming language being intimately involved, or should another way be chosen?

In terms of technical detail, an object database can be built with schema construction tools independent of an object programming language, and with query languages that can deliver information elements to languages such as C++. But considering such technical details before looking at the big picture is putting the cart before the horse.

First, attention must be paid to the *macroscopic* picture of database organization and its flexible restructuring as the ongoing application demands. Say that there are distributed databases along the lines shown in Table 4.1. Most of them are heterogeneous: An asset accounts application will need to bring together objects from databases 2, 13, 6, 5, 10, 9, and 15, in that order, and a liability accounts application will involve objects from databases 3, 12, 7, 14, 11, 1, 8, and 4.

Another application may address balances and rates, entering or querying current, historical, and/or budgeted data for each account. The object-oriented implementation may have to deal with ad-hoc queries or with database updating through a self-prompting process.

Cross-database queries may focus on average balances and rates for each account—or specific details. Objects can be used to generate comparative reports as well as in the calculation of trend and seasonality factors.

Parallelism will play a determinant role. In an applications perspective like the one we just saw, as well as the one we examined in Chapter 3, queries will be fed to all processors in parallel, and the response from each processor will be monitored. Computer addressable memories make feasible parallel search of all objects in the database.

Another major factor relating to query response, visualization, and user interfacing concerns language design and links to application code. A critical requirement is to provide as much power and flexibility as possible, so that the solution will be usable with a wide range of implementation, representation, and interaction styles, not all of which may be envisaged at the time of original design.

Best results can be achieved by designing a system that is conceptually

Table 4.1   Accounting Databases in a Distributed Environment

Capital and equity	Capital and surplus; capital notes; undivided profits
Cash and due from	Cash reserves; other banks; Federal Reserve; corporations; work in process
Demand deposits	Banks; individuals; businesses; others
Dividends and taxes	Common dividends; state taxes; federal taxes
Federal funds and repos	Federal funds sold; reverse repos
Loans	Commercial; real estate; installment; bank card; bankers' acceptances; overdrafts; other loans; loan loss reserve; unearned income
Money market and time deposits	Money market CDs; six-month CDs; large CDs; other CDs
Noninterest Expense	Salaries and benefits; information technology; occupancy expense; furniture and equipment; other noninterest expenses
Noninterest income	Trust department income; service charges; commission income; loan fee income; other income
Other assets	Property and equipment; other nonearning assets
Other liabilities	Deferred taxes; accounts payable; accrued expenses; accrued payables; other liabilities
Savings deposits	Regular savings; premium savings; NOW accounts; super-NOW accounts; IRA fixed rate; IRA floating rate
Securities	U.S. government and agency securities; municipals; money market deposits; treasury bills; trading accounts; Eurodollar deposits; others
Short-term borrowing	Federal funds purchased; Federal borrowings; different repos sold
Tax credits	Investment tax credit; carryforward tax credit

powerful, flexible, and extensible, thus minimizing possible future problems which cannot be foreseen. It is further promoted by using an appropriate

- Knowledgebank management system (KBMS), which handles the *intentional* database, using artificial intelligence concepts and constructs, and

- Database management systems (DBMS) that address the more classical extentional aspects of accessing and manipulating information elements.

Contrary to the general acceptance of relational database management systems, there is no consensus on the proper model for an object-oriented DBMS. One of the reasons is that this sort of DBMS is only now emerging; another is that object-oriented approaches are seen as a set of concepts drawn from several areas in information science, which researchers adapt to their ideosyncrasies and that of their problem domain.

Something similar can be said about object-oriented methodologies. There is precious little of this type of methodology available in commerce—and the same is true of development environments, though some (e.g., Ptech) are beginning to emerge.

There is, however, a need to consider the features that should be available in an object-oriented DBMS and its associated development environment. One important factor is the need to handle compound electronic documents, particularly those stored in a distributed database: Documents have a sequential organization that helps locate information, but the logical path for a reader is a hypermedia network that can scan the entire set of documents from reference to reference.

Every document reader, and the same reader at different times, may follow an entirely different path even when exploring the same topic. Hence we need technology that is able to organize heavily referenced databases in an effective manner, and object orientation is the way to do this.

The above discussion brings up the concept of hypermedia, which we discuss in the next section, but it also helps to underline that if the various object-oriented DBMS currently being developed or used are only a different sort of relational DBMS, they will hardly be worth the effort.

The needs of the 1990s and beyond will focus on the handling of compound electronic documents and multimedia, not just data. Any object-oriented DBMS that is data-centered is doomed to failure. Another challenge is that this new generation of DBMS must be fully networked in a manner absolutely transparent to application developers and users—but not necessarily to database administrators.

Object-oriented concepts can be helpful in a networking mission in the sense that they assist in organizing database contents into discrete *nodes* of information, where each node is considered as analogous to a short section of an encyclopaedia—virtual links are used to join these sections to one another to form the document as a whole, and the reader can browse through connected nodes simply by making references which deliver the next node.

This concept of organizing and retrieving information distinguishes the solution we are contemplating from other forms of storage searches. It provides direct, computer-based links to instantiate complex associative structures—a process that has important implications, as we will see in the following section.

4-3 HYPERMEDIA AND SEMANTIC MODELING

A *hypertext* document is a collection of nodes interconnected by links. The *nodes* contain objects, their information elements being images, voice, data, text, graphics, or other items such as animation sequences and interactive video. The links assure direct connection between specific source and destination nodes and, as the preceding section suggested, are interactively instantiated at user request.

The process is shown in Fig. 4.1 where the link labeled A has been activated by, say, a pointing device. Such activation causes window B to be displayed, followed by windows E, C, and G, each filled with information from the objects identified in the database. Since this presentation covers image, text, data and sound recording, it is *hypermedia:* The nodes are used to store information elements, with links between them that represent associations between objects; the user interface enables movements between concepts following runtime associations. The simplicity of this model is very appealing in terms of implementation.

Informal browsing permits the traversing of the database by following relationships from one object to another. This allows a user to find information, for instance, by browsing a class hierarchy or a version tree. Implementation requires meeting three goals:

1. Closing the semantic gap
2. Supporting navigational aspects by traversing relationships
3. Providing easy query access by selecting classes and their instantiation

Closing the semantic gap is fundamental to browsing, and browsing plays an important role in learning; we often rely on exploratory searches when acquainting ourselves with a new subject. However, as can be seen in the example in Fig. 4.2, a mechanism that supports navigational aspects calls for a nonlinear, graphlike structure where:

Organizational perspectives dominate and may be hierarchically expressed.

Each organizational entity is expressed in an object form.

The runtime instantiation of these objects is presented in the form of a logical expression for machine processing.

The nodes and their segments contain information elements.

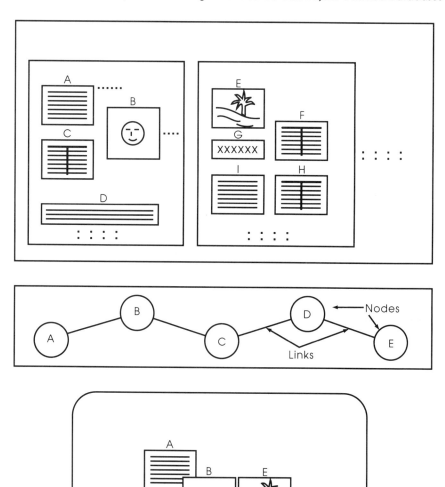

Figure 4.1 Networked objects in a multimedia sense.

The edges indicate relationship, such as annotations and references between nodes.

Links may be both *from* or *to* a node as well as within a node. With hypermedia, the nodes contain multimedia information elements, most so-

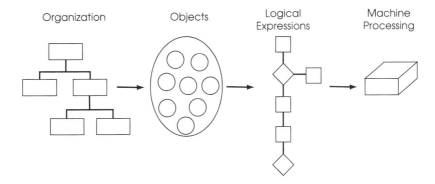

Figure 4.2   Successive steps in the composition of a semantic model.

lutions having extensible node and link types, and providing facilities for creating or linking nodes and browsing the graph. Hypermedia supports queries and can be enriched with versioning and context mechanisms.

A complete hypermedia system provides facilities for creating and editing nodes and links to form hypermedia documents, allowing any node to be connected to any other in a complex network. As Chapter 1 emphasized, such a network may well be expressed in a hierarchical form, but the hierarchy is short-lived and made only in response to requirements imposed by a particular instantiation. We also saw in Chapter 2 that such logical expressions may be in response to an ad-hoc query and also be subject to versioning. Either sunset clauses or garbage collection will do away with those objects whose real-time window has closed.

User-friendly and flexible interfaces must be provided for as long as a logical expression is active. These should assure a wide range of facilities to help retrieve other objects covered by the architecture of the hypermedia system.

A flexible interlinking of information elements aids exploratory browsing. It is also useful for integrating unstructured or semistructured information, and contributes to the goal of reusable software.

Hypermedia capabilities are very important with ad-hoc queries, whose programmatic interfaces go beyond the structures that a present-day database management system handles—such as those expressed by hierarchical, network and relational models. Such capabilities can be assisted through

- *Semantic* data models, including entity-relationship, which can assure more flexible data structures, and
- *Object orientation,* which helps provide facilities for storage, retrieval, and concurrency control.

Further progress requires the effective use of word objects that can be interpreted in a wider sense, so they can have polyvalent meanings within specified boundaries of the real world that defines the target system. This is the broadest possible concept behind objects denoting facts, physical or abstract entities, and relationships between any of these, but also the necessity of considering aspects of modeling—syntax, semantics, and behavior—in an integral manner.

For these reasons, semantic modeling and the associated notions we have mentioned have become an important force in the development of knowledgebank management systems (KBMS). They are an attempt to represent the meaning of an information element so that external schemata can be effectively expressed and object-oriented solutions can be more easily implemented.

Through semantic modeling, appropriate integrity constraints can be maintained, constructs can be clearly viewed as syntactic representations of an object within a target system, and inferences can be made to aid user interactivity. Also, ambiguity and fallacious associations can be avoided even though the operating environment is fuzzy.

4–4 THE OVERRIDING NEED FOR SOFTWARE REUSABILITY

Object orientation is an approach rather than a specific language construct. As we have seen, objects are designed as system components, but tools must also provide for handling *relationships.*

We have said that the object packages an entity (the information element), the operations applying to it (rules), and message-passing capabilities. Basically, the object is defined by its *behavior,* which is reflected in the object class, the set of instances of an object type.

But the handling of relationships and the manipulation of the objects themselves call for linguistic supports. The primary objective is to create a platform that allows a range of applications to be developed quickly and reliably, at low cost.

For instance, a linguistic construct such as a shell may consist of an object-oriented core, an evolving development database, a knowledgebank, and an application support environment. The core would incorporate the programming language, compiler, runtime utilities, and similar facilities.

Typically, the set of tools included in the shell is aimed at assisting the application developer in specifying requirements and in configuring the application within an object-oriented life cycle. This includes the need to select pertinent objects from the development database, design new objects, and configure the applications.

While these requirements are necessary, they are not sufficient. One of the overriding needs today is to be able to save, reconfigure, and reuse the modules of the applications that have been developed. We will require more of this facility in the future.

A cornerstone of this facility is the existence of features that permit the creation of multiple versions of a business model to reflect changes over time. New versions may be in design while older ones are in production, and any newer version should be able to include elements of older versions without the need to revalidate or reapprove their more detailed program-matic interfaces.★

Other issues pertinent to object-oriented solutions, such as procedural abstraction and data abstraction, help to promote program modularity, lead-ing to the development and acceptance of reusable code. By separating the specification of what is done, hence the abstraction, from how it is done, that is, the implementation, object-oriented programming provides the modularity necessary for programming solutions that present significant ad-vantages over those we have known and used in the past.

Still, the most important contribution of object-oriented program-ming is software reusability, which has become an overriding requirement of information systems. Reusability has been an elusive goal for many years, but today's object-oriented approaches bring it nearer to realization.

Software reusability has two inseparable requirements. One is know-ing how the various reusable parts can be isolated; the other is learning how those chunks can be composed together into new applications. To help in the study of different composition mechanisms, some researchers classify them into two categories, vertical composition and horizontal composition.

Vertical composition includes all mechanisms where a component ex-presses directly its dependency on another component. Vertical composi-tion has the drawback that reusability is one-way. While an object can re-ceive messages from any other object or procedure, when it sends a message it must know its destination exactly. This means that the reusable chunks must exist prior to reusing them, and the programmer needs to know the names, types, and semantics of such components.

The concept of verticality comes from the image that program chunks are piled on top of each other. Hence no higher level can exist without an underlying component. While vertical composition is far more common than horizontal composition, it is also more rigid.

Horizontal composition, on the other hand, supports independence be-tween components, which lie around in a flat manner—giving the appear-ance of horizontality. In this case, program structuring is done through binding operators providing interfaces, such as the fork and pipe operators in the UNIX shell. The interfaces serve to connect the standard output from one process to the standard input of another process.

★See also the discussions of temporal semantics in Chapters 12 and 13.

Horizontal approaches provide a binding mechanism that avoids the need to express directly which other components an object is depending on. As a result, such bindings are indirect and communication is flexible enough that a whole range of protocols can be implemented. Horizontal composition, however, is not possible in all situations.

4−5 THE DESIGN OF REUSABLE MODULES

The design of reusable modules is necessarily an iterative, evolutionary process, which can be assisted by object-oriented approaches. The methodology we have chosen for software reuse promotes a new way of thinking about system design. Software is built by composing prepackaged components, provided we assure a mechanism for organizing and decomposing programming products into encapsulated components—that is, objects and classes—and a mechanism for incrementally modifying characteristics such as inheritance, metacommands, and dynamic binding.

The potential for software reuse is both defined and constrained by object-user compatibility, as well as the ability of objects to fit together in a comprehensive and compatible manner. An able solution would support the extension of business modeling concepts in whatever direction a particular user might find important.

Modular modeling is a young discipline and may evolve in unpredicted ways during this decade. Therefore the solutions we provide must be able to support experimentation and evolution by their users. They must rest on sound theoretical premises while affording a development consistent with the growing needs of the user population.

Object-oriented programming reduces the cost and time required to produce complex applications by supporting the development of reusable software that is easier to enhance and maintain. It also makes it simpler to model real-world entities, because of its ability to imply relationships among objects, and among operations that can be performed on objects.

Using a high-performance, object-oriented database management system can reduce the time and cost of development, with the DBMS taking responsibility for data management and freeing the developer to add functionality and value to the software. This in turn reduces the effort necessary to manipulate complex, heterogeneous databases and at the same time improves modularity and extensibility. It is therefore not surprising that object-oriented techniques are gaining support in a variety of applications where developers have discovered the limitations of conventional procedural paradigms.

As we have noted, object orientation frees applications, particularly complex applications, from record-based data. This is indispensable for two- and three-dimensional graphical images, and for multimedia applications that include voice, image, text, data, and graphics. It is for this reason that object-oriented databases offer an ideal substrate for applications such as mechanical and electrical engineering, architectural design, construction engineering, and mapping purposes such as exist in topology, logistics, finance, and medical imaging, as well as computer-aided software engineering.

The contribution of object solutions to the implementation of a strategy of reusable software has much to do with language schemata, which dominate database usage. Within a database schema there exist different language views. The intersections between the views contain objects that can be reused by, say, two different languages. This, however, does not happen often.

The database schema is reflected in all application objects that were built by one particular language. A language view includes all those objects that were constructed and can be reused in that particular language.

For example, Fig. 4.3 shows the intersection of schema 1 and schema 2, corresponding to two different DBMS. DBMS 1 supports languages A and B; DBMS 2 supports languages B and C. Languages A and C have no view intersection. The common area of B and C is that of objects that can be reused by either of the two languages.

These notions are fundamental to the design of reusable modules. From a data structure viewpoint, the scope of DBMS schema and language view is a virtual homogeneity. Object solutions assist by intersecting application schemata within the language view.

An interesting question in the context of software reuse is the management of *polymorphism* (defined in Chapter 2) and the associated recognition of concept equivalances between different languages. A good way to proceed is to look for semantic equivalences: The database administrator (DBA) re-

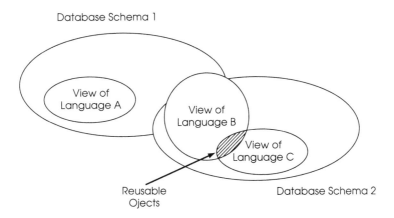

Figure 4.3 Database schemata and language views.

trieves the concepts of languages that are already known, and compares them with the concepts of the language to be added to the system, creating a profile and reuse capability.

Another vital aspect is comparison between language concepts already known to the system and new ones. This helps in understanding polymorphism and concept equivalences. It can also provide an automated support of reuse definition.

A valuable extension can be the inclusion of a world model about language types, as well as a reasoning mechanism to perform language views in the sense of polymorphism. Such an approach will permit the system to make decisions about parametric and inherited polymorphism, while more classical conversion routines merely support an ad-hoc approach.

4–6 SOFTWARE REUSE AND CULTURAL ISSUES

One of the leading American service companies mentioned, during our May 1991 meeting in Dallas, that by far the major issue for a change to object orientation is *cultural*. Part and parcel of this issue, which has a great deal to do with productivity, is to accept the principle of software reuse.

Leading-edge companies know by experience that software reuse is far from being a catchword or a miracle maker. Everyone, from computer specialists to endusers, must understand the benefits to be obtained, focus on the principle of reuse, and do so even if, because of past habits, this is difficult.

Some people say that, particularly in an interactive environment, software reuse is a work of art. That may be so, but art has its principles. Object orientation and knowledge engineering are two of them.

Another necessity is to identify code that is common across applications and therefore should be reusable. This can be done, but there are difficulties to overcome, including problems such as deadlines.

The policies we establish for software review must account for the fact that we need both to *deliver* applications faster and to *reduce* application development time and cost. The tools we choose must meet user requirements, building applications that are resilient to change and at the same time produce higher-quality software.

The principle of software reuse permits us to protect existing investments without compromising future progress. Many leading companies have chosen object orientation to take maximum advantage of reuse. There are implications deriving from this policy decision, as a senior corporate executive suggested:

1. Establishing a corporate class library, as a central location for storing object definitions

2. Managing the growth, maintenance, and use of the corporate class library, as a major corporate resource

3. Making it easier for everybody to reuse rather than rewrite software

4. Having both information elements and instructions accessible as one scalable logical entity to the developer

5. Supporting in an able manner the chosen object-oriented development procedures

6. Seeing to it that any chosen object development process and methodology supports the corporate class library in an efficient way.

Present-day realities are different from those that prevailed 10 or even 5 years ago. For instance, in avant-garde companies information scientists and users are collaborating in software development through prototypes. By means of computer-assisted software engineering, they aim to integrate device capabilities and thus further enhance the popularization of computers and communications systems.

The time is past when only programming experts could write code for computers. Not only are endusers now programming in manufacturing, finance, governmental, and other organizations, but also home computers have become popular, widely spreading computer literacy.

A growing spectrum of individuals, other than computer professionals, use personal computers, workstations, and word processors incorporated in networks. They do so from their offices and homes. Various kinds of computers have been integrated into industrial and business chores as the informatization of society is expanding.

The challenges posed by this broadening horizon of computer usage have to be faced in a simple and sustainable manner. Object-oriented solutions can help, by promoting both simplicity and flexibility.

But corporate practices must also adapt to this new policy. One solution is to have a team of people who make reusable components, motivating them and providing them with appropriate tools—while realistically appreciating that there are, as yet, no ideal means for doing so on a large scale.

"We must focus on reuse, but the implementation of such policy brings major implications," said one of the cognizant people in the information technology domain. "We all agree that reuse is good and necessary but few throughout the organization are willing to productize and support a common library. Clear top management directives can make the difference."

Chapter 5

Why an Object Database?

5-1 INTRODUCTION

In an environment of major technological change, databases have been the foundation for managing corporate information resources. It is through database management techniques and products that organizations seize the opportunities offered by advances in computer processing—ranging from real-time transactional applications to trading operations, decision support, and experimentation on market conditions.

Successful organizations have always capitalized on data resource management, and they have done so in the context of migrating from classical data processing to more sophisticated applications domains. Quite recently, the focus has been on object-oriented modeling, a development that significantly alters the way business is done, enabling improvements in productivity and in methodologies that greatly affect the bottom line.

Object-oriented databases should be seen within this context. Part of the challenge is the ability to:

Define whether the changes are detailed or coarse

Effectively implement a highly distributed environment

Accommodate multimedia-type applications

Know what to do about recovery from crashes and other problems

Some functions that have been typically handled by DBMS must now be developed all over again because of the distributed characteristics of the environment in which we work today. The premise is that this can best be achieved with an object orientation.

The inefficient handling of distributed database operations has become a major constraint on dispersing functions and information elements as required by business perspectives. Object-oriented approaches may make this less of a barrier and improve networking database capabilities.

Some people may say that, except for a few examples, distributed databases do not exist yet. Such people think they are wrong. Big corporations have for several years struggled with a variety of different database systems from different vendors that have developed separately.

In general, these systems cannot talk to each other, which is the *heterogeneous* database problem. In all these cases, it is not the hardware that is important, but the software. Heterogeneous systems are in principle distributed—even if virtually so.

When two file management systems or DBMS (e.g., VSAM, IMS, DB2) are totally different and incompatible, then there is heterogeneity on the same engine. Therefore, it is much better to have a physically and logically distributed environment than an unmanageable mammoth with internal contractions.

Classical database management software does not provide for the possibility that reference information elements or invoked files may be on a variety of machines accessible through a network. As a result, the developer of a distributed application is forced to invest in the elements necessary to reach remote database functions, provide ad hoc the routines for recovering from network failures, and assure cross-node security every time the database network is revamped.

With classical records management approaches, the provision of such facilities time and again proves a serious barrier, adding considerable expense and complexity to the application, as well as requiring skills beyond those of most systems programmers.

An object orientation, by contrast, provides a direct and natural representation of rules and information elements in distributed business problems. The representation starts with the development of extensible and reusable modules as discussed in Chapter 4.

Combining object-oriented concepts with distributed database capabilities results in powerful systems that may become dominant in the 1990s. This is a necessary evolutionary step toward the implementation of intelligent databases.

5–2 A NEW LOOK AT THE DATABASE UTILITY

Together with networks, databases have become the single most important component in information technology environment. Integration requires sharing of multimedia (text, data, graphics, image, voice) system-wide. There are two types of sharing, referential sharing and concurrent sharing.

In *referential sharing,* multiple applications or classes share a common object. For example, the bill of materials is part of product design as well as of inventory control procedures and of acquisition lists. In banking applications, current account information is integral to demand deposit operations, but so are loans, securities, and foreign exchange.

In the transition from centralized to departmental processing and to personal workstations, referential operations are key to the effective distribution of computing resources. With referential sharing, hypermedia links can be used effectively to navigate between objects.

The second type of sharing is the *concurrent sharing* of objects within an applications environment. A great deal of activity by database management systems is dedicated to controlling concurrent access to databases by applications programs, terminals, or multiple endusers.

It is nonetheless true that, by and large, the appropriate tools are still missing. Operating system, DBMS, and network primitives—as well as utilities—are not presently in place to support a distributed object environment, or even a distributed relational world.

There are some exceptions to this statement. The AI-enriched UNIX OS, built by Carnegie-Mellon University Mach, can provide support for sharing objects over distributed sites. But an operating system cannot do everything, there is a whole world of basic software that should work in synergy.

Within this context, the mission of an object-oriented database utility should be that of combining the features of objects with traditional database capabilities. The goal is the structuring of referential and concurrent sharing of objects through the support of meta concepts, data abstraction, and inheritance.

The sales-inventory-production application shown in Fig. 5.1 helps demonstrate the referential and concurrent sharing necessary in a fabrication system. The basic input, sales orders, will be algorithmically handled several times in forecasting, inventory management, and production scheduling, providing generations of information elements. These operations will typically involve different functional databases, which may be heterogeneous. They will be carried out in a distributed sense, factory by factory, where more incompatibilities are added. Yet the distributed information elements must circulate freely in this network, the forecasting and planning algorithms must be valid company-wide, and management reports such as profit plans must be consolidated.

The distributed database system we develop must be able to handle both simple and complex transactions as well as analytical queries that typically need to access several, often heterogeneous databases. This means accessing a logical network whose nodes are served by different, often incompatible hardware, software, and data structures.

To operate such a system we need a mechanism able to regulate secu-

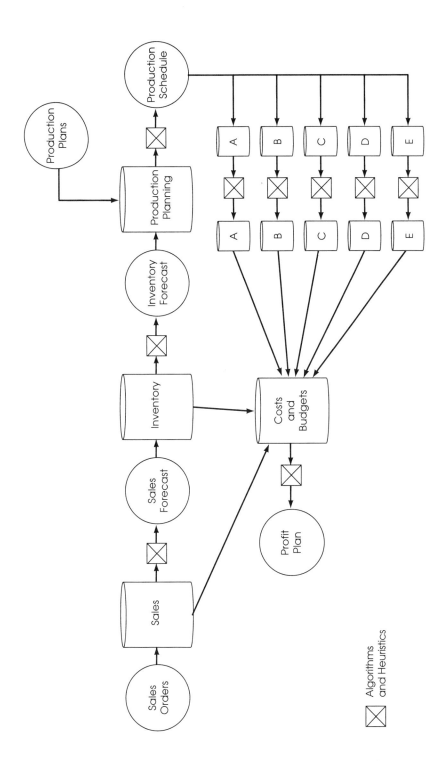

Figure 5.1 Referential and concurrent sharing in a planning system.

Algorithms and Heuristics

rity and contention. We also have to look in an integrative way into database contents—using an approach that is transparent to the user.

Among the functionalities to be added to the database utility are integrity, versioning, and control of a distributed environment of objects. The aim is to create a true repository of information elements shared by multiple platforms, by removing the semantic gap between an application domain and its representation. To reach this goal we must overcome some important constraints:

1. The heterogeneity in the design of information elements to be encapsulated within objects
2. The heterogeneity of programs running within the same applications environment
3. Internal cultural issues in system usage, which magnify and perpetuate these heterogeneity issues
4. Requirements for increasingly rapid transaction and message turn-around
5. The specificity of hardware and software characteristics, which add further to heterogeneity

The first and second constraints have rarely been accounted for in a rational manner. All software now in operation or even in development assumes that the schematic knowledge is the same. In reality, however, not only are databases different but also, as we integrate a variety of procedures, we find great diversity in data structures and handling approaches. This has significant consequences in information technology, as the most basic requirement, and the main problem, is *data access*—that is, not just accessing some files and doing table lookups, but implementing an effectively distributed and dynamic access database-wide sense.

Table 5.1 summarizes the results of a recent study that estimated the principal requirements of five different implementation areas. Two of these application domains require number crunching; three deal with long transactions; but all five need effective database access.

5-3 THE ROLE OF META-MODELS IN VIRTUAL HOMOGENEITY

Section 2 noted some deep-rooted incompatibilities in current database practices. Moving data in a networked sense and deciding which side will have computing responsibility is a dynamic problem, and few companies are prepared to address it. One major American corporation recently canceled a multiyear project to build a company-wide distributed database, not

Table 5.1   Principal Requirements of Five Areas of Implementation

	Clearing	Lending	Settlement	Cash	Reporting
Number crunching		X	X		
Long transactions	X	X	X		
Effective database access	X	X	X	X	X

because it could not achieve a unified design or meta-model, but because the network portion could not be made workable and efficient.

Object-oriented solutions can be of help in these cases, but the network and load-balancing problems persist. As emphasized since the beginning of this book, object solutions are not expected to answer all problems or to perform miracles. They should be looked at as stepping stones that provide some better tools.

We have also spoken in preceding chapters of the need to take the proverbial long, hard look. The first step in a successful database project is the *macroscopic* view. Yet most systems analysts become so involved in the details that they lose track of the project's overall design—and of its precise goals.

The realization of the existence of this danger has led serious researchers to the proposition that in order to manage distributed databases, we have to establish a meta-model underlying the system running the distributed database as if all information elements were in the same structure and format.

However, knowledge about meta-models applied within the context of distributed databases is still very weak. Though work in this direction started in the early 1980s, such work still proceeds very slowly.

One of the projects focusing on a meta-model approach, LOOM (University of Southern California, Los Angeles), divides the problem into two levels of reference: (1) *modification,* which is hard to do; and (2) *retrieval,* which is a relatively more easy proposition, though at times it can become complex too. LOOM rests on first-order logic, uses nonautomatic functions for default, employs fuzzy sets (possibility theory) as well as unitary predicates, and is object-oriented. The *default* layer is based on assumptions. A higher level is that of *constraints;* still higher are the *definitions.* A definition language addresses itself to predicates of arbitrary complexity.

The goal is to provide both an object-based approach and a much more flexible means of database manipulation than current shells can support. An example on the *definition level* is a certified check. The *constraint level* is the legend, "Not valid over $5000." The *assumption* is that the issuer was in the city where the check was issued. The *facts* are the amount and date.

This four-level default structure can avoid the trap that its component levels look like firm assertions. By contrast, the outer behavior layer is extralogical and, in the LOOM project, it is expressed through sets by using possibility theory. Its expression includes methodology, heuristic rules, operators, and search procedures.

Rules are the actual triggers. Instances can go in and out of a frame, a frame being like a query. Declarative facilities are added, as rules are procedural, not declarative. The methodology includes the notion of setting up a query by reformulation.

An integral part of this solution is a *classifier,* able to take two definitions and tell whether one specializes the other. Hence it analyzes the implications included in a statement. This is an important feature in multiple databases and distributed information structures. A distinction is made between handling

- *Data*—facts, values, episodes that change with high degree of frequency—and
- *Knowledge,* which tends to accumulate, but changes much more slowly.

The classifier can help organize the intentional knowledge in a hierarchy. It requires the notion of *inconsistency,* which calls for more semantics than is supported by current logic programming languages. As current research helps document, the mapping of different knowledgebanks in an object-oriented solution is one of the hardest tasks ahead.

The links and relationships among entities in the complex real world are represented and manipulated directly. This approach achieves its modeling capability through object-based concepts while trying to alleviate the mismatch between heterogenous programming languages and incompatible data structures. Most important, the method just described could not be used without object-oriented concepts.

$5-4$ APPLICATIONS DOMAINS FOR OBJECT DATABASES

Earlier chapters have emphasized a number of advantages associated with object-based solutions: reuse of existing software, care for life-cycle evolution, a mechanism for incorporating software quality objectives, as well as early elimination of unattractive alternatives. It was also suggested that a conceptual framework is of fundamental importance, and as we will see in Chapters 9 and 10. This is done through prototyping.

A conceptual framework is most necessary in connection with the design of object-oriented databases and their access through a query language or retrieval paradigm. For both queries and transactions, we need to understand the requirements posed by distributed resources, including a redefinition of concepts leading toward the integration of global database approaches with existing data processing procedures and their information elements (Fig. 5.2). The premise is that object-oriented solutions can help.

Provision also has to be made for algorithmic and heuristic processing, since current database languages provide little support for complex computations. Object-oriented approaches also aim to assure the necessary expressive power for performing complex computations associated with an application.

The need for associating specially adapted programming products to the object database metaphors has been present for some time. The problems that have been encountered with traditional approaches have meant that today the main markets for object-oriented solutions are:

1. Computer-aided design (CAD)
2. Computer-aided manufacturing (CAM)

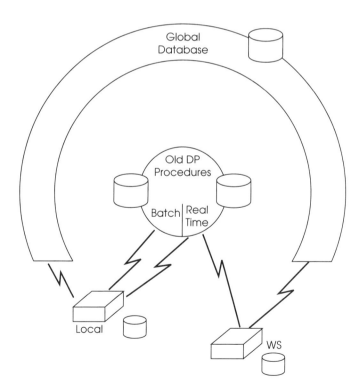

Figure 5.2   Object orientation in a distributed database environment.

   3. Computer-integrated manufacturing (CIM)
   4. Complex market-oriented operations (such as Forex and securities)
   5. Cross-functional projects (such as risk management)
   6. Cross-departmental projects (for instance, cost control)
   7. Cartographical implementations
   8. Computer-assisted software engineering (CASE)
   9. Office automation (OA)

Not only are the characteristics of these applications different from traditional accounting-type routines, but for some of them, such as office automation, there exist rather rich libraries of programming products that are
well accepted by the user communities. What particularly characterizes
these applications, however, is that they present stringent requirements in
terms of database manipulation.

   There is another fundamental reason why CAD, CAM, CIM, risk
management, cost control, CASE, and office automation applications tend
toward object-oriented, multimedia databases. They all require fast-grow-
ing amounts of computer storage, and the connections between the information elements in storage is much more complex than in classical data processing. In many cases, database size and complexity make it nearly
impossible to cluster related multimedia information elements (or even
data) in an effective manner through preestablished paradigms, as has been
done for nearly 40 years. A considerable amount of navigation is necessary
to access and update such databases—object orientation presents a demon-
strable advantage.

5-5 HANDLING AD-HOC QUERIES

Another vital reason for the growing interest in object databases is the fast-
increasing practice of *ad-hoc queries.*★ These can be handled only with great
difficulty, if at all, by databases that are heterogenous in general context and
hierarchically oriented in their design, or too dispersed in a relational sense.
But ad-hoc queries can be handled rather efficiently through an object orientation, particularly if the underlying layer is relational and the metalayer
benefits from knowledge engineering.

   Some people may challenge this statement, saying that it is not clear
why object databases are better at ad-hoc queries than well-designed relational databases. Others may add that object DBMS are not known for

---

   ★We do not mean to imply that object approaches can solve all ad-hoc query problems,
but as existing DBMS are increasingly unable to handle complexity, it is worthwhile to try
them.

speed in commercial environments, citing Ontologic's withdrawal of Vbase due to criticism of its performance.

Still other people suggest, not without reason, that the best-performing current object database management approaches often use a file server as an object store. They download a set of objects to a high-performance worksta-tion, which manipulates the objects and cuts down on network traffic. This, however, is not a very good solution for sharing objects that change a lot.

The message the careful reader will get from such statements is that we are far from having a unanimous opinion on what can and what cannot be done through object approaches. At the same time, however, many expe-rienced systems people are willing to try them, and they find both strengths and weaknesses in the results.

Object-oriented databases can also be valid means in applications that require information hiding and associated paradigms for manipulating data. In applications such as computer-aided design, object-oriented data models integrate object primitives to simplify the organization of and access to databases. The same is true of risk management.

As a matter of fact, the term object-oriented data model originated from work with CAD, and it was again in CAD applications that it was es-tablished that whether hierarchical, network, or relational, traditional DBMS:

Underperform in concurrent sharing environments

Lack the necessary modeling primitives and associated flexibility

Cannot help in supporting the growing sophistication of application perspectives

Relational approaches, for example, impose a normal form constraint: The object space must be mapped into a collection of tables (flat relations). As a result, much of the inherent semantics of complex object composition is lost.

As we will see when we discuss the need to go beyond relational databases, there have been several attempts to address this issue by introduc-ing semantically richer data models. Various postrelational models have been tried, including semantic data models, and complex object data mod-els, but the fact remains that in superimposing these concepts on old database structures we reduce both efficiency and flexibility—without nec-essarily obtaining the desired results.

This fast will be much better exemplified after the subject of object-oriented programming has been introduced, in Chapter 7. More precisely Object SQL (OSQL) by Texas Instruments, Hewlett-Packard, and others, will be presented as an example of the competitive advantages to be pro-vided, in a query environment, through an object solution.

Complex object data models aim at incrementally extending the relational approach so as to allow more expressible queries. This makes it necessary to introduce:

Tuple-level attributes and nested relations
An approach to tuple constructors
Sets of names, integers, and other atomic values
The concept of object identity

While these approaches and the options they present make feasible more direct representations in the persistent object space, they do not answer all object-related requirements. For instance, it may be desirable to have a relation nested within another relation. There have been a number of nested relational models, but none seems to have given a truly satisfactory outcome.

5-6 IS COMPLEXITY THE BEST SOLUTION?

The message of the discussion in Section 3 is that in building more general object models on top of a collection of basic types and using object constructors such as sets and tuples, we end up with very complex object data models. On one side, these extensions help modernize the use of relational databases, carrying them toward an object-oriented environment. But on the other hand, they complicate the representation process and subsequent object handling.

We have to return to the fundamentals in order to appreciate the possible effects of complexity. Data types are used to describe a set of objects with the same representation; typically, a number of operations will be associated with each data type.

The notion of an abstract data type extends the foregoing concept by making transparent the implementation of the user-defined operations associated with a given data type. Languages that support such approach are able to define data structures as well as the operations used to manipulate their instances. All manipulations of occurrences of a data type are done through operations associated with that data type; such operations should be simple in principle, which is not the case with the superposition of different approaches. We use objects to increase the simplicity of an implementation—both conceptually and computationally.

We should never lose sight of the fact that object orientation is a metaphoric design tool that seeks to naturally model real-world objects and processes with appropriately chosen configurational objects and classes. This makes it easier to construct systems out of individual components, without the complexities embedded in older, less elegant approaches. The appeal of object orientation is that it provides clearer concepts and better tools, facilitating the modeling and representation of real-life situations. But the advantages of this approach can be lost if we start with complexity in representation. Our goal is to see how otherwise complex problems can be expressed easily and naturally—not the other way around.

Therefore, the overriding need is for basically straightforward methodologies that allow construction of software systems from modularized reusable software units, which should themselves be simple and comprehensive. This is the real *raison d'être* of object-oriented databases and object-based programming.

In past years, complex object data models may have been necessary because of the need to use existing tools in serving the ever-developing goals in database administration and management. This, however, does not mean that all approaches are necessarily rational. At times they can be counterproductive.

Today we have tools, largely knowledge engineering oriented, that are able to remedy this situation. As an example, Fig. 5.3 presents a three-layered approach to the selection of tools, from shell to AI language and conventional programming routines.

If the aim of sustaining a simple and comprehensive approach throughout database design and software development is to be maintained, then we should use every tool at our disposition to reach such goal. One example is functional decomposition: What does the system *do,* versus what is its *function?*

Shell	– Rapid Prototyping – Saving Time, Labor – Paying In Cycles

AI Language	– Designed for Logical Processes
	– Little Support for
	  • User Interfaces
	  • KBMS/DBMS
	  • Development and Debugging

Conventional Language	– Use with Workstations – Saving Cycles – Paying in Time, Labor

Figure 5.3   Layers of reference in expert systems programming.

Within the perspective of a distributed databases implementation, the functional decomposition technique can help in upholding reasonable simplicity. It is based on (1) the identification of key factors entering the problem domain, (2) the interpretation of the problem space and associated hypotheses, and (3) its translation to solution space as an interdependent set of functions.

System design of a database environment can be seen as a set of these functions that operate on objects. In a global sense, this will require describing the interconnection of so far independently operating resources as well as providing programmatic interfaces for networking purposes.

Functional decomposition is more or less a top–down design methodology and, as such, it imposes some discipline. It has, however, the disadvantages that it takes no account of evolutionary changes, the system is characterized by a single function (a questionable concept), and it does not encourage reusability.

Such disadvantages run contrary to object-type implementation. Therefore, beyond helping in a transition period, functional decomposition may not be the answer to the problem on hand.

How conflicts between applications goals and design solutions take place is shown in Fig. 5.4. The database design process simultaneously addresses four different goals, which happen to be interrelated up to a point, and therefore influence one another. Further influence comes as a result of both testing and the evolution of new requirements.

In the specific case under discussion, the conflict that exists in terms of

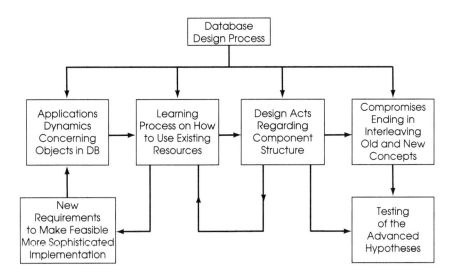

Figure 5.4   Paradigm of a structured approach to database design.

database design is between *simplicity* and *complexity*. It comes into focus in attempts to use the information obtainable from the object-based system and its potential refinements for implementation in a target system that uses already existing database components.

While this can be done in different ways, a layered approach using meta-levels is the best alternative. The Japanese Institute for New Generation Computer Technology (ICOT) has provided evidence that the conflict can be resolved by creating a two-layered structure that distinguishes between:

- *Intentional databases* (IDB), which have a knowledge bank with domain definition, rules, and heuristics, and
- *Extentional databases* (EDB), which can be flat files of objects whose behavior is commanded by the IDB.

This two-layered approach simplifies the whole issue of database management and permits effective integration of new and old components. The intentional database acts as a *meta-layer* to the extentional database. It imposes constraints and therefore rules of conduct, to which the objects in the extentional database must conform.

6

Object-Oriented Paradigms and Long Transactions

6-1 INTRODUCTION

As we will see in Chapter 7 when we discuss software solutions, an object program is a construct of interacting objects that encapsulate information elements (IE) and the algorithms that specify the behavior of the IE. Operations on an object can take place only through a well-defined interface to the object's behavior, the actual implementation of such behavior being hidden from every user but the designer and the database administrator.

The routines that act on an object are the primary means through which the IE, encapsulated in that object, may be manipulated or modified.

We also said that other objects invoke a given object's resources by sending a message, the target object interprets that message, and the appropriate action is performed.

This is the simplest form of an object-oriented paradigm. The evoked action (or method) uses known components: information elements and procedures, as well as encapsulation and interfacing.

Returning for a moment to the reference made in Chapter 5 regarding decomposition, a high-level analysis will be accomplished on an object-oriented approach not only in terms of objects, but also in terms of the services they provide. Each service will help define the properties and behavior of a set of common objects, or more precisely instances of classes created as a program is running.

This identifies another limitation of functional decomposition, which becomes obvious when we account for the fact that each object has the same number and types of fields, and differs from other objects only in the class of values stored in those fields. While class templates provide a basis for modularity, leverage is really gained by the ability to define one class of objects in terms of other classes—which requires new departures.

6–2 AN OBJECT-ORIENTED PARADIGM IN THE DATABASE

In order to capitalize on the leverage discussed in Section 1, through methodologies currently being developed for object-oriented databases, and associated programming approaches, several organizations have chosen the solution of (1) identifying existing library classes, (2) extending these by using inheritance, and (3) developing new classes as requirements evolve.

Objects descending from the same parent class are essentially compatible. Each understands the same messages as the others, yet each performs the task in its own way.

This modularity allows the transparent creation and insertion of new class instances into the program, but to be implemented in an able manner, it also calls for an object-oriented methodology, starting at the design level. This path is feasible, but there are problems.

One of the problems is that most of the object-oriented database design and development approaches available to date are not *generic,* having been structured specifically with some programming language in mind. Furthermore, most of the software tools being used are not truly object-oriented, and some key features of the basic paradigms, such as inheritance, are not addressed directly. These shortcomings have detrimental effects on both database management and programming.

A rational methodology will start at the database level, focusing on object-based paradigms. It will elaborate on classes and their characteristics, identify objects and attributes, cover operations affecting objects, establish visibility, and work out rational interfaces. These are necessary conditions for implementing a fundamental object solution, always keeping in mind the characteristic prerequisites of which we spoke in Chapters 1 and 2: Meta, inheritance, equilibration, data abstraction and so on. This is precisely what the IDB-EDB approach does.

As we have seen in the preceding chapters, some of the preconditions in an object-oriented environment stand at a system level. Others are more strictly related to design and implementation details. But together such preconditions help provide:

Direct support of object concepts
Development of sharable objects
Persistent constructs

Dynamic schema evolution
Queries on class lattices
Version management capabilities

The observance of such conditions is also crucial in multimedia applications. Flexibility and modularity are key, as the now-developing ad-hoc multimedia systems do not have a persistent object image, in contrast to more classical databases and their more elementary transactions, such as account balances in banking or inventory balances in manufacturing.

Sophisticated office automation systems were the first to see the need for polyvalence of the type we are talking. They did so by underlining requirements for an extensible framework able to support the capture, storage, retrieval, and visualization of information elements—and doing so interactively with an increasing content of multimedia information.

6-3 DATABASE-WIDE OBJECT IDENTIFICATION

The identification of appropriate objects within the database must not be limited to those singled out in the requirement-specification stage. Not only is it generally anticipated that well-designed object classes will be used repetitively, but also the identification of objects (and ultimately of classes) will de facto define the operations affecting these objects, the services they offer, and the varients they need to have.

Proper identification and classification has proved fundamental in establishing interactions between objects in terms of services required and services rendered. This is written in an any-to-any sense, that is,

Cross-database
Any object to any object
Any location to any location
Any time to any time

In a dynamic environment like those rapidly developing in databasing, we never know in advance which object will be needed at any given time. Hence there is a need for steady accessibility, valid notation, and any-to-any connectivity.

Object notation pertains to design level as well as to the classes of runtime objects prior to and during implementation. Interrelationships between design objects and classes can and should be represented through different stages of the life cycle.

Object identification should also account for the transition that has taken place in databases, which is reflected in Table 6.1. Such transition changes the frame of reference of what is and what is not a database, as well

Table 6.1   The Transition Taking Place in Databases

From	To
1. Computer words, fields, files, records	1. Objects and episodic memory structure
2. Hard data	2. Soft data (projections, extrapolations, forecasts and hypotheses)
3. Data	3. Multimedia (text, documents, data, image, voice, graphics)
4. Preestablished queries	4. Ad-hoc queries
5. Crisp queries	5. Fuzzy queries
6. Simple retrieval	6. Complex retrieval from distributed databases
7. Keywords	7. Memory-based reasoning
8. *As is* presentation	8. Analytical evaluation

as the ways and means to be used for handling the polyvalent database concepts outlined in Table 6.1.

Old hierarchical concepts in notation pertinent to the computer world—fields, files, records—do not constitute an efficient approach in object orientation. New solutions that make use of knowledge engineering and rest on classification are necessary.★

With regard to object-based solutions, in Chapter 1 we spoke of the distinction made by Dr. McLeod between *record-based* database models and an *episodic memory* organization. We should now add that the latter is not devoid of structure, but structuring involves only those objects pertinent to an instantiation, and it dissolves as fast as this particular instantiation ends.

An electronic funds transfer environment provides an example. Objects about client accounts and management accounts exist at headquarters and in branch offices (BOs). They reside in distributed databases and have to be instantiated both for transmission and for reporting reasons, as shown in Figure 6.1. This can be handled through massive, specialized code the way it has been done for over 35 years, or it can be approached in an object-oriented manner through proper identification and instantiation.

The second alternative is more efficient than the first because, in a distributed database landscape, unique and unambiguous identification is a de-

★See also D. N. Chorafas, *The Handbook of Databases and Relational DBMS,* TAB Books/McGraw-Hill, New York, 1989.

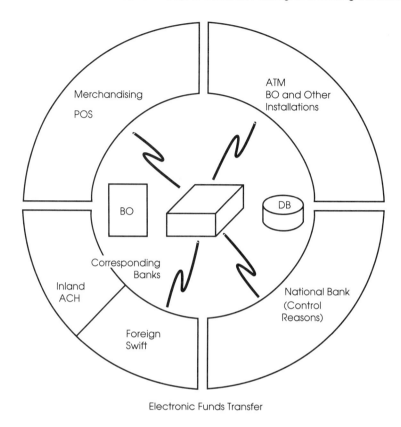

Electronic Funds Transfer

Figure 6.1 Communicating subsystems in a financial environment.

manding task using traditional methods. The organizational prerequisite is *object classification.* Once the classification is done properly, identification is fairly simple—provided we have clear concepts and the appropriate supports.

6-4 OBJECT CLASSIFICATION IN A DISTRIBUTED ENVIRONMENT

Classification and identification of all objects in a distributed database environment is a challenging job, but it can be done. A possible hindrance lies in programming languages. The decision of whether or not to represent embedded classes, and how to identify them, reflects the language being used. With some object-based programmatic approaches, no embedding is possible. To bypass this limitation, several approaches are possible:

Classes may refer to other classes, typically by using pointers and anchors.

Attributes of a given abstract data type inside a class amount to reference to an object, hence a single instantiation.

The class may define the implementation of that abstract data type. At the top level, an object of higher abstraction would be represented by a single piece of notation.

This approach has its limitations, particularly as more objects are identified within a detailed database design.

The handling of classes requires an iterative analysis of whether a new organization will be useful. This creates the need for inheritance diagrams, but helps assure that future projects can reuse the structure without having to redesign class and object relationships. The trick is to proceed cautiously and do the proper experimentation.

As Chapter 4 outlined, prototyping helps in providing constructive feedback, assuring that object identification requirements receive the appropriate documentation and clarification. Such feedback is made possible by object-oriented techniques, which help provide a more reliable and robust database structure.

As this discussion documents, methodological class design and rational system development go together. System development influences class design, while the latter affects implementation. This life-cycle perspective occurs for different classes at different times within an operational environment.

A process of consecutive refinement also has to be ensured. The specification of a class is itself a refinement resulting from the specification of the system, which describes the semantics of the class and the services it renders.

While classification should be system-wide, identification can start with the persistent objects that can be handled early in the development cycle. These may be presented to programmers as object classes to be handled at a rather early stage, with a degree of confidence that even if system specifications change, such classes stand a good chance of remaining invariant.

The fact that some classes can undergo detailed system design and be implemented on an *a priori* basis makes system analysis and database design a much easier process. Up to a point, this compensates for the fact that there is no single object-oriented model of software life cycle that has yet gained universal acceptance.

By capitalizing on the features and functionality supported through an object orientation, coordination between database design and system analysis can be encouraged. When this is done, the resulting artifact may be more robust and at the same time more flexible. The result is a more easily maintainable solution that is closer to the users' requirements.

6–5 TRANSACTION PROCESSING IN AN OBJECT DATABASE

It is hardly necessary to underline the need for consistency in the design of an object-oriented database. This is just as true of the availability of agile commands that are valid in a fully distributed sense as it is of the runtime (and compile time) description of the abstract data types used to identify solution space objects.

Careful study of object-oriented requirements specifications will help discover if there is a large degree of overlap between object design and systems design. One of the best approaches to controlling overlapping and possibly contradictory definitions is to establish projected data flows between active objects, keeping in mind that:

> The database is the root of the consistent object space.
>
> Both default clauses and constraints must be applied in a distributed database sense.
>
> Every object reachable from this database root must itself be consistent.

Using this approach, database management systems and programming languages should provide a basis for database-wide consequence, even if the DBMS and data structures are heterogeneous.

Instantiation variables should contain the names of all objects that serve as the roots of such consistent object space. Only objects thus specified can be shared and accessed through different transactions (or queries), with the user assured access rights in the database under authentication and authorization conditions.

These qualities are upheld through an object-type orientation, and have been found to be quite helpful in a query and/or transaction environment. Transactions are typically atomic, and their program is either executed entirely or not at all: *If* the user (software, terminal, enduser) performs updates to the persistent database related to a given transaction, *then* either all the updates must be visible to the outside world or none must be seen.

This consistency aspect and all related functionality must be supported by database languages and their primitives. But consistency per se is a meta concept.

Under these basic principles come the specific applications. How to execute an on-line transaction, in a classical sense, has been known since the late 1960s, with the first implementation of realtime in banking; it does not need to be repeated.

What should be emphasized is that even in an object-oriented environment with different database systems the actual syntax of the transaction as well as the begin, commit, and abort mechanisms may differ. Here, too, a consistency clause is needed, and in principle it is easier to implement within an object environment than otherwise.

Whether the overall intention and semantics of different applications are similar or dissimilar, some principles can be generalized. For instance, committing a transaction in an object environment is achieved by sending a commit message to the system, which, however, must be interpreted in a homogeneous manner. Among other things, syntactical differences lead to heterogeneity.

As in the case of functional decomposition, this type of heterogeneity can be counterproductive. Nothing we do should contradict one of the key reasons for moving toward object-oriented databases. They should provide a higher modeling capability with fairly homogeneous concepts, approaches, and results, while being able to assure integrative reference to the diverse, heterogenous, and incompatible data structures that have developed in the organization over time.

A great deal of the missing functionality in classical database systems is precisely this integrative aspect. It is not unusual for a major organization to find itself with 15 or 20 incompatible database approaches implemented and in operation, due to different

- Data structures,
- Database management systems, and
- Operating systems.

Any or all of these factors may be too diverse, too hard to maintain, and nearly impossible to put together. Database heterogeneity has usually developed into a jungle. The hope is that object-oriented database solutions will lead out of the jungle—which is not necessarily the right hypothesis.

6–6 MAKING SENSE OF DATABASE HETEROGENEITY

We have said the object orientation should not be seen as the way to solve all problems. This is particularly true when incompatibilities in database solutions approach and programming tools perpetuate if not accentuate damaging discrepancies. It is wise to take the proverbial long, hard look at object database solutions before making definite commitments, studying them in detail and establishing the reasons for heterogeneity, benchmarking them with transactions, messages, and ad-hoc queries, and making a factual and documented choice of tools and concepts, then sticking to it.

Under no conditions should there be one type of object-oriented solution for a transaction environment, a second for messages, a third for queries. If this happens, most of the benefits of the implementation of object-based databases will be lost.

Account should also be taken of the need for concurrency control within a given implementation perspective. In the typical execution environment, transactions run concurrently under a given DBMS, with multiple transactions being active at the same time. These transactions can access and update the same consistent objects, with a DBMS guaranteeing the handling of a given database and of the transaction results.

But in a distributed database environment, if transactions are allowed to run concurrently without any conflict resolution, there can be anomalies in both the database consistency and the transactions' execution. A similar statement can be made of queries and messages. This leads to the need to:

Specify object-oriented system requirements

Identify the objects and the services they must provide

Establish their interactions in terms of interfaces

Always observe inheritance relationships as well as the aggregation of classes

Since transactions are atomic, the design to be adopted must guarantee that partial results or updates that fail are not propagated through the object database. There are also several types of failures from which a system must recover, and in this regard much can be learned from what has already been achieved with more classical transaction processing.

By contrast, a new and important concept associated with object databases is the notion of *nested transactions.* In a nested model, each transaction consists of atomic subtransactions, which can as well be nested. For a transaction to commit, each of its subtransactions must also commit.

The meta concept holds, as with each nested transaction there is always a higher-level transaction monitor supervising it. Higher-level transactions can have a number of filial transactions, which might also have nested transactions within them.

The updates of the transaction tree become visible only after the higher-level transaction commits. The updates of the committed transactions at the intermediate levels (the leaves) become visible only within the scope of their immediate predecessors.

A system-wide "commit transaction" may ask the underlying system to commit its transaction(s), while the user might choose to continue the session after the commit. This will start a new transaction and create a new workspace. Alternatively, the user might decide to undo all the updates to the database and abort the current transaction through a message such as: "System abort transaction."

But the solution is not always so simple. A commit indicates success.

If a parent in a transaction tree has three children that are doing sub-transactions, what happens if two of them commit and one child is running on a node that crashes? The parent might find out about it and abort its own transaction, but two of the children are committed. They cannot be rolled back, so there must be a cleanup to correct erroneous data. A simpler approach is to use only phase 1 commits. But this does not serve for complex transactions.★

The best way to look at this issue is to appreciate that solutions within an object-oriented transactional environment are a composite of the best parts of applications we did in the past and of new concepts substantiated through an object orientation. The latter can enhance the sophistication of database design, and help in assuring reasonable homogeneity—provided we know how to use to advantage the object-oriented approaches that are available today.

6–7 HANDLING LONG TRANSACTIONS

The problem with long transactions has been touched upon in Sections 5 and 6. The notion of computer-processed transactions against files in magnetic storage started in the 1950s with batch programs. By the late 1960s it had evolved into on-line, real-time applications consisting of simple transactions of the debit/credit type, made with reference to a centralized database, with a number of relatively small number of files.

Debit/credit is a simple transaction and emphasizes one aspect of DBMS processing: completing an update against a database whose characteristics are typical of early DBMS implementation. Debit/credit contains a description of a simple banking environment with crisp rules for handling the transaction, and may include tables, usually stored in a record structure:

A customer account table containing the customer's balance

A teller table with balances by teller

A branch table containing balances by branch

A file containing a history of completed transactions.

As the implementation of information technology expanded and databases became distributed, this simple approach no longer worked. The tables might well be located in four heterogeneous databases. Furthermore, more complex transactions require more than one object from each database.

★This issue has been debated both at the International Workshop on Interoperability of Database Systems, in Kyoto, Japan, in April 1991, and in the International Symposium on Distributed and Parallel Systems, Miami, Florida, December 1992. No universal solutions have been reported, or even suggested.

Most important, not only the types of transactions but the whole information environment has changed. The resulting complex transactions can no longer be handled by a simple debit/credit procedure.

For example, in their role as financial intermediaries, banks can execute on customer order one transaction that involves purchasing securities in New York but debiting the client's account in Tokyo after converting debit dollars into yen. This is just one example of the growing range of long transactions—which take time to complete and address faraway databases.

The *long transaction* is both a concept and a mechanism in full evolution. Unlike conventional short transactions, the long transaction typically involves lengthy interactions with databases spanning minutes, hours, or even days, and covers an increasingly wider topology with different database structures that may well be heterogeneous.

A long transaction often includes many versions of data. Hence the wisdom of using *versioning* and *configurations*—embedded in an object orientation—to develop applications that have *no-conflict* concurrency control.

The mechanism for long transactions must have the ability to execute across heterogeneous databases. Among other issues, this brings up the question of how to organize queries into transactions, including messaging into this process.

For these reasons, object orientation is not just the better way but the only way to handle long transactions efficiently. In fact, the issue of long transactions has recently gained prominence because in a multidatabase environment, the traditional transaction model has been found to be too restrictive. Further, multidatabase transactions are often long-running activities.

Managing long-running activities by means of record structures and traditional transaction methods can lead to serious problems, such as low system availability and a high possibility of deadlock. Therefore, extensions to the now classical transaction model have to be made, including transaction isolation, the ability to handle subtransactions, and sophisticated recovery mechanisms.

The principles are known and simple. Far from being theoretical aspects, these paragraphs describe the bread-and-butter interactive databases of the 1990s. The projects a company does today should look to the mid-1990s, not to what might have been valid in the 1970s.

In an object-oriented distributed database environment, access to the database occurs within the framework of a long transaction and its subtransactions. Each subtransaction consists of a sequence of operations on the database done at an atomic level, but the long transaction as a whole has practically no limits as to the time spent on its completion, the topology of the databases being accessed, and the number of operations performed on the database.

Typically, within such environment, a session begins when a client application sends a log-in request, with work on the database accomplished within a transaction and the atomic units composing it. Database consistency requires that either all atomic units (operations) are performed, or none of them is performed. The end of a transaction is signaled by requesting a commit or abort of the whole transaction.

Studies done so far on the object approach suggest that it is superior to any other, including the relational, in handling long transaction requirements. When a log-in to the database occurs, the DBMS typically begins a session, starting a transaction by creating a private copy of the database. No actual data is duplicated, but a copy appears to the user with all information elements he or she is authorized to access.

Objects are shown as they exist at the beginning of the transaction. Calculations or queries based on the copy are valid for the life of the transaction. The only changes visible are updates, additions, or deletions the application program has made during the transaction's execution.

Handling long transaction requirements in an object-oriented fashion allows examination and modification of the database within the context of the local copy until the transaction ends with a commit, abort, or log-out. On an atomic basis, but also for the long transaction, *commit* signals the DBMS to update the database by merging all changes that have taken place.

Chapter 7

Approaches to Object-Oriented Programming

7-1 INTRODUCTION

Object-oriented programming is for systems specialists whose main interest lies in delivering working solutions. As a programming approach, it differs from other types of programming primarily in the need to thoroughly understand the *foundation paradigm,* by using object-oriented analysis and design methods.

There is synergy between an object database and the programming solutions to be followed: The two are strongly linked. A refining or overriding methodology makes it possible to reduce the amount of code an application needs. The approach is that of explaining how class characteristics and methods differ. The process of redefining and extending a class of objects in terms of another class is very important in terms of efficiency.

A programming methodology based on the use of objects puts strong emphasis on identifying what needs to be done before one can deliver a working object-oriented system. This includes everything from concept modeling to coding and testing, particularly *modeling,* which rests largely on

- Knowledge acquisition and
- Knowledge representation.

Object-oriented programming has a great deal to do with knowledge engineering: Fast prototyping is the method, starting with acquisition of the enduser's knowledge, in regard to information elements and commands needed to satisfy job requirements. We discuss prototyping in Chapters 9 and 10.

Able solutions require detailed exposure to the tasks of generating concept and event schemas by using object-oriented paradigms. We prototype these schemata through abstraction and we subsequently concretize our artifact by means of representation. We must also consider in advance the maintenance of reusable components, as discussed in the last sections of Chapter 4.

This concept fits well with the approach increasingly taken by the software development community: Objects are pieces of software that emulate parts of the real world. They can represent discrete items such as stocks and bonds, or global issues such as the economy as a whole.

Like their corresponding entities in the real world, objects can be constructed of other objects. A sales order, for example, is composed of a client name and a list of products and quantities. In contrast to a record approach, this incorporates manipulation rules and associated knowledge. There is also a public interface to the environment to which this object belongs.

Each object is identified by the system in a unique manner. Each object is an abstract representation of its real-world counterpart. Abstraction, however, has two elements: application independence, and representation. Both are open to modeling approaches that are becoming increasingly popular among software developers.

While modeling is the challenging problem, a similar statement is valid about making the transition from schemas to code. This has to be done in an object-oriented implementation environment using C++ (the de-facto object-oriented language standard today) or another programming construct.

7-2 WHAT IS OBJECT-ORIENTED PROGRAMMING?

One of the basic assumptions that dominated classical programming, but that no longer holds, is that computer applications are unique. This concept of "uniqueness" justified the use of slow and laborious "waterfall" methods of development. We have since come to realize that in software development:

Large numbers of apparently different applications perform very similar functions (the reason for the success of fourth- and fifth-generation languages).

Object-oriented techniques are well-suited to sorting common functions into reusable classes, as a way of allowing many applications (in similar domains) to share a large part of their code.

Reuse of object classes results in more flexible, robust systems and can significantly affect applications development.

Effective solutions, however, require standardizing the hardware and software platform, and ensuring that standards are observed as the applications environment expands. It also calls for a significant degree of interoperability among software modules. Open system approaches must be adopted, in which information and commands are continuously exchanged as the system adapts to changing requirements.

Object-oriented programming can be used all the way from the processing of information elements to the establishment of graphic and other interfaces. In the latter case, for example, it allows us to create new screens by providing descriptions of: what the images on the screen are to look like, and how they are to be organized.

An object-oriented graphics system knows about all the relevant objects (panels, graphs, tables, and so on) and about how they break down into classes and subclasses. As subclasses inherit properties, new screens with exactly the desired properties can be defined and rearranged quickly.

In this sense, object-oriented programming helps to maximize software effectiveness, provided the objects are fully integrated with the rest of the system. For example, if we enter values in a graphics interface by using a mouse, the results must automatically become available not only to the relevant tables but also to the entire network of relationships.

In this, as in all other applications, object-oriented programming aims for a logical grouping of facts leading to an agile knowledge and data representation scheme. Rules can be attached to objects so that whenever an object is used in an application, the rules associated with it are automatically executed. Hence there is no need to program these rules into each application that uses the object. This is basically an extension of object database concepts.

The key problem is identifying the *semantics:* What do we want to represent in the database? Where are the links between the information elements? What is the purpose of our application? Has the representation been studied methodologically?

7–3 ALGORITHMIC AND HEURISTIC APPROACHES

In Chapters 3 and 4 we saw that no methodology now available treats pure object structures. But there are methodologies in the domain of entity relationships that can be used for the purpose.

Considering objects as callable entities, we said in Chapter 1 that they typically include both commands and information elements. Thus, they allow more knowledge to enter the application programs, resulting in independent but sharable object structures being available for referential integrity checks.

The commands embedded in these objects may be *procedural* (hence algorithmic) or *heuristic.* In the latter case, intelligence-enriched objects have expert systems rules associated with them that automatically fire when the object is used. Because of this algorithmic and heuristic duality, object-oriented systems are capable to certain types of knowledge and data manipulation that conventional programming approaches cannot perform.

What is more, data validation rules can be attached to an object such as an inventory item or a banking account. For example, every time a lot is received or shipped, the data validation rules for an inventory item can be invoked automatically. As a result, the application program can be leaner as well as more independent of information elements. Furthermore, consistent data validity and homogeneity are ensured across applications.

For these reasons, an object-oriented programming style helps develop solutions to the problem of *referential integrity* even within a relational database. But such solutions are not free of problems.

Problems may arise from the fact that in the table-oriented structure of a relational database, a particular concept can be deleted from one table while dependent concepts stored in another table are not deleted as they should be. By contrast, integrative object-oriented approaches help solve this problem by attaching rules to the fields of the objects in reference:

Whenever an object is deleted, the rules review the database for references to the deleted item.

The rules also see to it that relationships are changed before allowing deletion of the original object.

The point is that a methodological approach supports integrative object-oriented solutions. It involves both programming languages and database systems, but also knowledge representation as well as more classical, procedural lines of code, as shown in Fig. 7.1.

Languages such as C++, Simula, Smalltalk, Eiffel, and Ada, among others,★ are suited to this type of object-oriented software development, but they are not going to do miracles. Much more is necessary than what current tools offer in terms of removing different burdens, such as user-interface consistency, from the application programmer.

Above all, an object-oriented methodology is necessary and must be able to apply standards and permit small groups of programmers to work on different parts of the system in parallel in a way similar to that of concurrent engineering. No doubt, the implementation of such methodology must be computer-based, which brings computer-assisted software engineering (CASE) into perspective.

★For instance, Objective C, Object SQL (OSQL), Object Pascal, Actor, Beta, Damocles, Object Designer (of the Ontos DBMS), and Common LISP Object System (CLOS).

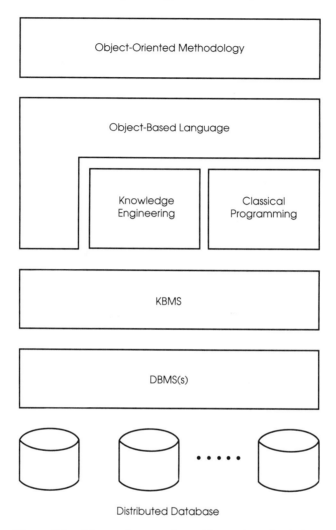

Figure 7.1   A layered approach to object-oriented solutions.

$7-4$ OBJECT PROGRAMMING AND META-PROGRAMMING

Object-oriented programming approaches typically utilize many different predefined classes of objects to represent common real-world situations. By reusing existing classes, systems can be assembled in much less time than it would take to program them from scratch. Such solutions are more robust because they are developed from proven components, and they lead to increased quality and reduced maintenance costs.

Object-oriented programs are easier to modify to meet changing business needs than are other programs. They also lead to flexible software and do so at a fraction of the time and cost of traditional program development methods.

Once defined, classes can be used repeatedly in the construction of new software. The result is a new approach to software development, with programs constructed by assembling existing, proven classes rather than re-writing procedures from scratch for each new application.* No recompilation of application code is required, while changes made by others are available at the beginning of the next software development task. When more than one class in the inheritance chain defines a method with the same name, the definition closest to the higher class in the hierarchy takes precedence.

Object-oriented programming stresses program decomposition based on objects, not functions. Code generation itself rests on data abstraction and encapsulation, permitting more flexible approaches than the waterfall method, as we will see in Section 6. Programming is based on concepts oriented to the application domain, while the new methodology permits mapping problems to solutions and promoting the identification of generic concepts within that application domain.

With this approach, modules can be defined more consistently among applications than with a function orientation. Primitives for defining classes and subclasses facilitate the development of reusable modules.

The features of the object-oriented languages (which we examine in Chapters 8 and 11) promote reusable software development. Such features include data abstraction through high-level definitions of a data structure, and information hiding by means of separation of public data from private data.

Inheritance characteristics of object solutions are conductive to *meta-programming* methods. These permit a higher level of abstraction as well as development of a translator to produce the source code.

With meta-programming, the programmer's effort is focused on the development of a high-level notation to capture the abstraction of the application on which he or she is working. This permits the use of a high-level notation and the construction of generators to produce the module by translating the notation into source code.

Meta-programming permits the combination of a variety of notations, each of which may capture the abstractions relevant to some aspect of the application. This is achieved by creating notations that are free of the syntactic and semantic constraints of a given source language.

Since the notations employed in meta-programming are suited to a given application domain, the process of describing an application problem in these notations is simpler and more free of errors. The encoding of an

---

*See also the discussion of reusable software in Chapter 4.

application into notation can often be performed by endusers who need not be professional programmers.

Capitalizing on these notions, a leading Japanese financial institution is in the process of developing precompiler-level commands—each class responding to the jargon and business habits of a particular group of professionals. This will both increase the accuracy of the programs and cut the development backlog.

As a program development method, meta-programming models a production process, combining software technology with process optimization characteristics. Subsequently, programs to realize that models are produced through *generators* whose mechanics are known from compiler technology.

Because the effectiveness of system design depends strongly on the amount of optimization that is performed, it is necessary to know the cost trade-offs of this approach. Hence, besides an object orientation, we need knowledge engineering techniques* to assist in the optimization process.

As a high-level descriptor, meta-programming permits changing a program within the limits of the code generator. This provides programmers with leverage but also forces them to think about the structure of the program and the process of software creation. As a result, it focuses attention on both productivity and product quality.

More particularly, an object-oriented programming methodology is useful in that it allows computer specialists as well as endusers to allocate resources properly during development, making the job of monitoring easier as well as fostering productivity and quality. Good monitoring prevents the misallocation of resources at any stage of the design process.

7-5 CONCEPTS ASSOCIATED WITH NEW PROGRAMMING POLICIES

As we saw in Chapter 3 while discussing architectural issues, the object-oriented solution we employ must facilitate the integration of modules developed by different groups and avoid duplication of effort. It must promote the synergy of development teams as well as create a system that is extensible and suitable for prototyping new applications.

At the present time, there is no object-based software capable of providing complete solutions. This is particularly true of linguistic constructs, which work all the way from prototyping to assembly-level code through the use of the appropriate compilers. As a result, companies and university laboratories have emulated such an environment by building some of the pieces themselves, adapting and integrating tools developed piecemeal by

*See also D. N. Chorafas, *Knowledge Engineering,* Van Nostrand Reinhold, New York, 1990.

others. This resulted in a layered approach that more or less permits programmers to develop applications conforming to object-oriented criteria but not necessarily obeying an integrative methodology from prototyping to fine-grain code.

The most successful solutions along this line appreciate the fact that for object-oriented systems to succeed we need many well-behaved, high-performance, useful objects. For most people, the emergence of objects able to provide their own documentation changes the definition of *what programming is.*

But it is not as easy as it sounds. One criticism of programs written using object-oriented techniques is that they tend to be slower than comparable conventional programs. Much of this view relates to historical speed problems in early versions of Smalltalk, where object-oriented code was interpreted rather than compiled. Another reason for this view of speed of execution comes from the fact that object searches in the database have overhead—but it should not be forgotten that they are much more flexible than relational-type approaches.

With the advent of more powerful search heuristics, object compilers, and associated optimization techniques, speed is no longer an insurmountable problem, though it is always necessary to prune and optimize reusable chunks of code.

In essence, the problem is not in programming objects per se, but rather in getting the right objects and supervising them properly. The growing experience with object-based programming affects computer usage patterns, more so as this type of software becomes an integral and important part of processing libraries.

A key issue in the change of images, and in some cases of culture, is that concepts associated with objects, such as inheritance, meta-rules and meta-data, message passing, late binding, graphical interfacing, and so on, are approached in a consistent manner. The same is true of public interfaces and private implementation parts.

Programmers considering object-oriented constructs should never forget that objects also have *methods* attached to them, within their private parts. These specify how certain operations are to be carried out in connection with that object. One example is communication with other objects, which can be done only via the public interface, through message passing.

Another crucial issue affecting programming approaches is consistency in the distinction between *passive* and *active* objects, as shown in Fig. 7.2. Consider, as an example, clients and loans. The client file is a passive object, whether it consists of data only, text and data, or other media. By contrast, the client–loan pair is an active object. It includes the loan as a file, and the loan as a process.

Particulars of clients and loans are read and attached to parent objects.

Entities

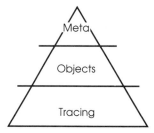

Inheritance, Equilibration

Figure 7.2   Callable objects and their background support.

Rules must be developed in a group fashion as far as possible, for instance: "No loans of less than $1000." Inheritance will see to it that all resulting loans are subjected to generally applicable rules.

As this example helps document, objects are things existing in the real world. Actions are also regarded as objects. Because of actions, objects change. The whole concept of object-oriented programming is included in this short paragraph.

The world in which objects exist is known as the *object world.* Knowledge in the object world is *object knowledge,* such as the management of multimedia information elements in the distributed database. *Meta-knowledge* provides:

Necessary conditions on objects

Limits, controls, and constraints

Relationships between object-covering action(s)

This type of approach frequently requires a large address space. The latter is an advantage because it allows the program to address many locations without requiring the hardware or software to do a lot of context switching, which slows down processing. Processing becomes simpler, cleaner, and faster if a large address space is available.

Fertile implementation domains for the approach we are discussing include information systems with complex, interlinking files operating in a global sense, environments characterized by widely distributed interconnected databases, as well as applications requiring system consistency under distributed control. Other examples include:

Problems needing definitions at a level below (more fundamental than) file consistency

Office automation-type implementation, particularly with multimedia requirements

CAD/CAM implementations with multiple simulation requirements

Securities, foreign exchange, and treasury applications executed in different financial markets and involving a number of instruments

The same is true of simulations of large organizations modeled on the basis of objects, messages, and transactions, and of complex software constructs built in a modular way with a variety of interconnecting capabilities—with causality being an important programming criterion.

7–6 A MODERN METHODOLOGY VERSUS THE WATERFALL MODEL

The nature and size of the problems we have been discussing suggest that programming solutions developed in the 1950s, when the challenge was smaller by two orders of magnitude, no longer work. New methods are necessary to solve the problems of the 1990s and beyond.

It is largely for this reason that object-oriented programming has become accepted as a valid technique for building modular, sustainable, and portable software that will also raise the level of programming expertise and enrich it through libraries of object classes. *Inheritance* and *parameterization* are the main mechanisms being exploited to enhance software reusability.

In terms of applications development, the object-oriented approach provides a mechanism for building reliable and easy-to-change programming products. In traditional programming the application system is built as a *waterfall* model in one monolithic block.

By contrast, object-oriented approaches look at an application as a group of communicating, *integrating,* and cooperating object structures. Such objects have local behavior, represented by their operations. The global behavior of an application is given implicity through *invocation,* provided there exists proper coordination and interfacing between objects. Parameters allow specification of the entry point of an application—that is, the operation that is invoked at runtime. Other parameters are bound to objects to be invoked in a given application.

Researchers in software development methods and procedures have come to the conclusion that the so-called waterfall model of system analysis, design, and programming has major limitations and inadequacies. A much better alternative to current methods consists of a cybernetic *meta-model* with an *integrative* framework, in which the emphasis is on the *evolution dynamics* of software products.

This approach defines the operational life cycle of programming products by levels, or *phases,* required for the new generation of computer applications. Each phase consists of successive milestones which may be repeated during design, depending on:

The learning process

The nonlinear structure of the phases

The levels of modeling

Coding practices and their automation

Sustenance rather than maintenance during the software's life cycle

Such a methodology requires simultaneous emphasis on both the organizational context and the application concept. Organizational solutions always affect software development. Only when organizational problems have been solved can the application concept be properly defined.

The interface between the prerequisite organizational solutions and object-oriented programming is *conceptual modeling.* It addresses both processes and databases, expresses assumptions, includes specifications, and defines the way they correspond to functional requirements in software engineering.

Processes, databases, assumptions, functional requirements, and specifications all influence one another. None can be defined on its own. As Fig. 7.3 suggests,

1. Conception
2. Specification
3. Design
4. Testing
5. Implementation
6. Maintenance

form a spiral structure that is essentially a *meta-model* framework. The more an object-oriented project moves out along the spiral, the more attention to detail and integration is needed.

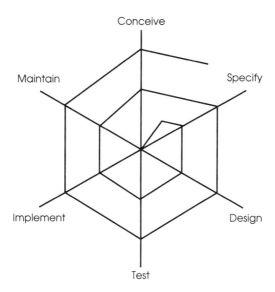

Figure 7.3   A meta-model framework for software evolution.

The meta-model framework starts with conception and specification. After these are done, the more technical questions can be tackled. The design and testing phases are where objects and object-based languages come in.

Evolution dynamics characterize such a framework for software development. They imply that programming products have a definite life cycle consisting of initial development, followed by implementation and sustenance. Such an evolutionary concept discards the old dichotomy between initial development and maintenance, providing a more realistic picture of what is happening in practice. In the background is the belief that:

1. The operational life cycle of an object-based artifact must be consciously designed.
2. The design process should be projected into object-based phases, following the order of the six modeling milestones we have seen.

Underlying this approach is the observance of successive milestones, with every generation in product development moving outward from the starting point, but utilizing already developed routines. After this cycle exhausts itself, the software design process is begun again.

The flexible structure of phases capitalizes on what object-type solutions can offer. It rests on an iterative structure that, as already stated, includes prototyping. It also helps in making some of the iterations explicit to support realistic project scheduling, cost estimation, and the performance of design reviews.

Chapter 8

Meta-Programming in an Object Environment

8-1 INTRODUCTION

A new generation of high-performance computing and communications (HPCC) systems, made possible by increasingly powerful semiconductors, places new demands on applications development.* This new technology provides previously unavailable opportunities in databasing and programming solutions for firms that know how to capitalize on it.

The new, very-high-level tools for analysis, design, and programming have arrived none too soon. Companies are under pressure by endusers to develop novel, advanced applications—fast. The more successful a company is in using information technology, the more this need is felt.

One of the best examples of a financial institution that has been able to convert to on-line processing all of its data handling requirements—thus eliminating batching—is the Dai-Ichi Kangyo Bank in Japan. Dai-Ichi has also "terminalized" nearly all of its personnel. Now the managers and professionals are pressing for analytical applications, and the backlog is mounting. It currently stands at 70,000 man-years, an astronomical figure.

Correctly, senior management at Dai-Ichi has come to the conclusion that there is no other way to solve this backlog except enduser programming—but not just any type of enduser programming. A new policy calls for the development of meta-programming-level linguistic interfaces. These will be professional or managerial functions that essentially talk the jargon of a given line of business. These meta-programming constructs will then be

*See also Chapter 22 on HPCC and its impact during the 1990s.

automatically converted into code through generators, as suggested in Chapter 7.

The satisfaction of new requirements and rigorous quality specifications are becoming a means for some companies to solve their database challenge, but also to increase their market share. The new opportunities are suited for mainstream software strategies in many branches of industry: manufacturing, marketing, finance, the service sector, as well as the government. During the 1990s, leaders and followers will be distinguished by the way they take advantage of such opportunities.

Cognizant American executives suggest that both software and hardware developments will be aiming to provide higher quality, tighter tolerances, more reliability, and greater nonstop processing capabilities. Japanese computers and communications manufacturers seem to lead in several of those areas—one reason being that they focus their efforts.

In this age of mass production, miniaturization, and enormous R&D budgets, *focus* has become the keyword. The message is that if we want to be successful, we have to focus on what we are doing. Software development is no exception to this rule.

As we will see in the following sections, object approaches can be of significant help in creating new software solutions, from conception to coding and maintenance. Novel tools, however, require the proper environment on which to function. Faint-hearted or half-baked solutions will not do the job.

8–2 OBJECT-ORIENTED LINGUISTIC SOLUTIONS

In general, the object approach offers more promise for computer software than alternatives such as structured, functional, or logic programming. Software development and maintenance could be well supported by the object paradigm, benefiting from code structuring and the sharing mechanisms that are possible.

Data abstraction, for example, is helpful in ensuring the coexistence of many different internal data representations. Reusable modules could be encapsulated in objects whose interface would be the same no matter what their internal representation is. Changes could be handled by active objects. Constraints and a graph-based data model could be seen as sets of objects connected in networks, with message flows and activities associated with the connected objects.

Concepts and tools are the means for reaching this goal. Many of today's object languages were created in the Simula tradition. On principle, they support pattern abstraction mechanisms. The objects of such linguistic constructs, such as the object language Beta, may respond to messages and execute as co-routines or processes. Supported features include generalization and integration of abstraction as well as of control structures—in short, the features we have examined in the first chapters of this book.

In an object language such as Eiffel (Integrative Software Engineering), for example, abstraction is a key mechanism. Eiffel includes constructs that fit the needs of abstraction, merging the concepts of class, module, reference semantics, abstract (deferred) genericity, inheritance, polymorphism, and specification through assertions. As a language, Eiffel supports:

Classes
Multiple inheritance
Polymorphism
Dynamic binding

It also features systematic use of assertions and other constructs to help in program correctness. Quality assurance is one of its strong points, but this is as true of object programming in general.

In Eiffel, multiple inheritance is treated as an indispensable intellectual tool for abstraction and separation of design factors. Meta-linguistic constructs, as mentioned in the introduction to this chapter, are also possible.

Eiffel is implemented by compilation through C⋆; however the Eiffel language itself is an original design and has no relation to C commands. Memory management is handled by a runtime approach that takes care of object creation and system-controlled deallocation. Garbage collection is performed incrementally by a parallel process that steals as few cycles as it can from application programs. Compilation is executed on a class-by-class basis, so that larger modules can be changed and extended incrementally.

Eiffel also contains debugging tools for runtime checking of assertions, as well as a tracer, symbolic debugger, and viewer for interactive exploration of the object structure. The language produces a message when an assertion is found to be violated. This supports the process of equilibration, whose importance we have stressed.

Another object-oriented language with strong feature of knowledge representation is Quixote, which was designed by ICOT in collaboration with Kobe University and the University of Kyoto. This is an integrated linguistic construct that brings together the deductive and object-oriented database language Juan with the knowledge-representation language Quint.

Quixote handles object identity and parameters in situation theory as well as complex objects and feature structures. The basic equation is

Feature structure = complex object logic + abduction

⋆As we will see in later chapters, this is one of the real advantages of object-oriented shells. Another example is Ptech, which permits rapid prototyping and then automatically compiles into C.

where *abduction* stands for the Bayesian concept—for instance, "It rains, therefore it is cloudy." Among its features are semantics, object syntax, and paradigms. Paradigms are expressed through deductive objective database concepts.

Quixote features inheritance characteristics and uses a constraint-logic programming language on labeled graphs. Its paradigms are based on modular and situation-theoretic programming. The syntax rests on:

Basic objects (a lattice of basic concepts)
Object terms (defined by basic objects and variables)
Attribute terms (with constraints on object terms)
Inheritance (based on type hierarchy, rules, programs, and databases).

The syntactic module reflects a situation or world with parameters. The semantic domain includes a power set of labeled graphs as well as a class guaranteed by solution lemma. Quixote supports an ontology of objects:

Property within a module
Object identity (OID) within a database
Database name over a range of databases

ICOT has used Quixote to construct a new information processing system using objects and knowledge engineering. Among the applications are legal precedent databases, molecular biological databases, and natural-language processing solutions. The objective of the applications that have been undertaken so far has been to show the effectiveness of the deductive databases that have been developed, as well as the management of knowledgebanks and knowledge representation languages.

8-3 OBJECT SQL (OSQL)

The proliferation of object-oriented database management systems has created the need for a standard database language. Most people agree that such a language should combine the best of object-oriented and traditional database programming, and should focus on the underlying execution model. There is less agreement, however, on how much standardization is needed. Should there be only a standard syntax for basic data definition and data manipulation statements, or should standardization cover much more than that—and if so, what else should be included?

A standard syntax for basic data definition and data manipulation statements is the option chosen for Object SQL (OSQL). OSQL, based on research performed at Texas Instruments and currently supported by object DBMS such as Versant and Hewlett-Packard's Open ODB and Pegasus, is a high-level language for developing object-oriented database applications. It assures database interfaces with modeling constructs able to match real-life situations in expressing the needs of business and technical applications.

Since its design phase, the objective of OSQL has been to combine traditional advantages of database programming with the benefits of object programming:

• Inheritance,
• Encapsulation, and
• Extensibility

For instance, declarative queries, views, access control, and multiuser concurrency control. The aim was to provide the best of two worlds, integrating object programming and classical coding.

OSQL is based on a functional language approach, with access to data and operations provided by a set of built-in functions. Appropriate supports help a database application programmer to define types and associated operators. Included are special language constructs (statements) for data definition and manipulation. To shorten the learning curve for current SQL programmers, these are intended to resemble equivalent SQL constructs as much as possible.

Parts of the OSQL language are implementation-dependent, including constructs for specifying the implementing of foreign functions, and facilities for physical schema definition, data structures, and access methods. In its fundamentals, however, OSQL is a functional language with special syntactic forms which, as we have said, resemble those of SQL for common database functionality. Within the realm of the object orientation, basic constructs of OSQL are

type (class)
object
function

The developers emphasize that OSQL is not tied to a specific programming language, nor is it intended to replace other programming languages in the development of database applications. But for database-intense programming, it can be used in combination with other programming languages such as C++ and Smalltalk, providing the benefits of SQL-type declarative data definition and manipulation.

Among the goals of OSQL are object-oriented features such as an intuitive model, code reuse, extensibility, associative access, integrity constraints, query optimization, and alternative views of data.

Some meta-programming concepts are included, as the developers considered OSQL to be a semantic *superset* of SQL. Features of current database technology, such as multiuser access, multilanguage access, and security, are also available.

As a rule, when a given object language is characterized by flexibility and modularity in its design and object evolution, new features can be added to sustain meta-linguistic capabilities. Interfacing, however, is an important factor, and that is why OSQL has been chosen as an example.

In a runtime environment, objects should typically have implicit interfaces expressed by their visual presentations and their physical significance. A design is a set of elements associated according to implicit and explicit rules, in a part–whole hierarchical fashion. Rules are maintained in an object dictionary.

8-4 OSQL PRIMITIVES AND FUNCTIONS

OSQL statements provide for definition, implementation, and deletion of types and functions. This facility corresponds roughly to tables and views in SQL.

A fundamental OSQL primitive is function invocation. Many features of the language are provided by a set of built-in functions. Linguistic constructs are assured in the form of OSQL statements for common data definition and data manipulation.

An OSQL function may take an object as an argument and return an object as a result.

The argument object must be an instance of the argument type specified for the function.

The argument and the result may be an aggregate object.

Functions may change the state of the database as a side effect of their execution.

Functions perform database updates by updating other functions. Functions that perform in this manner are said to have *side effects.*

A function whose body is defined by an OSQL statement may query and update the database. If the defining OSQL program is a query, the function is called a *derived* one, and can be thought of as a view of other information elements.

If the defining program contains a statement other than a query, the function is a *procedure.* A foreign function is implemented by a program written in a general-purpose programming language, such as C. The extension for the foreign function is determined by the defining program.

The implementation of the foreign function must adhere to certain interface conventions that are implementation-dependent, but beyond that, the implementation is a black box with respect to the rest of the system. Foreign functions do not have side effects on the database, though they can change the state outside the database.

The extension of a function may change with time. For some functions, this is explicitly accomplished by updating. Only those functions for which update semantics are defined by the system can be explicitly updated. The associated semantics define how such updates are mapped to underlying storage structures that help maintain the functional extensions.

In the OSQL domain, a distinction is made between a function's declaration and its implementation:

The *declaration* defines the signature of the function and the constraints on its extension.

The *implementation* reflects the behavior of the function.

The implementation of a function may be changed without affecting the applications that call the function. This provides a certain degree of data independence.

To improve data independence, declaration and implementation of types and functions are separated. Hence the implementation of a function can be changed without altering the applications. There is a correspondence between the former procedure and the separation between physical and logical database schemata.

OSQL supports variables to which objects can be assigned. Variables can be used as temporary placeholders for results by function calls. *Local variables* can be declared inside function bodies; *session variables* are global and do not require explicit declarations.

Function resolution features late binding semantics. Through them, a specific function to be invoked is selected based on the type of the actual argument at the time the function is executed. This has implications for derived functions and procedures.

OSQL supports discretionary control through function invocation. Its two basic privileges, CALL and UPDATE, are granted separately for individual functions. The grantee is said to have call authority and update authority on the function. The authorization model is extended to include privileges for executing these statements.

The user who creates the function is its *owner* and has call and update authority on it. The owner can grant and revoke basic privileges to other users, transfer ownership of the function to another user, as well as delete the function.

Privileges are explicitly granted to specific *groups*. Group members are either individual users or other groups. Groups are organized in a hierarchy. All privileges granted to a group are inherited by the set of users defined by the group.

OSQL also provides statements for creating and deleting users, changing their password, creating and deleting groups, adding and removing members from groups, granting and revoking privileges to individual users and groups, and changing the ownership of functions. All this makes the language fairly flexible and applicable for database management implementation.

OSQL has, however, one major disadvantage, which it inherited from SQL. Originally designed by IBM and released in 1979, SQL has severe limitations when used in a modern transactional or complex query environment. Some of these limitations are inherent in the relational model. For transaction applications, hierarchical and Codasyl databases outperform relational DBMS. IBM still suggests the use of IMS fast track rather than DB2 with a heavy transactional load.

A few years ago, for example, a vendor suggested to a leading financial institution, which found itself obliged to reprogram a big chunk of its applications library, that the language of choice should be SQL. Elaborate study indicated that the use of SQL would *double* the number of cycles needed, and therefore require double the computer power and associated costs. Management correctly killed that vendor's proposal.

Other SQL limitations are inherent in the language itself. They have to do with the way it was designed but also with the fact that there have been so many mutations that created incompatibilities. For instance, there are SQL incompatibilities in the IBM product line: DB2 SQL, SQL/DS, SQL OS 400, and SQL OS/2. Other vendors tried to change SQL to market it "better"; OSQL is an example of the result. And ANSI found that SQL does not handle transactions, hence the new version SQL 2 (released in 1992); and it does not process interactive graphics, hence the work on SQL 3, which is expected in 1995.

In none of its versions is SQL able to handle the breed of voluminous multiprocessing decisions that must be made on the fly. This also creates a networking problem, with a major difficulty being that a query formulated at one node must be optimized for performance over hundreds of nodes and be intense in communications exchange as well as database accesses.

8-5 DYNAMIC PROCESSING OF OBJECT PROPERTIES

The traditional approach to characterizing a class of objects is to regard the objects as composed of properties that are related in certain ways. One of these relations is hierarchical, though the hierarchy of objects and subobjects may not be very deep and is instantiated rather than permanent.

An approach based on the relation of objects to properties is quite satisfactory for describing objects composed of well-defined and precisely described characteristics. Its limitations become apparent, however, if we try to apply it to even a simple class of real-world objects, where, even if the parts are well defined and conform to the norms we have seen, it is by no means easy to identify the constraints on property and relation values that characterize a given object class. Hence the wisdom of using knowledge engineering approaches as suggested since the beginning of this chapter and in the preceding ones.

Understanding the development process, planning the object-oriented project, choosing tools, getting training, properly structuring the prototyping process are all interconnected tasks which can only be handled in an able manner if we have the proper methodology. The same is true of designing, coding, establishing design reviews and testing procedures—all being prerequisites for building flexibility and extensibility into our solution.

The same statement is true regarding the use of techniques for questioning the domain expert in order to acquire his knowledge, analyzing scenarios for applying expertise, and defining domain concepts. The proper methodology will look into:

- Requirements,
- Project tasks,
- Milestones,
- Resources, and
- Deliverables.

An important mission is that of elaborating the *semantic relations* of these five issues, defining semantic networks, and establishing concept hierarchies.

Building the declarative component of a conceptual model helps in clarifying the object-oriented solution we are after. Figure 8.1 gives an example of a reasoning system for dynamic processing:

- The *object class* is the entity type of information elements in the database.
- The objects are the *entity instance* of those information elements.
- The object properties reflect the values of the IE as created through a meta-object approach.

The application may be, for instance, pattern matching with new instance-creating objects. New instances may be effected through *actors,* a term intro-

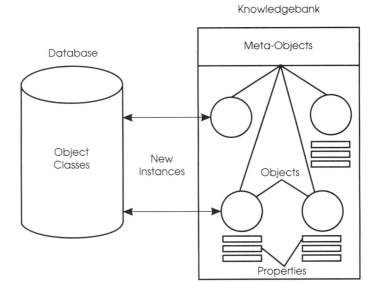

Figure 8.1 Objects and meta-objects: a way of looking at databases and knowledgebanks.

duced in the early 1970s by Carl Hewitt at MIT. As a term, *actors* is used to describe the concept of reasoning agents whose action is eventually developing into a model of concurrency.

Actor-type languages give special emphasis to developing flexible program structures. They also simplify our reasoning about programs. This enhances our ability to understand the properties of software, providing clarity in the structure of the code, and also helps create a dynamic processing environment, refining some of the concurrency aspects.

A necessary complement to the use of actors is the concept of *demons,* as introduced in Chapter 2. Demons are critical in distributed programming applications and therefore in object-oriented programming. Demons permit handling processes in parallel, with actors attaching themselves to objects through concurrent elaboration, subsequently joining their solutions in order to obtain a formal or technical resolution to the overall problem. For example, suppose that in a certain application, processing of new information begins with receipt of a sensor report or message at the monitor. Then

1. The report is parsed and injected into the database.
2. The information is then classified and routed by demons.
3. Actors suggest possible interpretations of the information.

In this example, a demon is like an interrupt handler in an operating system, because it performs no action until (and unless) a specific situation is encountered.

In addition to actors and demons, some extensions are required to satisfy the needs of an object-oriented approach, including:

1. A uniform methodology able to start a process from its static context and proceed through the executable program phase.
2. Features for suspension, resumption, and termination of processes.
3. A means of managing messages for cooperation and communication between objects.
4. Ability to handle distributed object base facilities, including entities such as named pipes, files, devices, and so on.

The system must be able to keep track of entities that have been managed in the heterogeneous database, common entities in a cross-database sense, and links among entities. It must also elaborate and follow authorization and authentication requirements commensurate with the level of security that has been selected.

Primitives deal with the notion of a program in execution, defining how a process can be started or terminated, how it can be controlled, how parameters can be passed. Supervisory processes must establish the relations between a running program, its objects, and the environment within which it executes.

Facilities must also be provided for defining and controlling access rights, and for identifying objects and actors and the way the latter manipulates the former. A similar procedure is needed for the interactions between a process and its surrounding resources.

Communication primitives typically deal with the way a process can access the contents of objects kept in the database. A mechanism must be provided to allow different processes to communicate with a high degree of cooperation and synchronization, exchanging information and proceeding to effective execution.

8−6 AN ARTIFACT IN THE OBJECT ENVIRONMENT

Object-oriented programming presents a significant contrast to the better-known (since the early 1970s) process of structured programming, which decomposes an application into functions. A major disadvantage of this method is that such functions bear little or no resemblance to the underlying concepts. By contrast, object-based programming is semantically oriented, so it stresses meaning.

A program modularity based on concepts is much simpler to comprehend. However, one of the unanswered questions so far concerns the criteria that define (not just describe) an object-oriented language. The software development community has not yet established the linguistic criteria that will make an object orientation feasible. Many people have opinions, but few can support them.

We do know that we need languages able to map reflective processing characteristics. Current programming languages have few facilities for a comprehensive, integrative approach to:

> Control over a reduction process
> Nonmonotonic reasoning
> Semantic representation
> The handling of viewpoints

A meta-compiler is needed that has reflective, self-referencing capabilities. Besides object orientation, it could include forks, pipes, semaphores, curses, demons—something of a more enriched, networked version of UNIX. Equally necessary are KBMS to manipulate intentional databases and act as a meta-layer over relational DBMS.★

Typically, this environment will handle objects, messages, methods, classes, and meta-classes. Among these add-on features should be object graphics tools for diagramming class relationships, including inheritance and encapsulation, as well as support for workspaces, views, browsers, form editors, debuggers, notifiers, and inspectors.

We are assuming here that encapsulation and hierarchy can significantly aid reusability in an object-oriented design meta. Another goal is to represent time and space dependencies with objects,† where knowledge is expressed that asserts properties of objects and inheritance relationships between classes of objects.

Descriptions denote a class of objects in terms of their attributes and their relations to other objects and their descriptions. Available functionality should permit classification of objects according to their properties in a multiple inheritance network. This will aid in the organization of knowledge and eliminate duplication because shared knowledge is specified only once.

The ability to extend the number and type of the attributes of a descriptor is useful when the knowledge about the object domain can be acquired only incrementally. It should be possible to obtain solutions by

---

★See also D. N. Chorafas and H. Steinmann, *Supercomputers,* McGraw-Hill, New York, 1990.

†See also Chapters 12 and 13.

searching the database for an object that meets given descriptor characteristics. This process can be performed by wandering in the network of descriptions, following deductive rules for inheritance, and discarding all spaces that turn out to have contradictory properties. We thus have another justification of the statement made in Chapter 3 that an object-oriented machine will have a memory architecture that is large but also flexible.

8-7 PHYSICAL MEMORY, LOGICAL MEMORY, AND PROGRAMMING

It cannot be repeated too often that the concept of database management is inseparable from that of programming. Most operations during the 1990s, and therefore most implementations of information technology, will be database intense. Not only is database management, hence the *logical* memory space, inseparable from programming perspectives, but also the physical memory exhibits similar characteristics. This is the message of the conclusion of Section 6.

Memory size is needed to handle the myriad of structures that emerge and offer easy access to virtually any part of the integrated artifact consisting of:

Programming language(s)
Operating system
KBMS and DBMS
Application environment

Type checking is important to the security of such object-oriented engine. The nonprocedural nature of the object-type languages, and the broad range of meanings a single command can carry, can easily instantiate unexpected or unintended consequences.

When type-checking works, the artifact compares the types of the objects being added in parallel with the addition itself. If the type matches, no corrective action is taken and no time is lost, since the check is simultaneous with the addition. If the type does not match, an exception handler is invoked to ensure that no mismatch occurs undetected and that action is taken if necessary.

A system view involving several of the forementioned functional components in a networked engine is shown in Fig. 8.2. It reflects a networked object-oriented environment that communicates through the local network to which it is attached—or does so long-range by means of a front-end processor. Everything moving along this artifact is an object defined by its behavior along the principle of

Message – – → Action

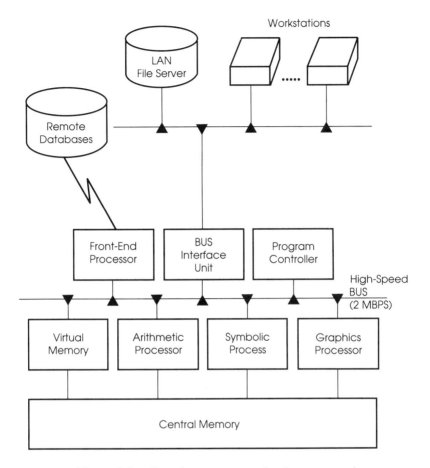

Figure 8.2. Shared resources on a local area network.

Classes can be combined through an inheritance graph, with real sets creating clones through a process of self-description.

The basic actuation mechanism is message passing. Communication defines the procedure of message execution as well as the system through which the artifact is run. The latter may be seen, for example, as an information utility, with programming tools capturing objects, processing them, and disseminating results.

A crucial component of such an environment is the existence of a central repository served through object-based solutions and manipulated by means of special software: A knowledgebank management system (KBMS) as the meta-layer, and a DBMS as the lower operational layer. The DBMS will access the object base in response to requests made by any of the environment's components. The artifact should manage these components in a uniform way, providing storing mechanisms, assuring convenient access means, observing the various dependencies that must be maintained, and accounting for the consequence of all changes.

The KBMS should allow the user to associate a number of properties with the contents of an object. These may be simple values referred to as attributes, or they may represent associations between objects. The power of a KBMS comes from its ability to designate an object by a *predicate* involving its relationships with other objects, rather than by a simple name, and the possibility of constraining certain structures through the introduction of schemas corresponding to descriptors of constraints, as well as properties of a collection of objects.

The values of the attributes that are associated with an object are used to record significant status data or to gain access to a given object. Both the developer and the user need to be able to define new attributes, while ensuring the integrity and consistency of the objects being manipulated. These are qualities that can be supported by an object-oriented programming language.

Chapter 9

Objects and the Process of Prototyping

9-1 INTRODUCTION

In the literature as well as in practice, *prototyping* has many different meanings. The sense of the word is literally *first of a type,* and it is this definition that concerns us. When we prototype, we build a real-life, working model in which some 80 percent of the needed functionality is provided by 20 percent or less of the complete code. This 80/20 rule is an application of Pareto's law, which says that about 80 percent of something represents 20 percent of something else. By building 80 percent of the functional requirements into the prototype, we get a quick glance at most of what is required. Fine-tuning and customizing can be done later, but meanwhile we have a working system on which we can experiment and which we can optimize.

The prototype may be an imperfect, unproven machine, but it provides a useful platform with which to experiment. We can test ideas, concretize our thoughts, evaluate our designs, make modifications rapidly, and generally improve the construct we have developed. Prototypes are conceptual modeling instruments. Using a prototype, we can:

Identify objects, classes, and structures
Develop a methodology for handling abstraction
Define subjects, attributes, and services
Test whether specifications are executable

Rather than jumping right into a study of functions and their sequencing, we first focus on objects and their instance connections as well as establish the proper messaging.

As we become more deeply involved in the object-based solution, we begin to discover nuances that even the experts may not yet have considered. This is one of the reasons prototyping is so important to the quality of an object-oriented program.

Critics of prototyping sometimes argue that prototyping lacks tightly written system design specifications, is mainly a demonstrator, cannot evolve into a production system, is merely screen and report design, or is just a simulation that can cope with data entry without actual database accesses and processing facilities. Prototyping, however, does all of what its critics suggest that it cannot do, but it proceeds by observing the 80/20 rule. In this sense, it is useful for its role in facilitating communication between system designers and system users. How well can an object-oriented approach provide for and be affected by prototyping?

9-2 THE ROLE OF PROTOTYPING IN AN OBJECT ENVIRONMENT

Objects can make a very valuable contribution, particularly when the prototype applies to a distributed database environment. An object orientation enables the designer to verify how the construct behaves, whether it responds in the intended manner, and what additional components or observations will be needed.

Conversely, as we have seen in the introduction, object-oriented systems require prototyping in order to be analyzed and studied in a rational manner. The facility is interactive and simple to use, so it is most valuable in application development. Through prototyping, classes, objects, inheritance mechanisms, meta concepts, and other elements may be defined, moved, deleted, have defaults sets, and have imposed validation rules.

A prototype allows mock-ups of system behavior (including interactive reports) to be defined, such designs being enriched with semantics. Prototyping techniques permit us to understand problem complexity and domain characteristics, provided that we capitalize on:

Lessons learned in how to structure the prototyping process

The ability to use conceptual modeling in prototype development

Facilities regarding the organization of multimedia data structures

The provision of interactive documentation with semantic modeling in its kernel

These issues are receiving considerable attention as the advantages of prototyping object-based solutions are becoming recognized.

Other advantages include better professional productivity and easy designer–user communication. The bottom line is efficient employment of human resources, as well as shorter implementation timetables and faster response to user requests.

As the introduction noted, the prototype may at first be an unproven, imperfect machine, but it is a very valuable one. It permits structuring the object domain through a model of the problem-solving process. A working model will not be perfect, but it will make it easier to correct specific errors and learn about the nature of the problems.

Following the loop of conceptualization, abstraction, concretization, testing, debugging, and refining the prototype is continued until the object-oriented system is satisfactory, or until we have learned enough to design a new version. This is the sense of the *meta-level framework* which, we said in Chapter 3, is largely preferable to the waterfall approach in software development.

Prototyping can follow structured lines, but ad-hoc methodologies are more popular with some software designers, because:

> Endusers find it easier to criticize and correct a working construct than explain verbally what is needed
>
> Designers see *their* prototyping solution as an elegant means to handle exceptions relating to information elements and rules
>
> The ad-hoc prototype keeps both parties interested in a dialog, which may otherwise not be the case.

In general, it is quite useful to get an object-oriented system working as soon as possible. A number of choices have to be made, however, regarding the type of objects to be used, their attributes, and their distribution. This process can be significantly assisted by experimentation, and the ground for experimentation is provided by the prototype.

9-3 PERFORMANCE, CONTENT, AND USAGE

In the course of software development, it is helpful to distinguish between *performance, content,* and *usage* characteristics as suggested in Fig. 9.1. Each of these main areas can be subdivided into component parts, all of them eventually converging toward the *target system.*

The classes may correspond to the organizational level of reference. The objects grouped in these classes will reflect:

1. Organizational concepts
2. Information elements and rules
3. Applications concepts

These three lines of reference define a universe of discourse. The meta

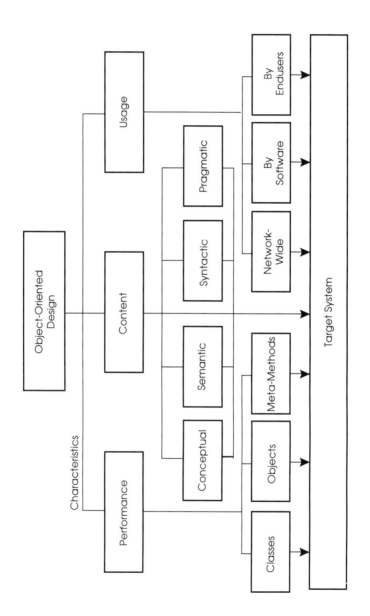

Figure 9.1 Underlying concepts in an object-oriented implementation.

122

method will define a higher level on a number of lower-level issues, including those of the data and rule types. All these lines of reference constitute the technical infrastructure that underlies the object-oriented approach.

Within the developing prototype, the various agents in the environment—*users, programs,* and *machines*—can be said to operate on entities that are known to the system and can be designated in it. The objects may be files in the traditional sense, record-oriented peripherals, communication channels, terminals; or the description of static and dynamic objects, including episodic memory IE and contexts of a program.

In a project management domain, for example, objects may represent information elements such as project milestones, tasks, committed resources, progression references, different values, or results obtained. Some may have complex relationships, such as, for instance, the documentation and source code for a program that contains several hundred modules, program fragments, configuration management routines, and so on.

A uniform treatment of the various classes of objects, and powerful mechanisms to store and designate these objects, are two important requirements that could be served through prototyping. The model allows the user to associate a number of attributes whose values represent specific properties, as well as express in a valid manner the relationships that can exist between objects.

A more detailed prototype will permit examination of the attributes and their primitive values which can be named individually. The same is true of relationships in which the objects participate. The latter permit experimentation on logical associations and dependencies between objects, making feasible a better structured but still flexible information environment. A prototype will be most helpful in looking into entities that represent composite objects, a notion that supercedes the traditional directory. Through it, we can establish explicitly a reference from one object to another.

Relationships may also be tested for attributes, which can be used to describe specific properties associated with missions. Another use of the prototype is to examine in more depth the designation of specific relationships, whether planned or ad-hoc.

All this means a significant role for prototyping in an object environment. Other issues have to do with timeliness of the development effort and the quality of the end product. We will look into them in more detail.

9-4 PROTOTYPE: A SOFTWARE EMULATOR

"The latest thinking in software engineering suggests that specifications should be interleaved with design rather than frozen before design," says Paul Abrahams, President of ACM. He adds that the tools we have available today permit interactive prototyping, making it feasible to:

Involve the enduser in the design process

Test and restructure the prototype

Shorten development times

Significantly improve software quality

Provide for better object-oriented approaches by acquiring both insight and foresight

The acquisition of experience through prototyping is very important, inasmuch as object-based reasoning strategies can be complex. The knowledge required may include spatial and/or temporal relationships,* and actions hinging on a great many conditions.

In certain applications, there are too many objects to handle and too much reliance on common-sense concepts, without the appropriate experience to back up the path we take in search of a solution. Twenty-five years ago, digital simulation was used as a working model. The aim was

* *abstraction* and
* *idealization*

of a physical system that we could study through computers prior to building the system itself. This followed a long tradition, from the 1940s when analog simulation was done through differential analyzers, to the 1950s with scale models, and into the 1960s with digital simulation of physical systems.†

As we saw in Section 1, prototyping is also a working model—but of a logical system. It is an *emulation* of the program's specifications, mapping the meta-rules in the design. It is a *dynamic specification,* not a static, rigid document, like classical system analysis.

Figure 9.2 follows a prototyping mission step by step. Once a network of objects has been constructed, the emulation can begin.

Emulation can proceed in two ways. With *synchronous* emulation, all objects may use the output values computed during the previous step as their input. The order of doing so is unimportant, since the object-oriented network being prototyped behaves as though all units update simultaneously, approximating parallel processing perspectives.

With *asynchronous* emulation, on the other hand, a fraction of the objects are updated at each step in, say, random order, and new output values are immediately transmitted to the other units. Synchronous emulation is easier to understand, but in a highly distributed environment, synchronous

---

*See Chapters 12 and 13 on spacial and temporal semantics.

†It has already been stated that Simula, a programming language developed for simulation studies, was the first object-oriented linguistic construct—and this was no coincidence.

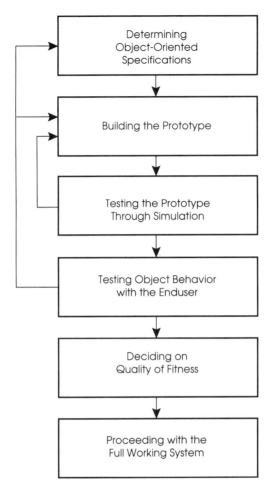

Figure 9.2   Prototyping an object environment.

updating with deterministic unit functions can lead to a confused outcome. It can result in oscillations in terms of system behavior, or may center on pseudo-problems.

In the general case, asynchronous emulation is more realistic, and more manageable. The object-oriented network is kept dynamic, and the prototype allows execution of user functions under real-life conditions. This is one of the reasons why there are significant benefits to be derived from prototypes of interactive systems: Dynamic object loading capabilities allow runtime redefinition of activation functions, and make feasible the construction of parts of the network as the results of the experimentation unfold.

The model we construct is a statement of a law of *object behavior.*

Within what the law of object behavior is supposed to represent, we should expect that the model predicts future real-life situations. In this phrase is embedded the very concept of experimentation, and the reference remains valid *if* these situations are governed by the mathematical laws we use in our model, *and* the population of objects does not change significantly, making the model invalid in a class sense.

The software emulator will help create a logical model, just as a metrics model can be formulated with the help of statistical or other appropriate techniques.

9–5 DO PROTOTYPES, NOT STEREOTYPES

The last sentences of Section 4 identify the main difference between *prototypes* and *stereotypes*. The former follow an experimental approach in the definition and handling of the problem space under consideration. They develop object-based modules, interface diagrams, and control flow capabilities, keeping every system component dynamic and changeable. By contrast, the stereotypes of classical DP programming languages fix the problem space in an inflexible manner. Their goal is code generation rather than the provision of an evolving problem solution.

According to the approach to be selected in prototyping, different types of models can be distinguished and experimented with. The three main classes of models are:

1. Theoretical
2. Data driven
3. Composite

Theoretical models are based on hypothesized relations among objects. Data-driven models rest largely on statistical analysis, with little concern for intuitive justification of the formulas being used. Composite models employ both approaches to determine the basic shape of a simulator or emulator. Data analysis helps specify the model's constants, while the theoretical background is instrumental in building into the model algorithms and heuristics.

Experimentation is a basic discipline in mathematics and in science. This statement is just as valid for object-oriented solutions. The three main features of the scientific method are:

1. The performance of experiments according to experimental design rules
2. The drawing of objective conclusions from experiments

3. The construction of laws to simplify the description of the conclusions reached from a class of experiments.

The classical approach in science is to separate theoretical and empirical solutions. The new distinguishes among three alternatives: Theoretical, experimental, and empirical—with emphasis on experimental.

By *experimental treatment* we mean the combination and testing of the factors that must be compared. This approach is as valid in relation to logical constructs in software as it is in physics—the latest breakthrough being exemplified by the object orientation. In the physical sciences, experimental results are reported in terms of frequencies, means, standard deviation, analysis of variance, correlation coefficients, factorial analysis, and test of hypothesis. In an object-based logical construct, experimental results must be reported in terms of classes, instantiations, inheritance, the meta layer, equilibrium, data abstraction, and the other fundamental criteria we considered in Chapters 1 and 2.

There are also challenges in the use of models. A major one is to conceptualize the idealized form, understanding the sense of approximations and distinguishing the relevant parts from the irrelevant.

Another challenge lies in the ability to separate the significant effects from the insignificant, summarizing and/or discriminating if the same reason accounts for different results, and understanding quantitative information in a qualitative way.

The ultimate challenge is in applying results obtained from experimentation in object-oriented real-world situations. This is the ultimate test of any science, and one of the cases where the means justifies the effort.

9-6 OBJECT-ORIENTED BLACKBOARDS

The *blackboard architecture* originally emerged from a continuous speech understanding project, Hearsay II, carried out at Carnegie Mellon University in the early 1970s. Today, blackboard-type solutions are pursued in a variety of problems, such as picture analysis, studies of protein structures based on empirical constraints, construction site layout, and object orientation associated with distributed databases.

Blackboard solutions can be useful in object-based applications because we are increasingly concerned about distributed information systems and their high-technology environments. A key advantage of a blackboard architecture is its ability to handle networked databases and workstations with processes operating in parallel.

Because networked information elements and rules interact among themselves and influence one another, we need a discipline that makes it feasible for them to be handled as self-standing but coordinated entities.

Object orientation assures this function. We also require a mechanism that permits objects to actuate one another through message passing, but that also informs and is informed of other objects' intentions. This is exactly where a blackboard architecture comes in.

Blackboard applications are particularly useful in knowledge engineering applications, but they have also been used for economic studies, business planning, risk evaluation, as well as computer-aided design, computer-integrated manufacturing, and other purposes, such as the planning of missions for autonomous vehicles and automatically analyzing satellite photographs.

Many of these examples are particularly well suited for an object-oriented implementation. Hence a study of the blackboard architecture is an integral part of object prototyping and programming, providing facilities that cannot easily be obtained otherwise.

The Crysalis project, at Stanford University, for example, addressed itself to the automatic interpretation of protein electron-density maps. It used a skeletonization algorithm to convert the electron density map to a line-skeleton representation, then partitioned the skeleton graph into chemical side chains and backbone elements. Rules and meta-rules were employed in an objectlike manner, to hypothesize and test atoms and "superatoms" based on the partitioned skeleton graph and the known chemical model of the protein under study. A blackboard architecture was adopted that included a hierarchically organized hypothesis of data structures, as well as support for the current hypothesis from the partitioned skeleton graph and chemical model.

The model used hypothesis toeholds to fire strategy rules and determine which task set to consider next. Part of the mission was to match task rules against the type (class) column of the event list, focusing on one event or object.

Subsequently, this model matched the hypothesis state and the *where* portion of the event to the rules, to increment the hypothesis and add to the object list. This cycle of operations was repeated until no further matches occurred, at which point the model returned control to the strategy-rule interpreter.

The blackboard solution was instrumental in helping Crysalis determine the three-dimensional structure of protein molecules. Problem sources can easily be expressed in an object form, whether they are due to:

Errors resulting from an incomplete or out-of-order amino acid sequence

Assumptions about *weights* for data quality and rule importance

Vague or uncertain *information elements* from electrodensity maps or other constructs

Nested *knowledge source activations* due to preconditioning

The blackboard architecture was of considerable assistance in providing an evolving communications solution for rules and information elements—therefore for objects—in stating of the hypotheses. This was particularly true in toeholding opportunities for accelerated development and testing of hypotheses, as well as in communications connected to the event list of recent changes by type and location.

9-7 USING THE BLACKBOARD FOR INTERFACING TO THE DATABASE

There are reasons why blackboard architectures are becoming an increasingly popular basis for the construction of problem-solving systems at large, as well as why object-oriented situations can greatly benefit from them. Typically, systems that stand to gain from blackboard solutions operate in domains requiring qualitatively different kinds of knowledge to be applied in order to arrive at a conclusion.

The metaphor on which blackboard approaches are based, as well as the structure of the blackboard database and its contents, are fairly easy to explain and comprehend. The metaphor is based on cooperative group problem solving, which is typical of practically all object-based situations. Hearsay II, for example, had a single blackboard divided into seven abstraction levels. Of these, the *database interface* level linked the system to a text database; this layer appeared at the top of the abstraction hierarchy, immediately above the *conceptual* level.

Since the Hearsay II blackboard is often taken as a reference standard it pays to take a closer look at it. It is arranged as a single, linear abstraction hierarchy as shown in Fig. 9.3. There are rules for accessing the blackboard:

1. A knowledge source has priority.
2. This knowledge source uses the blackboard to bridge two solution islands (or classes)
3. The user source writes before it reads
4. Access is ring-type, from left to right.

The *knowledge sources* of the blackboard architecture can be objects that behave with domain independence and use the blackboard as a structured database. Through this approach, they interact and communicate with one another.

A blackboard *monitor* acts as the system of traffic lights, and a *scheduler* activates knowledge sources and objects. The application of priorities or any other blackboard access rule requires the action of the monitor. Blackboard

Blackboard

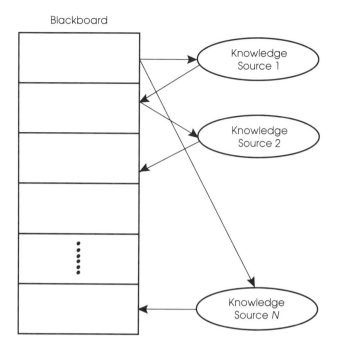

Figure 9.3   Implementation example with a blackboard architecture.

control can be provided by strategy, task, and object knowledge sources. In Crysalis, for instance, control focused on:

Clock events, rules to be processed at specific times
Possible problems, such as missing information
Expectation of different events
Objects writing information on the blackboard

The blackboard organization provides support for control in the form of an abstraction hierarchy, but it is the scheduler that enforces control strategies. The scheduler makes control decisions on the basis of the state of the blackboard and the applicable knowledge that is available at any point in time.

Blackboard schedulers can implement multiple strategies and are able to switch between strategies depending on the state of an emerging solution. Typically the scheduler maintains a control database, which records knowledge source activations in some form or another. The scheduler searches its control database to find knowledge sources that are applicable to the current state.

Knowledge source activations are created whenever an object is triggered. They record a variety of information about what caused the object source to trigger, such as details of the triggering event; where and when the trigger took place; as well as other data useful to the scheduler and its activities.

This discussion has emphasized the principles rather than the implementation details specific to a given situation. The details are an implementation's own characteristic values and therefore require a clear problem definition. Well-understood principles, by contrast, can be generally applicable.

Chapter 10

Prototyping
the Distributed Solution

10-1 INTRODUCTION

In an environment characterized by objects with communications-intense requirements, prototypes permit experimentation on networked solutions and evaluation of results to be expected. They permit educated guesses on the reliability of the outcome. Prototypes can be used to:

Check the validity of the global approach being taken

Refine original specifications

Integrate the objects being designed but also decompose them into finer components

Optimize and verify the developing design, leading to the derivation of needed details.

This process of design and verification is important to all implementations of information technology, but especially in a distributed environment. As we have seen in Chapter 9, the merger of object-oriented solutions and knowledge engineering presents unique opportunities for solving complex problems with distributed information systems. The blackboard architecture is only one example; we will see many more in this chapter.

Within limits, the prototypes permit us to activate the network, examine blackboard perspectives, link objects to one another, resolve incompatibilities, and evaluate the wisdom of decisions that have been made.

At the option of the designer, the prototype may focus on specific rather than general aspects, for instance, ad-hoc query handling functions, distributed concurrency control, or communications interfaces. But it may also be a global optimization verifier or a means of assuring conformity to original plans and definitions.

Since prototyping is computer-supported, it is faster than developing a classical system analysis on paper. And since the prototype is itself a fairly complete system according to the 80/20 rule, it can be run on the machine the final program will be running on, even though it is not optimized for runtime performance.

In other words, in contrast to classical DP approaches, which work on an all-or-nothing basis, prototypes offer insight into key features of the problem. Their strengths lie in the facts that they can be delivered early in the process of development, they are rapidly done, and their costs are containable.

10-2 PROTOTYPES AND SOFTWARE QUALITY

The best prototypes are focused. In an object-oriented environment they can be, for instance, constructed to help evaluate concurrency control on the network or to examine a distributed deadlock problem. A recovery system can be embedded in the model to preserve object integrity, with well-defined functional responsibilities.

In these examples, prototyping provides the designer with more options than simply observing executable specifications. It offers the benefits of early error detection at less investment than more classical approaches can provide, helping to answer questions such as:

What are the current latencies, throughputs, and reliability of the logical links between objects?

What are the existing restrictions in object-to-object communications due to external considerations?

Should we increase the execution speed of the network at the expense of reliability, or vice versa?

Is the operating software exhibiting unstable behavior due to some insufficiency? What is this insufficiency?

Similar queries can be posed with regard to process scheduling and workload balancing.

In an object environment, the finer programmatic interfaces cannot be worked out, much less performed, unless substantial amounts of information regarding the operating software and the parallel hardware are available.

Typically, this information includes details on program construction such as descriptions of the decomposition of the application code into processes—code modules and information elements—therefore, *objects*. Some details of these processes and multimedia information elements, as well as configuration data including the dynamic hardware and operating software states, must be made available in a fairly dependable form. Prototyping helps in doing this job well.

The availability of experimental results may mean a better-quality product at the end. Figure 10.1 divides the quality domain into four quarterspaces. In the upper half, the degree of disruption within an applications environment is average to high. A high degree of disruption is characteristic of monolithic designs applied to programming products and of throwaway software. These are the stereotypes we discussed in Chapter 9.

In the bottom half of Fig. 10.1, the degree of disruption tends to be low, because technical detail is embedded into a modular structure rather

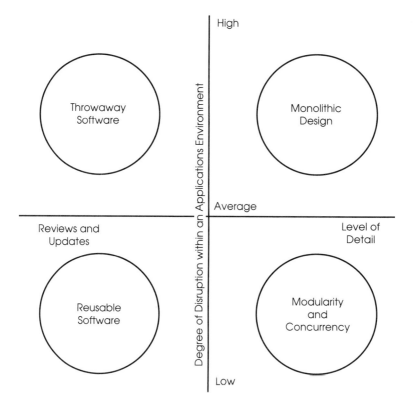

Figure 10.1   Quarter spaces of a quality domain in software engineering.

than being monolithic. In such an environment, reviews and updates can be simpler, faster, and more efficient, leading to reusable software. At the same time, parameterization and modularity help improve the level of detail.

Both types of results are attainable through object orientation provided that the criteria just mentioned are religiously observed. Throughout the organization, reusable software policies must be established and prototyping used consistently to model the environment under development.

Companies and professionals who have used such an approach have found that the constructs can be polyvanent. One implementation followed this scenario closely in projecting data structures for text-generation tasks, established sentence boundaries as direct correlates of text and data representation features, and elaborated generation goals implicit in the object-oriented program structure. Because of a priori experimentation, the resulting object-based programming product has proved adequate for some nontext computational purposes as well.

Experimental approaches are also instrumental in the selection of object structures and program components, as well as their dynamic substitution by others with different performance or reliability characteristics. Through prototyping, changes to component attributes that affect reliability or performance characteristics are studied beforehand, and the same is true of their interactions that affect, for example, time-out values used for communication among artifacts, or scheduling of tasks as well as their mappings to the different nodes of a parallel hardware.

A similar case can be made for the synthesis of specialized communication primitives for an application. The programmer (or algorithm) that decides, performs, or supervises object-related adaptations must have access to information that is not usually available but that can be emulated through prototyping.

10-3 GRAPHICAL APPROACHES TO AID HUMAN–MACHINE COMMUNICATION

As in prototyping, graphical knowledge-based tools permit a visual representation of an object-oriented environment. They also make it feasible to determine the structure of a domain:

Finding relevant objects—for instance clients, accounts, transactions—and relations among them

Establishing the attributes of each object: Name, sex, age, balance of account, type of transaction, and value

Breaking the reasoning down into stages, thus providing for further detail.

Experimentation helps in determining the structure of the domain, establishing an object-oriented working system, as well as testing, debugging, and refining the construct interactively. The same is true for graphical representation.

Since the 1970s, when methodologies were first created to help in software design, the role of *pattern recognition* has been appreciated, and system analysts have been advised to follow through with pictures. This is true of system component diagrams, interface diagrams, and control flow diagrams. In addition, system designers found it fruitful to draw plenty of pictures of their own, using icons* and lines between them as initial sketches of the problem space, and developing a pattern on how the different components interact with each other.

Such an approach is fully applicable within an object orientation. It should be followed consistently and should be computer supported, as there are a wealth of graphics software available that can be used to advantage.

To elaborate an object-oriented approach along these lines, it is necessary both to define the information elements and to determine the domain rules. Rules need a *structure* to fit into, and the more accurate the latter is, the better. Information modeling identifies and describes the object required to operate a business system, determining what types of objects exist and what facts are known about them. A graphical presentation helps in clearing ideas and concretizing concepts that might otherwise remain uncertain.

Objects may be customers, accounts, products, orders, or marketing plans that need to be identified, described, or recorded with their given names, synonyms, and narrative descriptions. Facilities must be provided to capture, store, edit, and validate the descriptors of these objects—and such facilities are greatly assisted through visualization.

Quite often, a graphics interface provides indispensable information on objects during emulation and simulation, and during the debugging process as well. It allows the developer to view and examine the object environment before, during, and after execution.

Each significant aspect associated to each object in the network can be displayed as a separate icon whose size, shape, or shading varies with its current value. As the simulator runs, the icons are constantly updated to reflect changing values. This gives an overall view of what the operating environment is doing. A graphics interface provides maximum flexibility to the user in determining how objects are displayed.

In addition to displaying and running objects, the graphics interface should have facilities that allow the user to display detailed textual information for specific objects, and to show network topology as well as log the simulator and graphics commands for later replay. It should be possible to

*Icons are familiar objects, hence easily recognizable by most users.

move freely all objects—icons, text, data, drawings—appearing on the display, as dictated by changing functional requirements.

10-4 DEVELOPING GRAPHICS INTERFACES

A graphics interface is a vital component of the prototyping process, and much of its power lies in its dynamic properties. In principle, representation schemes are evaluated on the basis of:

1. *Expressiveness.* Does the representation scheme make all of the important distinctions between the objects being represented? Can it support different specialized and ad-hoc forms of representation?
2. *Representation uniformity.* Can different types of knowledge and different classes of objects be expressed with the same general scheme? Is the representation scheme compact, clear, and at the right level of abstraction?
3. *Computational efficiency.* Does the representation scheme allow for efficient computation of various inferences required by the object? Is it easily modifiable? Who can proceed with the modification? And how should this be done?
4. *Multiple-level mapping.* Does the representation scheme allow the mapping of the same concept at different levels of abstraction? Does it permit meta-layers and inheritance?
5. *Logical consistency.* Are the different objects mutually and logically consistent? Is the representation scheme such that all objects operating in the environment as well as the associated desired knowledge can be easily accessed?

A proper representation scheme will be typically based on a detailed analysis of the necessary characteristics of various object sources such as situation databases, as well as functional knowledge pertinent to a target task. It will extend to inheritance mechanisms and blackboard solutions for sharing information served by structural descriptors and interfaces between objects.

A valid solution will capitalize on the fact that objects, relationships, and attributes have types which define their properties. *Object types* may be linked together by subtyping relationships that can be expressed graphically. The *object base structure* and its *integrity constraints* are represented by a set of type definitions for objects, attributes, and links. This is the *object base schema*. It is vital that a process operates with a set of definitions that constitute its working schema, established for a given process but also dynamically reestablished as the operational context changes.

A working schema corresponds to a description of certain constraints on the properties of a collection of objects and of relationships, as operated by a given process. It can also reflect the specificities of a given programming tool which has been applied to the objects and relationships in connection to a specific user or task.

Various users and tools might access the same objects, but see only the information that is relevant to them. This, too, can be mapped in graphical form. If the proper security mechanism is in place, the object base structure used by a tool or a set of tools will act as a gateway control. The latter can be and should be described in a separate schema definition.

$10-5$ THE ROLE OF KNOWLEDGE ABSTRACTION

Prototyping processes at large, and most specifically those connected with object representation, need *knowledge abstraction*. This is one of the areas that has not yet received the attention necessary for formal representation within an object-oriented environment.

The use of knowledge engineering brings competitive advantages to an object orientation. It provides, or alternatively enhances, a systematic methodology for handling abstraction or conceptualization of the problem space. It can also help in terms of class expressions.

Abstraction is the middle layer between the acquisition and the representation of knowledge, both being crucial stages in the development of an object-oriented system. *Acquisition* involves eliciting, analyzing, and interpreting the knowledge that an expert uses. The first phase of knowledge *abstraction* is idealization, followed by conretization through prototyping. *Representation* is the process of transforming the acquired knowledge into a suitable artifact or machine.

Knowledge abstraction may, for example, concern facts about entities that interact in a given object-oriented system. They define the types of relationships between different entities. For example, if each customer is assigned to one branch office for contacts and support, then there should be a fact about servicing each customer through a single assigned branch.

When prototyping, this type of fact must be recorded, indicating that each customer is associated with one branch and that each branch has a list of customers assigned to it. This type of reference is made at a level of abstraction describing the existence and type of an interobject structure.

The second kind of fact, pertinent to the subjects being described, provides some measurement of the entity (or object) and is used to distinguish one object from another of the same type. This is the role of *attributes*. Pertinent questions help to identify measurement facts in connection to attributes, within the prototyping structure.

This is true all the way from heuristics to algorithmic procedures. *Heuristics* is a conceptual approach based on trial and error. It is nonprocedural, involving vagueness and uncertainty. Heuristic processes typically reflect *qualitative* reasoning and (sometimes) quantitative results. Heuristic solutions can also imply classification order to achieve efficient search strategies. These can be expressed through an object shell.

An object shell is also instrumental in the development of powerful prototypes. Ptech, which we discuss in Sections 7 and 8 of this chapter, has been used successfully to conceptualize a distributed database structure, identifying all component information elements and their contents, the organizational units from which they descended and which are using them, and the way in which information elements link to processes and vice versa. This is one of the best examples of the way an object solution can help in knowledge abstraction, and it is not the only one.

To gain an appreciation of what object-oriented prototyping can do, and to obtain control of the method, a Swiss chemicals company started with a prototype that reflected the coarse grain, types, and relations regarding future information technology implementations. The result obtained documented the simplicity and ease of understanding of the requirements that were presented, as well as the associated constraints.

The second prototype, using an object approach, involved knowledge abstraction and considered interactive work with users—focusing on the design of a small database. Ptech helped to improve the system analysis timetable by 25 percent; but more important, it provided solutions that are factual, easy to demonstrate, and easy to prove.

On-line development contributed to easing the enduser-oriented applications backlog. What impressed the endusers most was the fact that this sort of database design, interactively done and immediately visualized, was far more comprehensive than paper documents. The approach proved to be much more factual than the manual work on information elements and structures that had been done till then.

Based on these results, another project was undertaken on integrative database design involving much larger perspectives. This covered different databases, though the most voluminous was one under IMS. Here again, visualization was key to the comprehensive presentation of the results. Quite important, as well, was the timeframe within which such project materialized.

In Sections 7 and 8 we shall see the features of Ptech that permitted this accomplishment. It should not be forgotten, however, that the big difference is, as always, the contribution of expert human capital.

10–6 GOALS OF KNOWLEDGE ELICITATION

In the preceding section we saw that the power and utility of an object-based environment depend on the quality of the underlying representation of knowledge. The example we considered was very simple, but knowledge elicitation is often a difficult and challenging task, which can be a bottleneck in the production of object-based systems. Techniques have been developed, however, to increase its effectiveness within a selected domain. These techniques come primarily from knowledge engineering, and should be capitalized on during the development of object-oriented solutions.

To a large measure, the same is true of object representation. In the latter case the designer can influence system behavior by making some of the following initial choices:

1. Formalisms for representation
2. Procedures with which the construct can operate on observations
3. Strategies for internal representation of external observations
4. Tools for the generalization of observations
5. Limitations due to the complexity of the learned object-based model
6. Representations of the object(s) structure

While the last choice above is served by object-oriented languages and linguistic approaches discussed in Chapter 3, the first five choices are higher layers constituting prerequisites to the last. Once should also consider going beyond point 6 toward the automatic generation of object models of an observed environment.

As far as the first five choices are concerned, experience from knowledge engineering can provide rewarding results. Without it there will be limitations of learning relative to one or another level of abstraction, for example:

Learning about objects, or even object classes, but not learning how to use object relations effectively

Learning about words, or syntax, or phonemes, but not learning about language

Developing specifications that rest on a conventional naive approach

Confusing data processing roles with an object orientation

Another way of saying this is that with object-oriented systems the pivot process of knowledge abstraction is full of difficulties. It is also not very well understood. We are still at a very early stage of development, where experience is still being gathered and general principles have not yet emerged.

This is true, but some of the reasons are historical. The first software abstraction, now called *procedural,* grew out of a fully empirical view of programming. Procedural abstraction is the isolation, either as subprograms or macros, of useful sequences of possibly parameterized computer instructions. Subroutines were invented in the early 1950s but were not appreciated as abstractions at that time. Nor have subsequent developments in computer programming elaborated in a rigorous manner the concept of abstraction within the realm of procedural approaches.

Some people might add that this is not entirely true: The original higher-level languages, such as Fortran, abstracted the semantics of primarily arithmetic expressions away from the machine and embedded access to them in the syntax of the new languages. Of course, arithmetic expressions often reflect problem-level relationships and the ability to express arithmetic operations directly in the syntax of a computer language. Hence, Fortran was indeed an important step. But it had to do with *procedures,* not with *knowledge*—and object-oriented solutions are nonprocedural.

Only the knowledge engineering-based, nonprocedural solutions have approached the issue of abstraction in an able manner. This has become key to the development of object-oriented environments, and to a large extent it conditions how successful we may be with their development and operation.

10-7 THE PTECH SHELL

Ptech (by Associated Design Technology, ADT) is an object shell that draws upon elements of class and on functional calculus, featuring a methodology for object-based design. It is a graphical modeling tool that can execute interpretively, permitting the user to test assumptions.

Typically, the Ptech shell supports a workstation-based environment that uses knowledge-based graphics to visualize processes and their operation. Manipulations of the graphics modify the process specification database, while changes in the database are reflected by the graphics.

After process descriptions are developed, Ptech can be used to check designs for conceptual integrity using examples with functional prototyping capability. Logical implications are computed and constraints checked in real time. The following characteristics underline the way Ptech works by means of events, event types, and operators.

1. An *event* is an actual change of state of an object.
2. An event is an actual change as the successful application of an operator.
3. An *event type* can be preType or postType, which are disjoint types.
4. An operator is a potential for change, a subtle but important distinction.
5. An *operator* may have multiple implementation methods.

The power of operators lies in the ability to refer to them without regard to their implementation. Correspondingly, the force of event types is due to the facility of specifying cause and effect of applications of operators. Operators may be applied in different ways, each application corresponding to an event type.

1. An *event* equals *object state change.* At any given moment, an object may have many concepts that are applicable. If so, their intersection is the state of the object—although that may change.

2. An *event schema* is a *process specification.* Ptech uses an event schema to prescribe the changes in state; each change of state of an object is an event. There are at least two ways to think about an event schema. One is as the process specification of an active object. The other is as a method or, more precisely, process rules. Such rules specify an implementation of some operator along with a method selection capability.

   The concept of operators and their reusability is quite important. Basic operators are: create object, classify, declassify, terminate object. These operators and many others are provided in Ptech libraries.

   Every operator has an argument set, each with a typing rule and cardinal constraints. In addition, there exists a distinguishing argument: the *given object* with a typing rule, the *preType;* and a *return value* with a typing rule, the *postType.* The goal of the operator is to take a given object, an instance of the preType, and effect a change so that it is an instance of the postType. Event type specifies a class of events regardless of the operator used to effect the change.

3. *Event types* and *guards* may participate in class expressions. A guard is a condition on a process rule and may be a complex Boolean expression. The conditional process rule will not fire if any guard associated with the rule is false. A guard is associated with an event type and is evaluated for the object. Guards may be composed using class expressions, and are defined in connection to event types. Syntactically, they are displayed adjacent to event types with process rules.

4. *Process rules* are specializations of the fundamental cause-and-effect relation. Syntactically, process rules are displayed as directed lines (with arrowheads) connecting event types and guards. A function is necessary when the process rule requires an event on one object to cause events on related objects.

   There are several sources of parallelism that can be specified in an event schema, for instance, independent process paths. Parallel process rules address the parallel invocation of an operator.

   The designer may not care to specify how an external event is implemented. He simply detects that it has happened. With these fundamental notions have been built the prototypes we discussed in Section 5, with regard to the Swiss chemicals company.

Quite importantly, when the prototyping job is done, the programming task has finished with it. Ptech, and a number of other meta-linguistic constructs,* use generators to compile on-line into C. This greatly simplifies the task of coding, improves programmer productivity, and upgrades the quality of software.

10–8 CLASSIFICATION AND METHOD SELECTION

Basic in any meta-linguistic approach are the concepts of classification and subclassification. Classification is the primitive relation. In an object schema, one of the most common and useful expressions is one that asserts that one concept is a subconcept of another—hence subclassification.

A *class partition* is a division of a class into disjoint subclasses. The superclass is the union of disjoint classes. As an extension of this concept, the class can have multuple independent class partitions, with the superclass being the union of the displayed classes and subclasses.

In terms of implementation, this affects software development directly. When argumented with a specific object, a function returns a class of objects. The class may contain one or more objects. The purpose of evaluating a function is to get hold of the object(s) to pass to an operator, and then to use these objects as argument(s) for invoking the operator.

When specifying a function, we may also wish to specify the minimum and maximum number of objects that the function may return. In Ptech, these are known as the *lowerbound* and *upperbound* cardinality constraints.

Like all object languages, Ptech supports a *method selection* mechanism. When the encapsulating operations on a type are specified, it is not the *how* a given operation may be carried out that is defined, but the *what.* How it is carried out defines the method for the operation, and is specified separately.

Ptech also provides a knowledge engineering approach for conceptualizing and defining processes. This involves a strategic-level discipline based on mission or value-added analysis, and a tactical level approach—essentially, analysis of events, triggers, and processes expressed as cause-and-effect networks.

Another vital component is a general conceptual approach reflecting the formal technology of conceptual schemata. There is also an embedded data dictionary facility.

As an integrated design, Ptech describes processes and databases at all levels of detail. Therefore, it can be used to exploit database structure and

---

*For example, Eiffel, discussed in Chapter 9.

contents. Implementation examples have used Ptech as an object-oriented software engineering tool, and in connection with code generation features.*

Thus Ptech can be employed as a front-end method that also adds value to implementations using relational technologies, but benefiting from object features. This is achieved through class expressions that allow the definition of classes in terms of other classes already in use, including relations as special cases of classes.

Functional calculus with temporal capability is used to express class membership, constraints, and rules. Nested transactions as well as dynamic classification and declassification are made possible. The same is true of schematic notation.

The object paradigm focuses attention on reusability by emphasizing abstraction. It provides simplicity but also upholds performance by maintaining integrity for more complex applications.

Concepts and operators of the problem domain are mapped exactly onto the programming language. As a result, there is one concept set for the expert of the problem domain and the software engineer.

The point is that software development can and should be automated through object implementation technology. Concepts specified by business people are automatically converted into code after prototyping, while knowledge-enriched, object solutions see to it that specification and implementation are unified.

The compilation of the Ptech shell into C++ solves the transition problem from system analysis to coding. Ptech's C++ compiler supports generation of class libraries, with methods for all of the basic operators and functions. This assures integrity as prescribed by the design phase. There are also optimization routines to achieve performance for generated applications, including support for logical and other constraints.

*Best exemplified by the Ontos object DBMS.

Chapter 11

The Nuts and Bolts
of Object Programming

$11-1$ INTRODUCTION

As stated in the Preface, software engineering and database management
have traditionally been separate disciplines. Originally, file management
database technology concentrated on static issues of information storage,
with programming modeling the dynamic software aspects. However, since
the development of relational database models and fourth-generation languages, the two disciplines have been moving toward systems that model
both process and data. This process has been furthered by object-oriented
solutions.

In addition to introducing dynamic concepts and their modeling, object-oriented databases represent a significant increase in our ability to capture the semantics of information elements leading toward semantic modeling.

1. An interest in object databases arose from application areas where
   traditional database systems fail to meet growing user requirements.
2. It became evident that, in order to exploit object databases properly, it
   is necessary to use object-oriented programming approaches.
3. It has been appreciated that since implementation requirements continue to expand, further new application areas call for an enhancement
   of object-type concepts.

Today we are beginning to appreciate that unless we have complete information, we cannot effectively automate the job which we are doing. Not only data, but also knowledge and rules regarding a given job, are part of the complete information requirements.

In a way, this sets the stage for a discussion of the nuts and bolts of programming within the context of an object orientation and most particularly of object databases. While one can think of databases as being independent of programming, this approach, as has been explained, is not advisable.

One of the main contributions of a joint solution to database and programming challenges is a valid way to *constrain specifications*. A *constraint* is a description of some relationship between two or more objects (factors, variables) that must be enforced. Because of their declarative nature, constraints are an attractive specification methodology: They permit one to describe what the relationship is, rather than how to achieve it; and they lead to a constraint satisfaction system that focuses on changes to variables.

Constraints are especially useful for specifying certain aspects of system construction, among the most important being the management of databases. Object approaches are rich in constraint specifications. In fact, a great deal of their power results directly from their ability to handle constraints.

11-2 BASIC CONCEPTS OF OBJECT PROGRAMMING

The first phase in developing a representation programming scheme for a slice of the real world is to project it as a collection of *objects* (named entities) enhanced by a collection of *relationships* among them. At any moment, the content of these collections constitutes a *state*.

State transformations occur through the creation or destruction of objects or relationships. This is the mechanism by which the databasing of information elements becomes inseparable from object programming. More precisely, it makes it feasible for programming and databasing to complement one another.

Object programming is distinguished from other paradigms in that it preserves the same decomposition throughout design, implementation, and maintenance.

An object-oriented programming system is an organizational framework for combining objects and operations and managing their mutual interactions. Correspondingly, object programming languages, such as the examples we saw in Chapters 9 and 10, support this programming paradigm.

An object-oriented language provides appropriate data structures and commands. And, as discussed in the introduction to this chapter, it imposes the necessary constraints on the usage of such commands and structures.

Evidence has already been presented in preceding chapters that object languages typically provide data abstraction, the class concept, inheritance, extension and intention, encapsulation, message passing, and methods. We also spoke of methods versus operations, as well as overloading and polymorphism.

For database applications, equally important linguistic features are object identity, extensibility, and computational completeness. These terms will now be explained; in the interests of simplicity, object programming languages will be loosely identified with Smalltalk.

As Chapter 1 explained, data abstraction refers to the use of abstract data types. In a programming paradigm, these help define an object in terms of its behavior, which is independent of the program manipulating it at any given time. Some languages provide a built-in hierarchy of objects, which can be used directly or can help to define new classes. Objects with similar behavior are grouped into a hierarchy of classes; the top of the hierarchy is the class object, and each class usually has a number of instances.

A programming function is a mapping between two classes, their domain and range. A class function maps from one class to a subclass of another, including temporal information,★ such as whether the function is to be evaluated at the current moment, at another specific moment, over a period of time, or permanently.

The grouping of objects into a hierarchy of classes and subclasses is a distinctive advantage, which allows an object of a subclass to inherit both storage structure and operations from its superclass. Programming paradigms both preserve and enhance this notion.

It has also been emphasized that inheritance is one of the most powerful elements of object databases; this is also true in programming. The feature that sets object programming apart from less sophisticated sorts of abstract data types is indeed inheritance—and with it, the concept of meta.

Inheritance owes a great deal of its importance to the fact that it enables creation of new classes of objects by specifying the differences between a new class and an existing class. This is much better than having to build the new class all over from scratch, and object programming capitalizes on this capability—but not in a uniform manner.

Some object languages organize the hierarchy as a tree, thereby allowing a subclass to inherit directly from one superclass, and indirectly from the line of its ancestors back to the object class. This is referred to as a *lattice*.

Other languages represent the hierarchy as a directed acyclic graph, thereby permitting a subclass to inherit from several superclasses. This is called *multiple inheritance.*

As with object databases, in object programming a class is itself an object that can have instances, namely, the objects that belong to it. Abstraction and encapsulation are used to formalize the notion of an object, which is made the central unit of modularity.

★See also Chapters 12 and 13 on spatial and temporal semantics.

Within this realm, a *concept* is a bundle of knowledge that holds for every object to which the concept applies. Objects to which a given concept is applicable are the extension of that concept, with the individual objects of the extension being the instances. This gives considerable power to object programming solutions.

Every concept has an intension, or definition, expressed, for instance, as a Boolean function. Acquisition of a concept requires that the analyst/programmer be able to determine when and where the concept applies, as well as when and where it does not apply.

This *intentional* approach to objects helps further explain a class as a *set,* the term used in mathematics and logic to refer to a collection of objects to which a concept is applicable. By consequence, the terms *class* and *set* are synonymous.

Every concept determines a class, as its extension. Concepts may be coextensive, in the sense of determining the same class.

There is, however, a difference when we talk of *types,* with emphasis on typing systems for programming languages. In a way, a type is equivalent to a concept, as just defined. However, not all problem domain concepts map to programming language types. In programming languages, if the type is an abstract data type, the instances are objects.

11–3 TYPING AND INSTANTIATION

A *type* is a set of data objects defined by a *predicate* that enables expressions of the type to be recognized. Clearly defined operations can be applied to this type to obtain meaningful results.

Types are used at compile time to assure that data structures and operations are appropriately paired. We have spoken of the difference between *types* and *classes* in Chapter 1, and also said that classes have more of a runtime role in creating and manipulating objects.

This approach helps in appreciating the close connection between object databases and object programming. A number of factors characterize the state of an object. Such a state may change, hence the reference to the state of an object as *at a moment.* There is great power embedded in this concept of *instantiation.*

Inheritance, which is one of the advantages of the object approach, is a flexible and dynamic process precisely because of instantiation. Without instantiation it would be nothing more than the monolithic hierarchical structure of other certain DBMS. Flexibility is vital in state changes, where events capture causal relations of object states over time.

Every object is endowed with a persistent private memory representing its state, together with a public interface in the form of a set of operators. This is the object's protocol, used to change its state or extract information by operating on its memory. Hence objects encapsulate both behavior and state, which again is a vital facility in software development.

Earlier chapters have also emphasized that message passing is a very important concept. In programming, objects communicate and perform all computations by exchanging messages, a message consisting of three parts:

1. The object to which it is being sent
2. The name of the message
3. A list of arguments (which may be empty)

The message instructs the object to change its internal state. Hence, associated with each message is a *method,* that is, a procedure for implementing the message. We have spoken of methods in relation to object databases. This definition is also valuable in an object programming context.

In object programming, as in databasing, a method is a *script* that specifies *how* an operation is to be carried out. It is best represented in the form of an event schema. A method consists of three parts:

1. The *name* of the class to which the method applies
2. A *message* format, including a name and parameters
3. A *body* of executable code to implement the message

Methods are defined for classes, not for instances. Each class object has a method dictionary of the specific messages that can be sent to its instances. Each instance knows its class; when it receives a message, it searches the methods dictionary of its class for the corresponding method. If the method is not found, the instance's superclasses are searched until the method is found. Alternatively, failure is reported when a class object is reached and the method has not been found.

Enriched with methods, the class functions as an object template. A new instance of the class is created by sending the class object some version of the built-in message mechanism.

At the same time, the class functions as an object warehouse. The collection of its instances—that is, its extension—is attached to it as a list. The programmer, or a knowledgeable user, can manipulate the contents of the warehouse by applying operations to all elements of the class.

Since classes are objects, they can be the recipients of appropriate messages. The corresponding methods are held in *meta-classes.*

The handling of complex objects is one of the major contributions of object programming. Their representation requires the provision of data types with a nested structure, which is not supported by relational approaches restricted to flat files.

Overloading of message names is analogous to the use of generic functions in procedural languages. This facility helps in sending the same message to instances of different classes and in evoking different, but appropriate responses.

Late binding provides vital functions both in databasing and in programming. In programming, it is a corollary of overloading.

Given the name ambiguity introduced by overloading, the system cannot bind operation names to programs at compile time, since it will not know the type of the object until runtime. Operation names must therefore be translated into program addresses at runtime. Binding at this level is generally dynamic.

In a system with object identity, an object has an identity that is independent of its value. This is important for sharing, updating, and manipulating persistent objects.* It also helps in:

1. Distinguishing between equality and two different representations of the same object
2. Handling semantic identity when components change, for instance, in the design process

The definition of *equivalence* is important among objects that look the same in the sense that all their components of primitive type are the same.

Another characteristic, *extensibility,* requires that a predefined set of types be provided by the language. The user has the means to define his or her own types. User-defined and system-defined types are treated uniformly. The meaning of *computational completeness* is that the query language can answer queries recursively.

11–4 ROLE OF A DATA MANIPULATION LANGUAGE

We have seen ample evidence that the management of information resources, and therefore databasing and applications programming, converges over a broad range of interests. They have a common ground. This, as stated in the introduction to this chapter, became pronounced with relational DBMS and their constellation of fourth-generation languages; it progressed further with object solutions.

Even before relational object-oriented approaches came around, however, DBMS were endowed with a data manipulation language (DML) and a data description language (DDL). DDL statements available to the programmer may be identified as:

*See also Chapter 1.

Control procedures that move data from a database to the user's work-station without altering their content

Data modification operations that cause the database to be changed in some way

Special-purpose statements that do something other than dealing with the information elements in the database

Data manipulation languages are not general purpose, and some cannot perform certain programming tasks, for instance, transitive closure, which leads to reformulating a query iteratively, each time from scratch. A DML can be used effectively for answering queries, but for deeper questions the programmer has to mix languages.

A problem arises from the fact that with elder DBMS the DML and the host language (such as Cobol) are incompatible. The result is an impedence mismatch arising from three conflicts:

1. Plain type mismatch
2. Set versus classical programming
3. Declarative versus procedural approaches

Type mismatch comes about because the type system of the host language and DML are not the same. Hence the programmer is responsible for converting when storing or retrieving information elements.

The contrast between set handling and record programming is seen with relational databases: The database unit is a set and the host languages unit is a record. Further, new applications use declarative rather than procedural programming, and these two programming styles are hard to integrate.

All this culminates in recurring programming difficulties and is a steady source of error. Object database management systems have not solved the problem as they should have done. Rather, the old weaknesses have been carried over.

The mismatch runs contrary to the stated goal of DML, at least theoretically. The original objective was

1. To extend host language capabilities to permit selection of record occurrences
2. To process data relationships in an able manner
3. To transfer information elements between the user's program and the database

Other things being equal, fourth- and fifth-generation languages perform better than the archaic Cobol, PL/1, and so on. Since the relational era, DMLs can rely in a more fundamental way on the host language to provide required data manipulation capabilities, but the symbiosis is not perfect.

Ironically, the mismatch went unnoticed for some time by the majority of designers of relational systems, yet it constitutes one of their major deficiencies. Even if fourth-generation languages and application generators have tried to close the gap, they are not the whole answer, besides raising difficult interfacing problems when programs written in different languages have to be integrated.

Progress is being made, however. With object solutions, a net advantage is provided by the single-language approach, with data and programs encapsulated in the same object, the programs being stored and manipulated as objects. Interaction with users can be handled through specific messages attached to objects, further removing the current relational need for separate language and DML.

While object-oriented shells and DML/host language/DBMS coordination are crucial, the same is true of the choice of a lower-level (assembly-level) language to handle the nuts and bolts of programming. Today, the emerging standard is C++. It can help both with object programming approaches and with parallel computing.

11–5 C++ FOR OBJECT-ORIENTED SOFTWARE

Contrary to the rather widespread opinion that object-oriented programming started with Smalltalk, Simula* was the first object-oriented language. In its original design, Simula was projected for simulating a simple form of concurrency; it did so using co-routines on conventional architectures.

Simulation is a good paradigm of an object-oriented approach. It is a working analogy mapping the entities of the real world into computer memory. In simulation, physical objects are represented by logical, computational objects. Thus there exists a direct mapping between physical and logical objects, which constitutes Simula's strength, as well as that of other languages that work along the same principle.

Simula and Smalltalk are only two examples of object-oriented languages. We have also mentioned Eiffel (one of the best recent developments) and Ada. Other examples are CLOS, Loops, Flavors, Nexpert Object (a knowledge engineering shell), and of course C++. However, none of these alternatives has been universally accepted, though C++ may be on its way to reaching that status.[†]

When Dennis M. Richie developed the C language at Bell Telephone

---

*Simula was developed in the mid-1960s at the Technical University of Trondheim, Norway. Smalltalk was created in the 1970s by the Xerox Appliance Park in Silicon Valley, California.

[†]ANSI has started working on the standardization of C++, and most computers and software vendors support it.

Laboratories, he stated as his goals economy of expression, control flow, data structures, and a set of operators. But then he suggested that C is not a very high level language. There is no analog, for example, of the PL/1 operations which manipulate an entire array of strings.

C is *not* an object-oriented language, but a nonstructured programming construct because "[the] absence of restrictions and generality makes it more convenient and effective for many tasks." The C language:

- Deals with characters, numbers, and addresses
- Incorporates recursive calls
- Features pointers
- Passes by value only (if pass by reference is needed, then it passes pointers)

The strength of C is that it lends itself to the development of well-written programs with straight-down coding, modularity, and good data-handling facilities. When used within the UNIX environment, a major plus is homogeneity between the operating system and programming functions: Every comment of UNIX is an instruction of C, and every instruction of UNIX is a possible procedure of C. The program is a function, and so is a file. The programmer should be careful, however, not to mix types in the routines.

Given the solid design background and the general acceptance of C, the lack of object-oriented features can be corrected. Parallel processing characteristics can also be added. This is what the Bell Telephone Laboratories did, in the early 1980s, when C++ was designed. This dialect:

- Provides data abstraction and object-oriented programming facilities, through syntactic extension to C, and
- Incorporates the class concept while remaining compatible with C in terms of syntax, performance, and portability.

Such choices have permitted an orderly evolution from existing C-based applications to the facilities offered by C++, assuring a transition for software and programmers' skills. It is, however, proper to keep in mind that, as embodied in languages such as C++, the object model is less rigorously defined and more complex than the relational model, but much more expressive, including the critical software concepts of inheritance and abstraction.

C++ is a multiparadigm language that permits use of object-oriented libraries. It is therefore becoming a major vehicle for the migration from traditional procedural programming techniques to data abstraction and object-oriented programming.

New syntactic constructs have been added to the C language that allow the programmer to define classes as well as instance methods. C++ can be used to send messages to objects. The goal is to give the software developer good resources to draw upon in making inheritance decisions when developing new classes.

11-6 EMERGING FEATURES OF C++

Though C++ is the emerging de facto industry standard* for parallel programming and object-oriented programming, the language itself is still evolving. Both C++ versions 2.0 and 2.1 have added significant functionality to the initial release through extensions. Some of the most notable new features have been in support of multiple inheritance, operator overloading, and parameterized types. In a more general sense, however, C++ developments aim to add functionality through class libraries rather than through language extensions. Work is also proceeding on more sophisticated compilers.

This evolutionary approach is favorable to analysts/programmers because C++ calls for updating skills but does not make them obsolete. It is also good for the company, since it assures a rather simple and cost-effective growth path if a major investment in C has already been made.

Currently available additions provide for encapsulation, polymorphism, a high level of abstraction, and greater reusability of code. One of the elements of the C++ design philosophy is to avoid paying for data abstraction at the expense of performance, while observing the basics of object programming orientation.

The importance of these features becomes evident if we take account of the fact that the entire process of software development, from design to testing, is greatly affected by language choices. The language we use influences our thinking, and this is just as true for abstraction, which allows a much closer correspondence between the problem domain and the solution domain.

Close attention must be paid, however, to how the conceptual features are implemented at the nuts-and-bolts level—for instance, the logic embodied in the default version of the messaging routine, the use of debugging and profiling features, as well as ways to customize C++ for different programmatic interfaces.

In its current release, the class construct in C++ permits programmers to define new data types completely, so that they operate as if they

*ANSI Committee X3J16 is working on standardizing C++, but AT&T's translator remains the current de facto standard. This translator is formally known as the C++ Language System, Release 2.0 for UNIX System V.

were directly supported in the language. Objects are instances of these classes, and the programmer can fully specify the functionality of the type mechanism.

C++ does not provide implicit dynamic allocation of objects, nor is there mandated support for garbage collection. Hence, if garbage collection mechanisms are needed, they have to be developed, this being made in a way transparent to users of the class.

There are limitations to the implementation of C++. The language supports the basic data types in C, so not all data types have an object orientation. However, the name and argument types of a function are included in its signature, so mnemonic names can be reused. The weakness is in the likelihood of name collisions when separately designed software modules are integrated into an application.

Because of the reasons we have discussed, a prototype specification must precede the use of a function, permitting the compiler to check the argument type. Ideally, applications will be of a parallel processing nature; C++ is successfully employed with parallel computers.

Within a parallel programming perspective, objects in C++ can be instantiated either implicitly or explicitly. The extent of an object is either static, automatic, or dynamic. C++, however, is not a distributed programming language, though it is used in connection with parallel processing. Eventually, there will be a distributed extension of C++ within the ISA (Integrated Systems Architecture) project. There is also a distributed Smalltalk, an extension of Modula, Amber (based on C++), and LII (Location Independent Invocation).★

While solutions of language extensibility such as distributed C++, distributed Smalltalk, and the like enable a reasonable level of reuse of existing applications, new linguistic constructs aim to make feasible fast prototyping as well as optimization in terms of implementation. In all likelihood, we are a long way from standardization in these efforts. Every time a vendor says "I have a better alternative," this means that it is probably incompatible with what already exists.

11-7 PROGRAM DESIGN WITH C++

In C++, a class can have public members that are available to clients and derived classes. Language facilities help in defining protected members available only to derived classes as well as private members connected to the implementing class itself.

Another C++ feature is the keyword *friend*. It helps to designate functions that are allowed access to private class members but are themselves

★Other examples of approaches with new languages are Emerald and Comandos.

nonmember functions. In terms of mechanics, a C++ programmer begins to write a program by:

1. Building a conceptual framework of the problem domain
2. Identifying concepts and deciding on how to represent them
3. Specifying the operations that can be performed on instances of a given concept.

Any external function typically interacts with an object by issuing function calls. This has been a well-established procedure since the late 1950s, and it has been used with both external and internal subroutines.

A programmer designing a C++ application needs first to identify and understand the concepts required by the application, in order to create hierarchical classes. A class hierarchy in C++ is composed of original classes and its derived classes. An *original* class defines a fundamental notion, which a *derived* class then refines by providing additional members. This mechanism permits derived classes to use the capabilities of the original class, the latter being extended so that the programmer does not have to rewrite it to add new features.

Programmers must ensure that original class functions have generalized functionality. This is necessary to prevent unexpected behavior in the context of derived classes. Furthermore, it should be possible to provide each derived class with its own implementation of a base function.

A principle in C++ holds that a concept does not exist in isolation, but is related to other concepts. This principle is supported by inheritance, which is basically a compiler-enforced organizational notion.

For design purposes, it is wise to note that C++ supports multiple inheritance, permitting a derived class to inherit the attributes of more than one original class. The use of multiple inheritance may further increase code reusability and program flexibility.

In support of multiple inheritance, C++ promotes the concept of polymorphism, which allows a programmer to have the same interface to different objects. A consistent interface helps produce different results, depending on the object type.

In connection with object databases, we have seen in Chapter 2 that polymorphism is associated with late binding, which refers to the attachment of member functions to an instance of a class and calls to functions. This is basically an evaluative process that may occur at either compile time or runtime. Polymorphism is implemented in C++ as the combination of virtual functions and derived classes. As a rule, the later the bind, the greater is the flexibility of a program.

There are also functions that C++ does not support, and for which a shell should be used. An example is help in the specification phase and generally in the process of software development. Experience with higher-level tools shows that they become accepted only if they provide natural means of exploitation of their facilities, and they require a minimum of training effort on the analyst's part. Both characteristics are fully supported by modern shells, such as Ptech, which we examined in Chapter 10. Ptech demonstrates the services a shell can offer. When this or a similar shell is used, it matters little if C++ does not support some process specifications directly—as long as the chosen shell automatically compiles into C++.

Another domain where C++ does not provide facilities, but specialized tools do, is *animation*. Visualization of the inner working of a process in action has been employed in programming for designing, developing, and debugging programs, as well as for monitoring their performance.

Animation can help the user as well as the programmer to understand and remember the functionality of a program. Algorithms are not the only things that can be animated. Control flows and data flow graphs are other examples of artifacts that can be animated so that their nodes are highlighted during execution.

The use of animation in system specifications is a good way to reduce errors in the requirements phase, ensuring that the behavior of a system has been properly modeled. Accompanied by graphics facilities, a working model of a system is more comprehensible to endusers, enabling them to interact with the analyst more effectively.

In terms of program design, feedback from animating a requirements specification can be used for its refinement. Animation can help in discovering and weeding out errors that can cause serious problems at later stages of development. Furthermore, graphical animation of a model may be used for demonstrating different aspects of functionality in the process of specifications.

In conclusion, object programming is a different culture than that known from old-time Cobol and related languages, which more or less followed the same path. It permits embedding powerful features, but their exploitation can be effective only if the human capital is up to the job.

Chapter 12

Spatial and Temporal Semantics

12-1 INTRODUCTION

Embedded in object-oriented solutions, as we have said, is the concept of data abstraction. It has also been demonstrated that objects have varying levels of granularity, which relates to, and up to a point commands, their *specificity*.

The explicit *semantic primitives* are another basic criterion of the object-oriented environment. They underlie the concepts of classing, inheritance, and versioning. Semantic database models map into themselves the semantics of an application environment, creating the corresponding schema and making the database more useful as well as evolvable. Instead of having a modeling concept based on the *logical record,* as is the case with record structures, semantic models typically represent the applications environment acting as a collection of entities, or more precisely, episodes. The aim is to provide a business system description that is independent of any specific data processing implementation. This will allow running programs against different database systems, identifying relationships between entities in terms of *partnerships.*

A partnership is based on the fact that one object has a relationship of a defined type with one or more other objects. This is the meaning of dynamic binding—though such a relationship may be temporary, resulting from an instantiation.

A number of factors must be considered when a partnership is identified. Each entity type, for instance, must state whether its episodes may have one or more partnerships of the same type at the same time. It is also necessary to define whether such dynamic bindings are optional, or whether at least one must be present to satisfy given requirements.

Each of these partnership sets is like an eye by which the world can be seen from that object's point of view. This is very useful in modeling certain business situations, particularly where the concepts of *temporal* and *spatial* relations are present.

We need concepts and tools that are able to provide manipulation and display capability for spatial and temporal object databases. They should support a standard set of graphic object types (vector and image), which can be used to implement the intended application sets, as required. Their development and usage is distinguishing those companies that are moving forward.

Temporal and spatial objects may be displayed by graphic, icon, and text presentation methods. In the case of spatial objects, for example, maps consisting of any subset of objects in the database may need to be not only displayed but also saved as objects for future reference. It should also be possible to select objects graphically, thus generating new map classes.

Spatial and temporal data models can thus be viewed as a language able to reflect and handle classes, types, and subtypes, as well as partnership interrelationships. Behavioral encapsulation, however, requires more, and the more comes by way of temporal and spatial semantics.

12–2 TIME AND SPACE

Time and space are the two pillars on which rest the basic concepts not only of information technology but also of most man-made events and artifacts. They are the frame of reference within which something exists, happens, acts. Temporal semantics exist in relation to a period characterized by given conditions with events associated to the action taking place.

Time is a point in duration, a moment or instant. Something has happened or is happening at a given time, and this something has semantics attached to it. These semantics become associated during suitable, proper, favorable, or convenient moments—and to a large measure they are expressed by *viewpoints.*

Facts can be grouped into collections or viewpoints, which represent different situations and their evolution over time: A new situation can be mapped by a new viewpoint, allowing one to analyze and reason about temporal processes, but a viewpoint can also represent a hypothetical situation in the search space of a problem.

Space is defined as distance, extending in all directions without visible limits. This is stated in the sense of a conceptual, continuous, expansive process within which all material things are contained. But space is not necessarily boundless.

In mathematics, space consists of a set of points or elements assumed to satisfy a given group of postulates. This happens within a concept of space we exploit, for instance, three-dimensional space.

Another important concept is *computer-generated space.* In a physical construction, the manipulation of space is an architectural goal; but manipulation of space in the sense of computer memory means a totally different thing to the specialist, who thinks in terms of *logical space.* Both physical and logical space have significant roles in man-made systems. What we often fail to appreciate is that a program's logical space abstracts from the physical space, then becomes alive and capable of variation by way of logical constructs and object representations.

Mathematically speaking—or, more precisely, in a *conceptual* sense—space, and therefore the domain, can be *finite* or *infinite.* The geometry codified by Euclid was an explanation of the world and therefore an excellent example of finite space. However, Descartes and the mathematicians of the last three centuries defined new relationships that led to infinite space.

The origins of *mathematical space,* hence the conceptual issues associated to domain definition, lie in analytical geometry, as does our X, Y, Z coordinate system. In contrast to the geometric example, a Cartesian space can be continuous, its lines composed of an infinite set of dimensionless points, each corresponding to one real number.

In *computer memory* this correspondence is more appropriately made in terms of objects and classes. The coordinate system maps real-world episodes, such as the *synergy of risks* shown in Fig. 12.1. In this representation, the axes of reference are markets, corresponding banks, and currencies. The space defined by every pair of them is, going counterclockwise, exposure, dealings, loans, and investments. Episodes relate to and characterize every planar coordinate, the latter being presented in the partnership of the two main axes of reference that envelop it.

12-3 FINITE OR INFINITE SPACE?

In mathematics, the Cartesian approach transformed the whole concept of finite space and eventually did away with it. With points defined by algebraic relationships among their coordinates, the solidity of ancient space dissolved.

Finite space is expressed by virtue of the figures occupying it. Their definition establishes the domain, and vice versa. *Infinite space* is expressed through algorithmic or heuristic relationships. This concept did not exist in the ancient world, as at that time mathematicians knew only what they saw and grasped. Only during the last three centuries did mathematicians learn to work in wholly *abstract regions* of infinite space, which can be of n dimensions, where n is greater or much greater than 3.

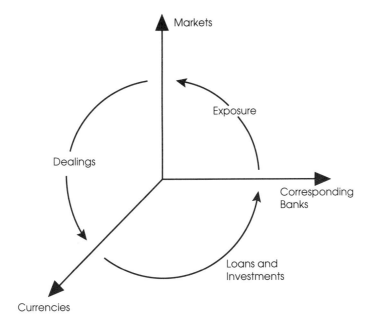

Figure 12.1   Synergy of risks in a financial markets environment.

Both concepts, finite space and infinite space, come into perspective when we talk of abstract data types subject to an inheritance mechanism—hence *objects.* For this reason, the conceptual database model must provide a specification that simultaneously accommodates and integrates physical and logical ways of looking at computer storage. Conventional database models fail to achieve this goal adequately.

Within this frame of reference can be located the concept of *relativism.* A database model must facilitate:

The description of relevant entities in both the finite and the infinite environments

The identification of collections of these entities, and their relationships (or associations)

Structural interconnections among such collections and the objects they contain.

Relativism may be supported through knowledge-enriched programmable interfaces able to reflect the manipulation of objects for application extension. It should be definable both graphically and by text.

Allowing entities to represent themselves in the defined space makes it possible to reference them directly from one another. This requires greater freedom than is available with record-oriented database models, where it is necessary to cross-reference between related entities by means of specific identifiers.

In the polyvalent space of an applications environment, both endusers and application programs should be able to reference and manipulate abstractions and symbols. This requires internal representations able to facilitate computer processing, leading to the need to go beyond data abstraction and include knowledge encapsulation as well as extensibility. In other words, the able manipulation of an infinite domain implies the ability of representing expertise, as well as that of inferencing and doing hypothetical reasoning.

12 – 4 STRUCTURE AND BEHAVIOR

When we talk of tackling issues related to time and space, the synthesis of object and rule processing can provide distinct advantages. Among these advantages are the ability to augment the content of rules through association with objects. This makes it possible to refine knowledge about the application beyond than what rules alone can do. It also helps advancing a helpful distinction between *behaviorally* oriented object solutions, which focus both on rules and information elements—hence *intentional* constructs—and *structurally* oriented approaches, where the information elements dominate—hence *extentional* environments.

On many occasions, object databases need this dual solution and therefore must go beyond the more classical abstract data types that prevailed around 1980. Rules, for example, help in adding deductive database capabilities, as we will see in Chapter 13, after we have discussed distributed database structures and their primitives, as well as object-oriented DBMS.

What we mean here is that our methodology must go beyond the sense of an abstract data structure, adding behavior as a way of representing *external* actions resulting from the environment in which the database system operates, and *internal* attributes such as triggers, rules, and derived data that relate to issues of conduct.

Through the duality of structural *and* behavioral solutions, applications programs can exploit data abstraction, inheritance, and encapsulation principles. They can also handle knowledge in a more efficient manner than is possible otherwise.

Enhancing objects with rules provides a more powerful paradigm for reasoning about them, while rule-based approaches can be expressed more clearly and concisely. This can be seen in Fig. 12.2, which contrasts older abstract data-type approaches to today's rule- and knowledge-based solutions, which can accommodate behavioral characteristics relating to action.

Present developments take place within this universe. This is true of operations as well as of equilibration, with *object equivalence* being *behavioral,*

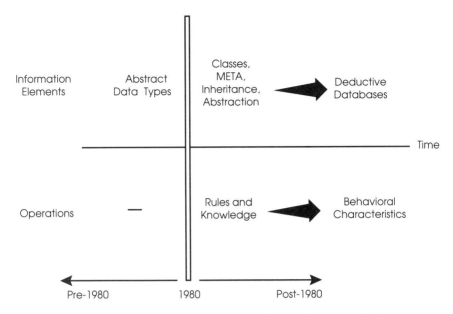

Figure 12.2   Pre- and post-1980s concepts in an object-type implementation.

therefore examining obtained results and defining if they are equivalent in terms of conduct, as well as *structural,* in the sense of comparing two objects and deciding if they are structurally the same.

Behavioral equilibration is a fundamental faculty in terms of implementating distributed concurrency—for instance, deciding whether distributed transactions can be factored in, and what sort of central specification of information is required for that purpose.

This particular concept goes beyond viewing a database as a collection of entities that correspond to the actual objects in the application environment. It permits effective organization of such entities into classes that are logically related, by means of *interclass connections.*

The behavioral approach helps underline that database entities and classes have attributes that describe their characteristics in relation to other database entities. There are different ways of defining interclass connections and derived attributes:

Some correspond to the most common types of information redundancy appearing in database applications.

Others help integrate multiple ways of viewing the same basic information.

Still others provide building blocks for describing complex attributes and relationships.

An example of the last is *polymorphism,* which assumes that types of objects can *change,* as well as that objects can be members of multiple classes. We have spoken of this concept in Chapter 2.

Polymorphic processes as well as their impact have to be managed at the *meta-data* level, including perspectives relating to application programs. The same is true for handling extensibility, as a way of building new abstractions, or following the evolution of the model itself by adding new code; and *referential integrity,* as an extension of the notion of abstract data typing, through the use of surrogates for an object.

Extensibility and referential integrity tax the analyst's ability in terms of determining the information content of the database, locating the appropriate schema. They also underline the need for a readable description of database contents, organized in a way that a user (person, program, terminal, host) can identify and comprehend.

Both notions can be instrumental in bringing into focus the fact that when we deal with *computer-generated space* (program space), there exist at least two levels of reference:

One is *physical:* an array of pigeonholes (or cells) that can be recorded in a linear or spatial fashion.

The other is *logical* and is exemplified by the type of structuring we do as well as the objects supported in the logical database, and their semantics.

Dual reference is made in this connection to the semantic schema, as it consists of objects and knowledge or procedures—application events.

Instantiation is a key to this duality. A set of instances is classifiable, and is associated in connection with each class. Among others, this is true of *descriptor objects* (atomic alphanumeric strings), which generally serve as symbolic identifiers, and *abstract objects* (nonatomic entities). The latter are defined in terms of their relationships with other objects through *interobject mappings,* hence by means of attributes.

12–5 COMPUTER-GENERATED SPACE

Attributes associated to a computer-generated space are fundamentally mappings from one type of object to another, and are typically connected to a given type. The object of an attribute domain has a specific value, which is a subset of the value type of the attribute and/or its range. This can be defined as a unique identifier, whether single- or multivalued. A type designed to represent a unique object has no multiplicity; a type that represents a set of similar objects has multiplicity.

Subtypes, abstract object types, and descriptors can be defined by specifying *predicates* on the values of attributes. Constraints on attributes are present in a semantic database model and can themselves be single- or multivalued.

Typically, within a computer-generated space, a number of semantic integrity constraints must be embedded as an integral part of a semantic database model. This is also true of relationships between subtypes, leading to the four-component model shown in Figure 12.3, where object computation and reflective computation interact with one another through knowledge-domain and control-action intermediaries. The interfaces can be rule based, represented through the knowledge domain itself and/or the control structure.

Such a schema helps integrate the dissemination and manipulation of objects, treating information elements as instance variables while nodes are arranged in an instantiated class hierarchy. Methods for learning, executing, and unlearning rules are a vital complement to such a process.

An important method in this regard relates to the idealized manipulation of computer-generated space, leading to a *logical geometry*. While it can reflect a wide variety of problems, this approach also returns to the finite-space concept of antiquity.

In a sense, computer programming merges both the ancient geometric constructs and the now classical analytical disciplines. Since computer space is both physical and logical, we can merge into our practice a great number

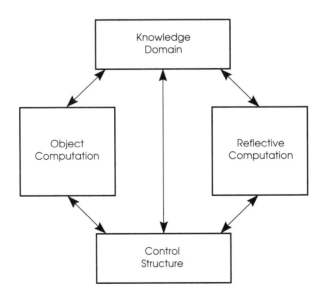

Figure 12.3   Basic components of a relational approach to object usage.

of past traditions without losing the pragmatic point of view. This becomes possible, however, only if we preserve the notion of polyvalence and that of layered representation of systems functionality. For instance, a rule can be examined in the three-layered structure shown in Figure 12.4:

1. Goal expression (meta-knowledge)
2. Trigger definition
3. Action body

Through the use of demons, nodes continuously monitor trigger conditions to associated rules. When a trigger is satisfied, the proper conditions are executed.

Such actions can be local, temporal, or spatial. Both are communications oriented, existential, and can be learning intense. Basically, they are of a supervisory or housekeeping nature.

It is appropriate to keep in perspective the philosophical issues associated with this concept. If the post-Renaissance mathematicians and the physicists of our century put forth the idea that space can be manipulated, it was the ancient mathematicians who taught us about geometric changes and expressions.

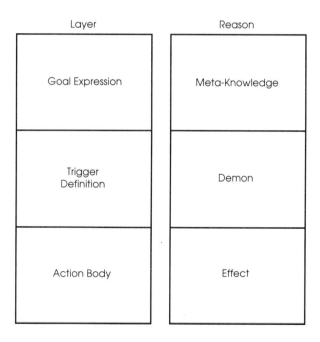

Figure 12.4   Representation of a rule in a layered structure.

12-6 LOGICAL AND PHYSICAL SPACE

We do not always appreciate the fact that it is precisely the aforementioned powerful concept of the ancient mathematicians that permit us to live in two worlds simultaneously: space as a logical entity, and space as a physical fact. Let us also note that the logical space we conceive in a computer-related sense is much easier to understand and express than the one in the atomic or cosmic physical universe, because it is much less sophisticated than the wholly abstract space of those universes. The logical space of a computer-based environment is the *domain,* and it is manageable as long as it is kept within finite bounds.

The origins of logical space date to the paging system, which led to virtual memory in the late 1960s. Paging built on the concept of physical memory that developed during the late 1940s and through the 1950s, and was characterized by addresses. The bridge between the two concepts, paging and addressing, is provided by the fact that solutions necessary to approach physical memory are logical in their nature. They were therefore a forerunner to the logical space approaches.

For storage and retrieval purposes, words or bytes in the physical space are numbered. This number is their address. At the beginning, and for more than two decades, numbers have generally been assigned serially and typically run from zero to the memory capacity of the machine.

This was a very simple solution but also an ingenious one, as it made each word or byte selectively available to the central processor. In other terms, it made the word or byte an *addressable entity*—and by extension an *object.*

In this sense, memory addressing has been the link between the physical space and computer programming. Computer designers in the 1950s distinguished between one-, two-, and three-address machines. With the one-address approach, for example, each programming instruction had an *operand* or command portion, and the *memory address* from which the information element would be taken. What was not appreciated at the time, but is today, is that the numbering or addressing of physical space derives from analytic geometry and at the same time its abstract notions are as old as Descartes.

This process has been useful for putting the physical memory space at the disposal of a logical process, and it opened wide vistas in reshuffling, manipulating, and optimizing the basic characteristics of computing machinery. But as memory space expanded, addressing solutions had to become much better organized in order to be more controllable. Schema presentation and cross-indexing were tried. A cross-index of schemata amounts to a *semantic data dictionary,* which identifies the principal features of the application environment, maps these features in a retrievable form, and catalogues their relationships for further use.

Ideally, such specification and documentation should be independent of the DBMS that manages the information elements. The external views of the information elements employed by programmers and endusers should be defined in terms of it, while a mapping from it to physical file structures helps establish the internal schema of the database—or, more precisely, storage and representation.

Chapter 13

Handling Temporal Databases

13-1 INTRODUCTION

The development and use of *temporal databases* will become increasingly important to computers and communications operations. An example is network systems, especially those providing for planning, provisioning, and maintenance capabilities.

Network objects may be circuits, switching centers, monitored variables, services, and so on. The relationships between them change over time. Hence control systems are needed to store the current state of the network, historical information, and future planned evolution of the network. Addressing the latter two issues requires temporal data modeling that adds a time dimension to the stored information. Such a process is greatly helped by an object orientation.

A number of data models have been proposed along these lines. Bellcore, Piscataway, New Jersey, U.S.A., for instance, is developing a model for the temporal dimension that incorporates the entity-relationship data model and its semantic extensions into conceptual design. Research projects at Bellcore specify a temporal query and update language. They identify temporal constraints supported by the model, and address the issues of indexing temporal data and processing temporal operators.

While network design is well launched in the direction of object-oriented databases with temporal capabilities, we also need concepts and tools that will provide manipulation and display features for spatial and temporal object handling. These concepts and tools should support a standard set of graphic object types (vector and image), which can be used to implement the intended application sets. Their development and usage distinguishes leading-edge companies from those that are stuck in outmoded ways of thinking and of using information technology.

13-2 MODELING TEMPORAL DATA

The modeling of temporal data cannot be dissociated from the fact that physical memory is finite while logical memory tends to expand. As a result, databases are pruned and tuned to carry more and more information elements. As new values become available, existing ones are discarded from the database through garbage collection or the use of sunset clauses. However, as we saw in Chapter 2, many applications need both current and past information elements (IEs) and possibly future ones as well. This is the concept of soft data, which we discussed in Chapter 5.

A database that maintains past, present, and future IE contrasts to the snapshot solution we have been practicing for four decades, and is known as a *temporal database.* A temporal database will typically contain:

> *Hard data,* consisting of past events and their values
>
> A *data input* stream from the environment
>
> *Soft data,* consisting of projections, extrapolations, interpolations, results of simulations, and hypotheses

Hard data, the data input stream, and soft data are interrelated not only because they share the same computer-generated space but also because they are connected by *temporal semantics.*

Different kinds of logic have been developed to express the semantics of time. One kind includes a number of classical first-order predicates with temporal components, for instance,

> A *temporal* realization *operator* that relates assertions to temporal entities
>
> A binary *reachability predicate* that connects temporal entities to other temporal entities that occur after them in time

Temporal databases and their semantics are very important, as new database architectures are dynamic and include both temporal *and* spatial relationships.

Several factors affect the nature and value of a temporal (or spatial) relationship. Seven among them are most important:

1. *Direction in time* (or space), which can affect both the development and the relationship in time (space) of different processes, including the

definition of which one comes first in the temporal (or spatial) dimension

2. *Pattern in time* (or space), the arrangement of occurrence of processes and their components, from the specific spacing to the pattern they exhibit

3. *Duration*, the length of time over which a process continues, as well as the moment it forks into another process (son) with inheritance characteristics

4. *Position,* the temporal (or spatial) location of a process among its peers, superior or subservant processes in an absolute, cardinal scale, including the prevailing order in time (or page)

5. *Number in time* (or space) of different processes going on in a given system or between its subsystems, as well as the frequency of repeated processes

6. *Containment in time* (or space), identifying whether or not given process(es) occur(s) among subsystems (or components) within specific periods of time (or space)

7. *Communication,* focusing on information exchange occurring in a specific timeframe among processes, causing a change in the system or any of its subsystems and components

All seven factors reflect the fact that the activities of any organization are an ongoing process. As a result, information needs and multimedia handling capabilities should be considered in a time (and space) perspective.

13–3 DECISION SPACE AND OBJECT ORIENTATION

The message of Section 2 is that data models must address issues of processing and maintenance of temporal data, with the solution to be adopted providing a time-processing sequence. In a real-life applications environment, such a perspective in time may, for instance, concern any or all of the axes of reference shown in Fig. 13.1:

New business lines and new services to be added for existing lines

New customers for existing products and services

A new infrastructure, such as a system-wide change of both non-intelligent and intelligent terminals

The need to sustain the temporal aspects can lead to other commitments. For instance, with knowledge-based systems, supported temporal

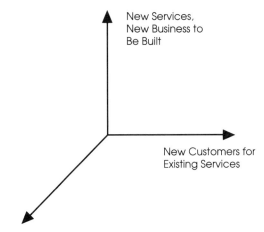

New Services,
New Business to
Be Built

New Customers for
Existing Services

Easy Change from Nonintelligent to Intelligent Terminals
New Communications Concepts and Possibilities

Figure 13.1   An applications-oriented decision space for object implementation.

entities, relationships, operations, and constraints must capture the semantics of time needed by applications programs.

The solution should embody the pertinent objects in a conceptual schema expressed in meta-model form through temporal primitives. Two main directions can be followed to handle temporal information elements:

1. Develop a new more powerful model able to integrate the time dimension

2. Enhance existing data models to reflect the time dimension in a comprehensive, coherent manner.

Included among the enhancements will be the process of time-stamping associated to the stream of data input and the use of query languages that can support temporal relations. A growing number of applications—for instance, stock market and foreign exchange trading—are becoming increasingly dependent on fine-grain time stamps.

Since these requirements will evolve with time, solutions must be open-ended so that new constructs and new functions can be added for completeness, user convenience, and efficiency. In doing so we must account for the difference between special-purpose solutions that include ad-hoc representations of temporal information with no attempt at integration with existing representations of nontemporal information, and models that perform such integration by extending and improving existing data and/or knowledge representations.

Modal operators are interpreted using a reachability relation. Different modal logic results from various assumptions about the properties of the relation and the nature of the state universe.

For simplification purposes, in most temporal models time is assumed to be linear and discrete. Events are associated with a start-point entity, end-point entity, and an interval. A principal goal is support of a number of different query types.

Different ways of mapping modal, temporal, and dynamic logic based on points and discrete linear times have been proposed by several researchers. They have been advanced in connection with proving the correctness of transactions against databases, or to formally define dynamic integrity constraints. Results, however, have been so far experimental rather than applications oriented. Even so, these models are helpful in supporting formal reasoning of the type we will need in the coming years.

Another class of logic used to model time is *intentional.* Its interpretation assumes a universe of states and a universe of constants. Individual variables are assigned functions and function symbols reflecting transitions from states to functions.

In most current temporal models, dates and clock times are considered to be *the* primitive temporal entities. Also, spatial relationships are often not recorded independently, but derived from the numerical information inherent in concrete representations. As projects move from theory to implementation, we can expect a new generation of application concepts to be born.

13-6 PATTERNS IN SEMANTIC REPRESENTATION

Whether knowledge is formal or informal, it is always based on the contemplation of something in accordance to a principle or a pattern. In a scientific sense, this process becomes formalized into a *method,* that is, an established procedure whereby:

Information flows within a problem area, or from one area into another.

Rules, and therefore knowledge, are related to a given processing pattern or housekeeping requirements.

Rules and information are conditioned by a principle that helps explain, or at least represent, a given meaning in a comprehensive form.

Knowledge sources frequently transform entries at one level of abstraction into entries at another level; some operate from the bottom up while others work from the top down. Either way, they tend to aggregate several lower-level entries into a smaller number of higher-level entries.

The higher-level entries are meta-levels that provide specialized constructs capable of mapping applications—for example, handling text objects, forms, and messages; or supporting certain actions and defining specification of information processing routines that form a given environment.

In research related to conceptual database design, software requirement specification tools have been devised that operate from the top down. They are intended to accommodate users who are not necessarily experienced in using object orientation and its analytical mechanism. A process of adaptive control, like the one shown in Fig. 13.2, can help by

Prototyping a fundamental knowledge structure

Improving the understanding of storage, search, and retrieval mechanisms

Ensuring pattern matching and recognition capabilities

The meta-layers look at patterns, links, relationships, and interdependencies that permit identification of the system by definition and classification of single events. This layered structure is represented and controlled through the use of meta-levels. In this context, *object-oriented* and *semantic* representations refer to characteristic mechanisms but also to a class of models.

This background leads to an *episodic memory* organization of objects in

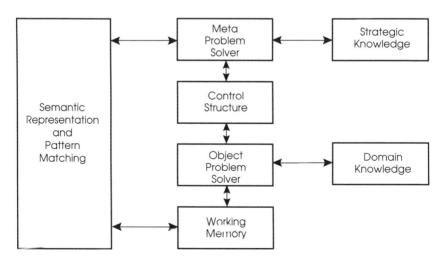

Figure 13.2   An object-oriented approach to problem solving.

contrast to the classical *record-base* model,★ emphasizing features associated with semantically expressed databases. Episodes include:

Atomic (primitive) data values such as strings and numbers

Abstract objects representing entities in the real world

Intangible concepts and patterns as well as other representation constructs, some of which are ephemeral

Relationships among such objects, their identification, and classification, can themselves be considered as episodes and patterns in the database.

Primitives should be provided to support object classification, as well as structuring and semantic integrity. Abstraction mechanisms address features of instantiation, inheritance, equilibration, and aggregation. Their roots lie in semantic primitives and data models that benefit from knowledge-based representation techniques.

The result of using knowledge-based representations is a simple, object-oriented distributed database model that can be used as a foundation for constructing higher-level semantic constructs. Temporal and spatial patterns can help in describing a small set of primitive operations that allow location, manipulation, and retrieval of database objects, supporting a basic kind of conceptual database evolution as it occurs in many application environments.

Through this procedure we are practically aiming at the development of a comprehensive picture, for instance, adding an interpretation of trends and changes that must be watched as they reveal a pattern and its underlying characteristics.

Intuition and memory often depend on a pattern representation, and so do our different moves and actions. Said Judith Polgar, the 13–year old who won the women's chess tournament in 1988 in 17 moves after sacrificing a queen and a knight, "It was a home variant . . . I caught a view of the board and the mate pattern was familiar."

Perception followed by cognition are the fundamental steps in receiving a stimulus and in interpreting it; also in gaining insight in terms of possible orientation. The mind patterns create coherence by recognizing schemes, developing frames, leading to concepts.

This helps in elaborating an object-oriented environment, for instance, knowledge-based graphics to visualize processes and their operation.

- Manipulations of the icons help modify the process-specification database, and
- Changes in the database can be easily reflected by the graphics.

★See also the distinction made in Chapter 3.

After process descriptions are developed, a spatial, temporal, or other pattern-oriented approach can be used to check designs for conceptual integrity by employing a functional prototyping capability. Logical implications of an object-based environment can thus be computed and constraints checked in real time.

The identification and recognition of patterns is guided by *meta-patterns,* just as we speak of meta-knowledge in terms of taxonomy and classification. This, too, is a knowledge engineering concept that has been used in object-oriented environments.

13 – 7 PATTERNING AND FUZZY ENGINEERING

Pattern recognition is not an exact science, and pattern interpretation involves many fuzzy engineering concepts. Patterning always occurs on curved surfaces. The same process (but not necessarily type) seems to occur on the surface of the earth as on the shell of a turtle—and both are rich in fuzzy notions.

Object-oriented approaches, particularly the exploration of spatial and temporal relations, can be of great help in the fuzzy engineering domain, because fuzzy models deal with an idealized abstraction, and inference permits dealing with uncertainties.

Handling *uncertain data* is an opportunity for discovery, provided we have the means to do so. Hence the interest in fuzzy sets theory, which provides a method of treating essential subjective information—ill-defined and ambiguous elements.

Ambiguous and ill-defined information is typical of human cognition and reasoning: We see words and numbers and try to derive a pattern out of them. Different types of work are done in each hemisphere of the brain, as shown in Fig. 13.3: The left hemisphere is more logical and works in digital fashion; whereas *intuition* is the mark of the right hemisphere, and processing is analog.

Pattern recognition is done by the right hemisphere. In this process, fuzziness defines a state of mind that says: "I may not know exactly what I want, but I can describe the process of a weighted decision."

The fuzzy sets are *qualifiers.* Their proper place is as an intermediate layer between known modeling solutions and the systems architecture we build.

The importance of this approach is underlined by the fact that few real-life business decisions can be described with yes/no answers. Usually, they involve a pattern construction that most often is characterized by fuzziness. To reduce this fuzziness and find a pattern, we need access to impressive amounts of information elements that are best handled as *objects,* not

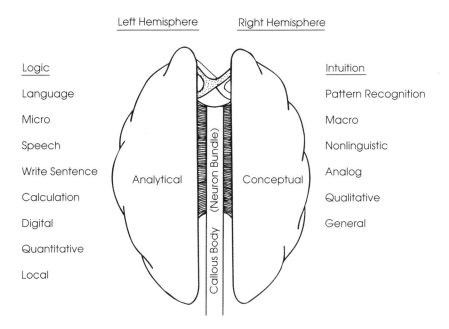

Left Hemisphere		Right Hemisphere

Logic

Language

Micro

Speech

Write Sentence

Calculation

Digital

Quantitative

Local

Analytical

(Neuron Bundle)

Callous Body

Conceptual

Intuition

Pattern Recognition

Macro

Nonlinguistic

Analog

Qualitative

General

Figure 13.3   Information processing in the brain (cerebrum).

through inflexible and cumbersome file structures. Objects can be of much greater assistance in appropriate reasoning that integrates vagueness, uncertainty, and imprecision into our conceptual process.

> *Imprecision* refers to lack of specifity of contents of an information element—for instance, an inflation rate between 5 percent and 8 percent per year.
>
> *Vagueness* results in lack of sharp boundaries of an object, whether they are denoted by approximate numbers or by words. For example, if we say, "A low inflation rate is good," then the inflation rate is context dependent, but ill-defined even in a single context.
>
> *Uncertainty* refers to our partial ignorance of specificity of a certain information element and its description. For instance, the probability of getting a 6 by throwing a fair die is $\frac{1}{6}$. There is no certainty that a 6 will show up.

A point often missed, however, is that, with the given state of knowledge, imprecise statements and vague patterns are more common than known statements or known patterns. We have to live with the uncertainty that certain situations exhibit, but we can improve upon it by:

Having access to rich databases

Using the appropriate concepts and tools

Developing and using the right models

For these reasons, fuzzy adaptive control has become a successful application of fuzzy theory, and it is used in many real-life systems. Its rules are good for knowledge representation, that is, encoding knowledge by means of representing pairs of a reference model for a process and its controller. In order to realize robust control, this approach:

- Adapts control gains using some useful process reference models that are given in fuzzy rules.
- Employs object-oriented solutions to databasing and programming to gain greater accuracies and flexibility.

This dual approach helps in evaluating a process output and connecting it with some suitable reference model. An example is Japan's Fuzzy Associative Memory Organizating Units System (FAMOUS), which employs fuzzy associative memory and can create automatically membership functions.

FAMOUS has three features: a fuzzy knowledge representation by means of causal relations; inheritance in knowledge realization by means of associative memories; and fuzzy inference by means of association. In terms of implementation, this fuzzy adaptive control is useful for simulating nonlinear systems and controlling stabilizers as well as the necessary temporal database.

This and other examples suggest that spatial and temporal databases have rich implementation domains. This is even more true when object-oriented models are enriched with knowledge engineering and employ high technology both for databasing and for software.

Chapter 14

Beyond Relational Database Management Systems

14-1 INTRODUCTION

Since the late 1970s, when the first commercially available relational DBMS were announced relational technology has been seen as the force shaping the future wave. By the late 1980s a wide range of relational database management systems were available, facing data processing departments with some of critical questions:

1. Are relational DBMS oriented toward high-volume transaction operations, or are they intended just for use in information centers?
2. How can available DBMS be evaluated so that the right choice is made for our organization's particular requirements?
3. How can the productivity benefits of relational DBMS be obtained while avoiding the potential pitfalls, including degradation of high-volume production performance?
4. How can programmer productivity benefits be obtained from fourth-generation languages, and what is their impact on the demand for computer cycles?

In many cases, sometimes superficially but sometimes in a more fundamental manner, the costs, rewards, and risks of relational systems have been analyzed, their performance capabilities investigated, and advice given on how to select a relational or lookalike solution. Most users, however, would like to see a complete and comprehensive functionality, but are not sure if this is possible. Many questions still remain unanswered.

Some issues are far from being settled. Therefore the statement that in more than one aspect relational approaches may have run their course may come as a shock. Yet there is substance to this argument: Relational approaches are reaching their limits.

As object-oriented solutions come into being, pushed by the growing needs of a global database environment, an increasing number of organizations are finding that requirements have outrun what can be provided by a simple set of relations. Features are asked for that are not available in a relational model, but that are essential to the handling of multimedia, long transactions, and other increasingly complex tasks.

$14-2$ MULTIDATABASES

Conceived in the 1960s, hierarchical and Codasyl DBMS became obsolete by the late 1970s, when management information requirements demanded a degree of flexibility that these constructs could not handle. Relational DBMS, developed in the 1970s were sometimes discarded in the late 1980s because they could not meet developing multidatabase requirements.

A *multidatabase* is a collection of independent databases that cooperate in sharing information elements (IEs) while preserving the autonomy of each local database. Such a system needs mechanisms for:

Providing every database with an integrated view of the global database

Supporting the exchange of IEs between databases

Maintaining the integrity of shared information elements in the multidatabase

An *integrative view* of a multidatabase calls for solving issues associated with schema integration, leading toward either tightly coupled or loosely coupled federated solutions.

Tight or loosely coupled approaches, each with its own norms, are necessary for cooperation among databases in processing queries and transactions. These norms provide every database in the network with a mechanism to:

Support the specification of multidatabase queries

Display the results of these queries in the specific format of each database

Handle transaction requirements, including those posed by long, complex transactions

Make feasible an integrative approach so that database heterogeneity is seamless to the user

Organizations request database integration, users want seamless implementation, and vendors promise solutions they find difficult to deliver. Among queries to which answers in most cases are quite fuzzy, are

Is the goal complete transparency?
What is the price of such transparency?
Should the solution be implementation independent?
What are the alternatives?

Before making a choice, we have to ask what the impact will be on other issues we are confronting. Just as important, we need to know the types of prevailing heterogeneity in the database environment as well as the technical and operational reasons for these differences. For example, differences may be due to:

Hardware
Operating systems
Communications protocols
Data structures
DBMS being used

Since the late 1980s, software researchers and developers have been working on resolving such heterogeneities, but generally applicable results are not yet widely available.

14–3 KNOWLEDGE ENGINEERING AND SEMANTICS

One of the main difficulties in overcoming heterogeneity in a multidatabase environment is the differences in the semantics of information elements. Therefore, part of the effort has been directed toward the use of knowledge engineering★ to provide self-describing semantic data models.

Figure 14.1 shows one of the approaches being followed in constructing a semantic data model, which then uses the model to describe itself. Access to a data dictionary is important, and the same is true of constraint analysis, including real-time update of views.

Knowledge engineering can be instrumental in bringing out, and eventually ironing out, differences in an environment with multiple DBMS. Pass-through capabilities aim at providing seamless access to incompatible DBMS purchased over a period of time, which may be different

★See also D. N. Chorafas, *Knowledge Engineering,* Van Nostrand Reinhold, New York, 1990.

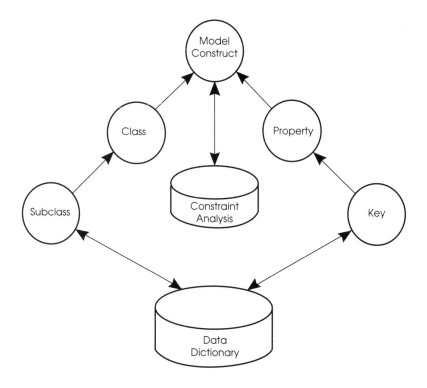

Figure 14.1   Self-describing semantic data model.

due to changes in data management technology, or simply to lack of coordination between database management efforts.

Besides heterogeneities due to differences in DBMS, there are also incompatibilities due to differences in data models as well as at the system level. Each DBMS has an underlying data model that is used to define data structures, establish constraints, and handle language aspects. Heterogeneous data models are characterized by incompatible structural primitives. If two representations have the same information content, it is easier to deal with differences in the structures. But if the information content is not the same, then it may be quite difficult to deal with such differences.

Just as crucial is the ability to handle a number of incompatible constraints within the context of a multidatabase. The same is true of differences in query languages: Incompatible languages are often used to manipulate data represented in heterogeneous data models. Even when two DBMSs support the same data model, differences in their query languages, or versions of it, can contribute to heterogeneity.

Incompatibilities in the system aspects of the DBMS also lead to heterogeneity—for instance, the way of handling transaction management primitives.

Most important, however, as the preceding paragraphs (and Fig. 14.1) have emphasized, *semantic heterogeneity* should be taken into account. Semantic heterogeneity occurs when there is disagreement about the meaning, interpretation, or intended use of the same or related information elements. It is important to reemphasize this point, because in general the problems associated with semantics are poorly understood.

Detecting semantic heterogeneity is difficult, since typical DBMS schemata do not provide enough semantics to interpret data consistently. Heterogeneity due to differences in data models also contributes to the difficulty in identification and resolution of the semantics issue.

14-4 COMMODITY SOFTWARE
FOR HETEROGENEOUS DATABASES

At the present time there is no commercially available, truly distributed relational DBMS—or for that matter any other type. This statement is true in an integrative sense, and in contrast to approaches that distribute a given database and its control mechanism across multiple geographically dispersed machines—but without providing all necessary services to sustain a global operational environment in a dynamic sense.

Nor is there a DBMS offered as commodity software able to handle multimedia databases, the way we are increasingly operating.* Since the late 1980s, some approaches have become available, particularly for engineering databases,† but these do not provide a solution for large distributed structures with rich primitives.

The generation of object-oriented DBMS that is just beginning its useful life can relieve such constraints. Already, prototyping and programming tools associated with these DBMS are available. Others are still under development, while interfaces are being built for still other object-oriented tools that have come to the market.

Since everyone is still at an early stage in terms of knowhow about effectively employing an object-oriented DBMS, both vendors and users tend to stay with specific implementations such as concurrent engineering. They are not yet ready to tackle vast and taxing areas such as heterogeneous databases.

Heterogeneity is more effectively approached through the strategy of

---

*See also D. N. Chorafas and Steve Legg, *The Engineering Database,* Butterworths, London and Boston, 1988.

†Although some of the developing object DBMS do handle this requirement, for instance, Hitachi's *Mandrill* (see Chapter 20).

deductive databases,* which is also a solution that goes beyond relational DBMS. But we have already said that object-oriented approaches and knowledge engineering are converging.

The lack of truly distributed database management systems and the limited functionality of relational DBMS in handling multidatabases are disadvantages of current systems. As we will see in subsequent chapters, object orientation can handle this job, but the DBMS presently available are not yet ready to meet the requirements of very large networked databases. Further, they are rather diverse in the approaches they take, they do not yet address in a rigorous manner a distributed global database environment, and they still lack the necessary primitives to handle diversified, heterogeneous databases. There are exceptions, and we will be discussing them in later chapters: Hewlett-Packard's Pegasus and Versant Star.

A solution to database heterogeneity is a pressing problem. To appreciate this, we should keep in mind that large users of database management systems typically run five, six, or more different, nonintegrated data structures and half a dozen or more incompatible DBMS. While these users are increasingly convinced that they should go beyond relational solutions, they do not see current commercial offerings as the answer. Hence they are still searching for solutions.

14-5 ARCHITECTURING A LONG-TRANSACTION ENVIRONMENT

A prudent way of approaching the problem of heterogeneity is to architecture a transitory approach that rests on three pillars, as shown in Fig. 14.2. These pillars are linked together through specific goals:

> One aims to bridge the gap between present and future applications.
>
> Another focuses on operating the current database resources under more efficient conditions.
>
> A third is to create an environment that facilitates the handling of multimedia.

In engineering a valid solution, account must be taken of the fact that different applications have different performance requirements and associated bottlenecks. We need a set of mechanisms for tuning performance around developing requirements, including control over the logical and physical clustering of objects as well as handling optimization requirements.

Optimization is important because performance was degraded when we passed from hierarchical and network to relational DBMS. The same

---

*Originally promoted by ICOT in Japan.

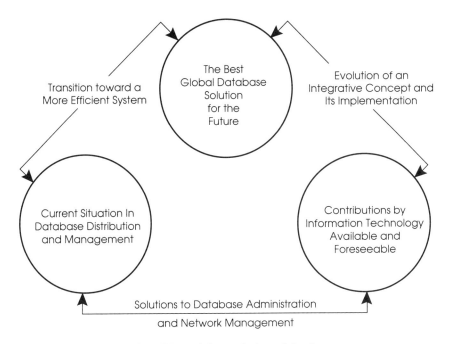

Figure 14.2   Pillars of the evolution of database concepts.

will most likely be repeated with multimedia and with the management of massive database structures, particularly in heterogeneous environments.

As a consequence, it is not surprising that companies are eager to find new and better solutions. Many do realize that object-based DBMS are not going to solve all their problems, but they are willing to try some precise applications to test the potential benefits. Others see the limitations of relational database management systems as well as the possibilities of the object database concept of single-paradigm programming. The more forward looking capitalize on the fact that the single, uniform paradigm of object databases can be used for design, programming, and IE access. This uniform paradigm is a key factor in providing new levels of performance, productivity, and functionality, setting object databases apart from relational solutions.

The message is that while object DBMS are not ready to perform far-out goals, such as the effective integration of heterogeneous databases, they may effectively reach more focused aims. After all, a basic query in management is: What are *our* alternatives? Have we studied them? Tested them? Exploited them?

Standards organizations, such as the American National Standards Institute (ANSI), through its Database Systems Study Group (DBSG), are working on these problems, but is not wise to depend on standards organizations for program solutions: Their goal is to normalize, not to create new products.

The DBSG advises focusing on database technology, starting with the fundamentals and proceeding with database management all the way to security and protection. Part and parcel of this approach is the concern about what to do with heterogeneity in multidatabase systems.

A number of organizations, among them DBSG, are correctly addressing other problems connected with the use of multidatabases, for instance, moving away from record-based approaches toward object-oriented ones for reasons of:

Enduser visualization,

Multimedia (text, data, graphics, voice, image), and

New forms of storing and retrieving information.

For instance, work in this domain is being done by the SQL Access Group, which is working on productizing a remote data access (RDA) protocol as well as on ANSI SQL, SQL 2 (for transactions), and SQL 3 (for objects, multimedia, and visualization). This is seen as necessary in order to accommodate the now-developing requirements of database usage across an expanding topology, with increasingly ad-hoc queries and the handling of long transactions.

The concept of *long transactions* is fairly recent. It is an outgrowth of the fact that in a multidatabase environment, the traditional transaction model is too restrictive. There is also the fact that multidatabase transactions are often long-running activities.

Managing long-running activities by means of traditional transaction methods can lead to serious problems, such as lower availability and higher possibility of deadlock. Therefore extensions have to be made to the traditional transaction model, including the requirements for transaction isolation and handling of subtransactions.

There are a number of problems, from splitting of a long transaction into subtransactions and the latters' serialization, to assurance of reliable updates in the face of crushes. Object approaches can be instrumental in the handling of long transactions, particularly during a transition period during which new concepts and transaction models will be worked out.

14-6 WHY ARE COMPANIES INTERESTED IN OBJECT DBMS?

The first four sections of this chapter identified shortcomings of relational approaches, some of which are due to a fast developing applications environment that makes relational database facilities too restrictive or even unable to meet the new demands in data management. This leads us to question why companies are interested in object DBMS.

Large user organizations are eager to obtain results from object-oriented approaches because they are concerned about efficiency issues which affect both professional productivity and costs. General Dynamics, for example, has launched a project aimed at creating a consolidated product database through object-oriented computer-integrated manufacturing (CIM). McDonnell Douglas is working on knowledgebank integration also using an object database.

Other projects focus on product definition through object-based approaches. Some are geometric modelers, and we have already spoken of DARPA's concurrent engineering effort. There is also an understanding that classical approaches have reached their limits:

An IBM study recently demonstrated that, to represent a single transistor through flat files, it is necessary to create 12 relational tables.

A study by Ontologic with 500 objects involving the Ontos and Oracle DBMS showed a 100:1 efficiency gain in searching an object database versus the alternative of searching a relational one.

A similar experiment by the South Carolina Research Institute concluded that the same set of multimedia searches averaged 2 minutes with an object-oriented DBMS and 2 hours with a relational construct.

Other experiments have documented that, for complex applications, object databases are much faster than nonobject databases. Part of the reason is that a very important factor in designing and building high-performance database applications is the ability to define performance-related characteristics that focus on computer usage patterns rather than provide definition in function of the application code itself.

Both for globally distributed database structures and for multimedia solutions, we need a wealth of semantics in connection to the information elements we store, as opposed to the rather limited semantics of the filing-cabinet approach. This is what most current DBMS offer, including the relational ones.

A key problem with the filing-cabinet, and by extension record-based solution to data handling, is that only with difficulty can it indicate where and how information elements are related to each other. Cross-indexing through pointers and anchors has been used for decades, but it is inflexible and not particularly efficient.

Object DBMS present other advantages besides avoiding ineffective linkages. As we will see in Chapter 17, Ontos offers the possibility of logical clustering and *caching:*★ Performance is improved if all information ele-

---

★From the French word *caché,* which means hidden (from the programmer's view).

ments required by an application are brought into central memory in a single disk access. As a result of this operation, subsequent processing accesses IE in central memory, with favorable performance results. Also, logical clustering overcomes the fact that the physical central memory available on a machine is limited, or that the virtual memory paging system will reach its limits if the application grows too large.

Stated in a different way, caching control can be provided through object-oriented approaches by means of logical clustering, which defines a group of objects that should be moved between secondary storage and central memory as a single unit. The content and size of such clusters can be changed, through software, to reflect usage patterns.

14 – 7 INTEGRATIVE CAPABILITIES AND SEMANTICS CONTENT

Attention should be paid to the importance of dynamic system adjustment to evolving requirements and its impact on the efficiency of a distributed database setting. Though the mechanics of this operation relate to knowledge engineering, there have been enough examples to document that object orientation and knowledge engineering complement one another.

Earlier we introduced the notions of *intentional* and *extentional* databases. The terms may be new, but some of their applications have been around for years. A primitive form of intentional database is *logic over data,* and it has been used with disk controllers for many years. Efficiency can be obtained in one workstation or file server through logic over data. This efficiency will be multiplied many times over in a myriaprocessor setting involving distributed databases, hosts, and thousands of workstations.

Since we already know that centralized databases limit the flexibility, functionality, and number of users, by increasing response time, we should bet on distributed resources. But, as stated, agile software for globally managing a distributed database does not yet exist—object-oriented logical clustering is just the beginning.

There are exceptions to this statement. In the early 1980s, Ingres presented Ingresnet, which featured network-wide demons. This implementation, however, was not particularly successful. In the late 1980s, IBM promised a golden horde of functions with its Repository and SAA, but none of the advertised functionality is yet supported, and it may take another dozen years to come.

Also in the late 1980s, several different vendors advanced the proposition that they could perform miracles in terms of distributed database management by using UNIX. This argument conveniently forgets that UNIX lacks the primitives for handling databases, let alone fully distributed and object-oriented solutions.

Another deficiency these various suggestions and offers have in common is that they are based on the record concept, with its filing cabinet approach. Both are devoid of powerful semantics; they are notions from the past that are used in the present without much alteration to fit the new environment. This means a lot of problems.

We have seen a number of reasons why half-baked approaches should not be adopted. We do not automatically solve our data management challenges simply by providing the infrastructure for storage and retrieval of objects. But such work assures the necessary basis for new departures.

One of the major contributions is a semantics orientation. The lack of appropriate semantics becomes more of a handicap as we begin to appreciate that, if done properly, a semantically rich distributed database management system can accommodate a significant number of computers, memories, and users.

Semantics is one of the reasons why, in the early distributed designs, most information elements were stored under local control. As we now talk about global approaches, we must find generalizable solutions, and these could be provided by object orientation.

There are other advantages to be derived from semantically rich distributed databases, which are waiting to be exploited. Redundantly stored information elements:

Increase system dependability

Help in overcoming local component failures

Provide a ground for parallel processing

Assist in decreasing response time

In a distributed database system, if one computer fails, the surviving machines merely continue accessing information elements. The same setting responds to the growing requirements for data sharing, which further leads organizations toward geographically dispersed information resources.

At the same time, there is growing interest in integrating information elements among a firm's different operating units, and meaning—semantics—can lead to integrative solutions. Still, in spite of what has been said about object linguistic supports, the commodity software is by and large missing. But when it comes, it will be semantically based.

14-8 SYNCHRONIZATION OF UPDATES

The point has already been made that if we wish to progress *beyond* relational DBMS, we must capitalize on what has already been achieved with current solutions, whether hierarchical, network, or relational. A major challenge lies in the dimension added by a hierarchy of storage devices.

One of the key housekeeping chores in a global database, which has been poorly addressed by hierarchical, Codasyl, and relational DBMS, is *synchronization*. Techniques for synchronizing multiple updates can involve a lot of communications traffic between lock managers, entities in the network, and updating nodes.

It is absolutely necessary to check automatically that all information elements are synchronized, but as soon as communications are introduced, there are time delay problems.

The distributed database perspective also brings up other issues of which we have spoken in the preceding sections.

If the database administrator has distributed the database resources so that, most of the time, lock management is local to the objects to be updated, network overhead is minimized and a distributed locking scheme is efficient. But so far there has been no well-defined method to decide how to distribute the lock managers and their authority over information elements in a highly distributed environment.

To compound the lock problem, distributed schemes require a directory of lock manager locations to be replicated at every node. Not only must this information be reflected in the data dictionaries, it must also be consistent.

This type of directory assistance represents the establishment of a new distributed database within the larger global one. The irony is that such a distributed data dictionary has all the synchronization and communications problems of the larger global database structure. To overcome these problems, one approach reduces some of the synchronization communications by decomposing updating transactions, much as queries are handled.

Transactional decomposition enables the DBMS to determine both the goal and the subgoals of the transaction, and preanalyze how transactions can conflict. Preanalysis forms the heart of a concurrency control mechanism. Depending on the application environment, it might show that very little runtime synchronization is required, thus saving messages. This, however, is no universal characteristic.

In order to handle transactional decomposition, we have to be analytical. Such a process cannot be done at all through hierarchical DBMS and data structures; it can be handled very poorly by means of record-based relational DBMS. But object orientation can provide the necessary infrastructure.

We can benefit from object-oriented solutions by analyzing all possible transactions and subtransactions for potential conflicts. One approach toward simplification is to organize transactions into classes according to the objects they handle. Conflict graph analysis can be of assistance in determining the type of synchronization required for each class.

- This is feasible because two transactions that run in different classes have a high probability of conflict only if their classes conflict.

- Hence, at runtime, an object-oriented transaction module can select a class, at a local or remote site, in which the transaction fits, applying the appropriate type of synchronization.
- At the same time, to ensure reliability in distributed objects, preventive measures must be taken to verify that the global database does not become corrupted.

A database becomes corrupted when it acquires erroneous information elements. Erroneous objects are possible when, for instance, all parts of a transaction cannot occur at exactly the same time or, if deferred, within the preestablished timeframe (real-enough time versus real time).

The problem in a distributed database setting is that once one of the computers in the network initiates an update, it assumes that it will be done and is unaware that a remote machine failed before completing its work. Consequently, it may allow other transactions to read the now inconsistent information.

To prevent this corruption of data, demons supervising distributed database processes are necessary to monitor all sites and flag any failures: Monitoring processes should be sending requests for acknowledgement to the active sites. If a response does not arrive within a predecided time period, the demon declares the destination machine to be down and takes recovery action.

We have already spoken of the needed recovery steps and flagging as well as backtracking of transactions. Applied within a global setting, different schemes are based on synchronized clocks, majority voting, and protocols declaring referenced IEs in advance. They deal with data consistency, different types of failures, and incomplete transaction problems.

The message is that it takes a great deal of checking to ensure that no erroneous values are written into a distributed database. In addition to handling multimedia IEs, as well as the commitment, consistency, and recovery control already discussed, we must be able to uphold concurrent correctness. These are issues that confronted hierarchical, network, and relational databases in the past; today they challenge object-oriented solutions.

15

Limitations of the Relational Model

15-1 INTRODUCTION

Database management systems provide mechanisms for accessing and manipulating data created by autonomous applications. Their employment permits repositories shared by multiple routines, provided every application has a homogeneous view of data. Short of this, we are faced with heterogeneity problems in multidatabases, as we saw in Chapter 14.

Even different databases may contain related or even overlapping information elements. In the fine grain, these may be characterized by various degrees of heterogeneity:

They usually have different schemata.
They are distributed among different sites.
They are implemented using different DBMS.

As we have already discussed, one of the main problems of providing shared access to multiple heterogeneous databases is preserving their autonomy, ensuring they can keep their own data model, schemata, and their communications.

Communications autonomy means that the distributed heterogeneous databases can decide the extent of data that is exchanged with other databases. This is an integral part of execution autonomy with regard to requests from other databases in the network. It is also one of the domains where the relational model falls short of meeting requirements.

Multidatabases are the coming wave because the emphasis on communicating distributed resources has functional background reasons. As organizations grow and their computers and networks become more complex, so do requirements for information storage, retrieval, and manipulation. A growing range of on-line functionality has to be ensured automatically, unless we employ vast numbers of staff whose sole task is to store and retrieve information—with all the delays, errors, and costs that such manual operations entail.

While the concepts of databasing, datacommunications, and data processing predate the use of computers, it was the introduction of computing machinery that caused a reevaluation of how information is structured and handled. At the same time, industrial and finance organizations created the need to collect and process large amounts of data. These were too voluminous to handle in classical form and too cumbersome to be held in traditional, paper-based files. While numeric information was the first to be processed by computers, increasingly multimedia perspectives opened up.

As experience with computer databases grew, we found that each of our consequitive solutions to their management—hierarchical, network, relational—solved some problems but created others. At the same time, over the last 10 years the volume of data stored and retrieved increased almost exponentially.

Although hierarchical, Codasyl, inverted files, and other DBMS are still used and will be used for another few years. However, in the words of the executive vice president of a leading New York financial institution, "IMS is strangling the corporation." The same is true of other aged DBMS.

Clear-eyed companies are moving away from hierarchical database management systems. Some have chosen parallel database computers. Others are experimenting with object-oriented, client-server solutions. The more experimentally minded of these organizations have found that new departures are necessary given their heavy requirements. More precisely, they have found that there is little that can be gained from the transition from hierarchical to relational models, hence such a transition is really not worth the effort.

It is interesting to note that each one of the three prevailing DBMS approaches that predate the object orientation was at one time the market leader. But before too long, each model's ability to represent fully the necessary semantics and to handle users' viewpoints, not to mention managing the growing data volumes and the landscape of a distributed environment, was recognized as being limited.

15–2 STRENGTHS AND WEAKNESSES OF RELATIONAL DATABASES

Relational approaches became popular because the flat files on which they rest are simpler than other structures as well as more flexible. When, a dozen years ago, relational DBMS came to the public eye, they became a base for new departures. At that time almost everybody was frustrated by the inflexibility of hierarchical DBMS.

Another advantage of relational DBMS is that at least some of them are equipped with fourth-generation languages. Such languages were missing from both hierarchical and network-type DBMS. Systems experts and computer managers asked, "What are our alternatives?"

While these issues are real, it is also true that databases cannot be properly modeled by entirely separate islands of data. And relational DBMS do not solve that problem.

The real-life information elements that a company manipulates are often related to one another; sales orders are related to clients and suppliers, and therefore should be linked in the company's data repository. A simple flat list of bill of materials without the information necessary to connect them does not model a design project adequately. In the light of this, database systems concentrated on linking related records together, for instance, by adding pointers to records.

When the profusion of pointers became difficult to handle, network approaches with their master/member architecture tried to make life easier for the programmer. These efforts predated the relational offers and proceeded by reflecting relationships between information elements, at times even capturing some semantic concepts such as dependencies and simple integrity constraints. But other important factors in DBMS performance were not necessarily supported.

This history is important for a number of reasons, not the least of which is suggesting that what has been integrated into object-oriented solutions did not come out of blue sky but rather through mapping of already acquired knowledge and tools. What network and subsequent relational approaches failed to do was remove the inflexible record structure and its associated filing-cabinet structure.

Over years of implementation, the record/file-cabinet approach had led to a loss of data independence:

Pointers invariably involve ordering of records.

Index dependence relies on the programmer to refer to and retrieve information elements.

Access path dependence obliges a program to follow a chain of pointers or access path.

While data models based on relations did not suffer from storage dependencies, conceptually they still retained the file-cabinet structure. Moreover, as distributed database applications were worked out, a number of problems still occurred because of programming complexity. Practical considerations of accommodating worst-case situations led to excessive over-head, slow performance, and poor throughput.

Eventually, the challenges in developing distributed database systems fell into two classes: communications and database design proper. At this point, the limitations of record structure and therefore of record-based flat files became even more apparent.

Communications-related problems involve primarily the speed with which network links can operate relative to workstations, hosts, and database servers. Such problems can be partially alleviated by proper node and link distribution, but this is a nontrivial problem requiring multiple attempts to be resolved, some of which can be made only after the system is in use.

One of the major issues in designing distributed databases is communications problems because of requirements imposed on channel capacity. An associated problem is to keep the information element records at different sites synchronized. This in turn involves making sure that, during updates, flat files replicated at different sites remain the same. It also means that consistent relationships between different IEs must be maintained, and requires support for transparency of access queries—users should not need to know the location of their IEs.

Further problems include monitoring remote sites, deadlock detection and recovery, portability, and compatibility between different software and hardware platforms. The portability/compatibility issue arises because heterogeneous computers are usually present at distributed sites, and flat file/filing-cabinet approaches can do little or nothing to solve this type of heterogeneous problem.

Solutions typically require an orderly approach that first establishes a concept, then elaborates on it and polishes it—even changes it—and then transits to the next level and repeats the polishing steps. The procedure is shown in Fig. 15.1. As can be appreciated, such a procedure should take into account what is commercially available as well as what still needs to be done to improve commercial offerings.

However, in the majority of cases, instead of following a systematic organizational approach, companies tried to attack database design issues by using complex algorithms and lots of classical programming. By contrast, portability is being addressed in a rather limited form, while most firms pay only lip service to the need for normalization to ensure compatible data structures.

Little by little we also discovered that when records are the units of reference and the filing-cabinet concept dominates, relational approaches are *not* the simplest possible structure. While the relational model is indeed simple and features a small number of concepts, this simplicity cannot effectively capture the necessary range of semantics—meaning—representation. As a result, it leads to increasing complexity.

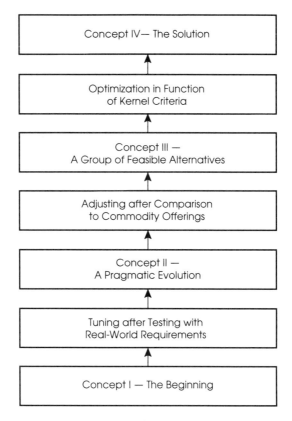

Figure 15.1   A step-by-step approach to problem solving.

15–3 CONTRIBUTIONS OF THE RELATIONAL MODEL

The limitations of relational technology and record structures become evident with the increase in the size of the distributed database resources. This was one reason why hierarchical and network DBMS solutions could not provide the expected functionality.

Casual users consider the relational model rather simple and easy to comprehend because they see the information in a relational database as a collection of independent records, which they look up as tables. This is a step forward from the older hierarchical and network approaches. With a relational solution, there is an improvement in runtime flexibility over hierarchical, network, and inverted files. Users can dynamically join together information from different tables, and applications can benefit from flat-file retrieval capabilities.

More knowledgeable users, as well as systems specialists, appreciate that the structure of a relational database may be altered dynamically, for instance, by adding a new attribute to a table. Older database technologies are much less flexible with regard to structure changes.

At the same time, however, sophisticated users and systems specialists understand that flat-file approaches lack other features that are just as vital today, for example, the ability to implement object-based referential integrity constraints. Also, referencing entities directly is a powerful and important quality of object identity, which relational approaches do not support on their own.

Others, however, would say that it is not impossible for commercial DBMS to enforce referential integrity. They have chosen not to do so for performance reasons. Any DBMS will pay a performance penalty to enforce it: Constraints are good, but they are not free, nor is referential integrity.

While experience is still being acquired, some information scientists are of the opinion that object approaches allow more integrity controls. Others, of course, think that this is not necessarily true. The latter point out that in a relational DBMS, only the system can create and update data. It controls the vertical as well as the horizontal. That is all that is needed, and one can build any kind of desired constraint on top of that power. But at what price?

In a model that features object identity, the branch office of a client is referenced and accessed directly by its semantic identity, instead of by an indirect identifier such as a branch office number. This sees to it that referential integrity constraints are not necessarily needed, provided the associated functionality is available.

By and large, object-oriented systems can support domain constraints using specialization through restrictions. A domain constraint is a specfication that attribute values must satisfy certain constraints. The most natural way to achieve this is to create a domain or a class whose instances are only those objects that qualify under given constraints. While some relational dialects reach this end algorithmically, object approaches allow more integrity controls because of the object's ability to create subclasses, often through separate constraint constructs. Integrity constraints with relational DBMS deal mainly with individual attribute values, yet much more general integrity constraints must be defined in a global database. These need to involve multiple attribute values or aggregates of attribute values. Arbitrary constraints on persistent objects must also be expressed.

In terms of design, the development of an optimal database schema for a distributed environment, with its associated subschemata and subsequent selection of a suitable set of database relations, represents in itself a major problem. This is an issue that has not been adequately addressed so far.

The optimization of database subschemata impacts directly on the running efficiency of an entire global database. Researchers have been working on the development of an appropriate methodology, but this is not yet available. Furthermore, with most of these efforts, the starting point has been a given set of relations and logical dependencies, or attributes and logical dependencies on which the design is to be based.

Most projects have been conceptually limited because they concentrated mainly on the forms of data that were modeled. Object-oriented modeling in contrast, stresses the importance of semantics. This is equivalent to *modeling the meaning* as opposed to modeling the data.

A fundamental weakness of a relational approach is that the semantics of real-life situations cannot be incorporated into the database schema. Hence much of the knowledge possessed by the database designer is not captured—but it can be mirrored into an object-oriented solution through knowledge engineering.

Furthermore, apart from being more limited in terms of implementation, within a global database environment the relational approach is by no means flawless. A fundamental weakness, for example, is that it is really too simple to reflect the complexities of a global approach. Real-world situations do not map well into a collection of simple, independent, record-oriented tables. As a result, we often have to distort the real situation to make it fit the relational model.

Another weakness of current implementations of relational technology is the lack of flexible ad-hoc queries able to deal with vagueness and uncertainty. SQL, which parades itself as the ANSI standard, is by no means an ideal way for handling ad-hoc queries; and it is totally incapable of addressing queries of a fuzzy type, yet the importance of the latter is rapidly growing.★

15–4 PREMISES OF RELATIONAL AND OBJECT-ORIENTED SOLUTIONS

One of the basic premises of relational models has been that moving the processing logic closer to the data will make it possible to simplify storage organization. The growth in database size, however, has meant that providing efficient access in a relational database requires sophisticated address and access structures based on pointer chains, hashing algorithms, and directories. In turn, these access structures have called for considerable skill on the part of system programmers. They also add to the overhead of the database.

Ingenious designers have produced some simplified representations. These permit viewing the data in close to tabular form, but the solutions being reached differ greatly in organization and performance. One reason for the difference is storage utilization, which involves manual tasks.

In designing a representation, decisions must be made on how a rela-

---

★However, the LIKE operator of SQL does not allow one dimension of fuzziness.

tion and its columns are identified, as well as how and where tuples (rows) are marked to indicate interest for further processing. For instance, a column value can be labeled with a name, delimited by special characters, or stored in a fixed position. Space can be reserved in storage for marks, or special marking memories can be provided. How these decisions are made determines time, cost, and overhead of storing a relation.

These references to the "fine print" of the implementation of relational solutions are pertinent not only because they identify divergencies and weaknesses, but also (if not particularly) because they bring attention to pitfalls. We may of course well repeat the same or similar pitfalls with object-oriented approaches, if we do not learn from past mistakes.

Another impediment to the use of relational database management systems that we should be keen to correct is installation cost and the amount of skill required. At present, the implementation of a complex DBMS such as DB2 calls for a staff skilled in the mechanics of the the DBMS itself, the operating systems, telecommunications, data management, and applications proper.

Object-oriented approaches, by contrast, should allow easy definition of databases and database applications. Without sacrificing function and performance, they should also provide sophisticated facilities that automatically handle system functions such as recovery and concurrency control.

To alleviate past deficiencies, an object-oriented DBMS should be easy to learn and use, permitting optimizer functions to improve performance. It should also provide complete independence between application programs and distributed information elements. Normalization is just as vital.

As Chapter 14 stressed, current practices are by and large characterized by DBMS heterogeneity. Currently, database management systems, of all types, differ in the way they organize records. They also differ in the way they support and activate relational operators such as sort, join, project, and select, which combine and manipulate various relations. This should not happen with object DBMS.

Another issue to consider is *navigation.* Relational systems have an advantage in that they require no extra navigation procedures. SQL is mostly relational calculus, which is declarative. Network, hierarchical, and object databases have hard links, which are often used for navigation.

At least one commercial object DBMS has a user tool called The Navigator. But object DBMS can also have declarative and functional tools. Any system with an explicit semantic structure can support navigation.

In real-life applications, the user needs to navigate through a network or hierarchy. For example, to find recent invoices of a customer, the user locates the customer account record, then locates the invoice records under that customer, and then moves to the accounts payable. A relational model may use a nonnavigational solution. In this example, an SQL program will be

```
Select
From Acct_Records
Where Acct_Num IN
        (Select Acct_Num
        From Customer_Accts
        Where name = "Paul Peters");
```

A non-navigational approach requests by name all account records pertaining to that customer and relies on the system to locate them. While navigation may not be inherent in nonrelational systems, some provide a navigational interface—which may be efficient or inefficient. But we do have *hypertext* and *hypermedia,* and hypermedia facilities should be embedded in object-oriented applications.

$15-5$ THE QUEST FOR RIGOROUS SOLUTIONS

Rigorous solutions and valid approaches in database design and the management of a distributed environment are not chosen arbitrarily, but consider at least five important factors:

1. Enduser needs
2. Available technology
3. System architecture
4 Database structure
5. The applications themselves

As shown in Fig. 15.2, these factors interact with one another. In a way they constitute a self-feeding cycle, which increasingly requires a higher level of sophistication.

In terms of enduser requirements, choices also have to be made with regard to the ad-hoc query language. Fuzzy engineering characteristics can help. One of the choices concerns runtime compilation versus interpretation. Compiling a query statement captures and preserves information that an interpreter must rediscover on each invocation. Interpretation, by contrast, presents the advantage of an interface that can help handle heterogeneous IEs in a more homogeneous form. Experiments, however, have indicated that compilation is almost always more cycle-efficient than interpretation, even for queries that are executed only once.

The system should also allow global optimization of the query and the consequent generation of an optimized code, which essentially means a minimum number of database calls and inputs/outputs.

Similarly, the solution to be adopted should be tuned by defining effi-

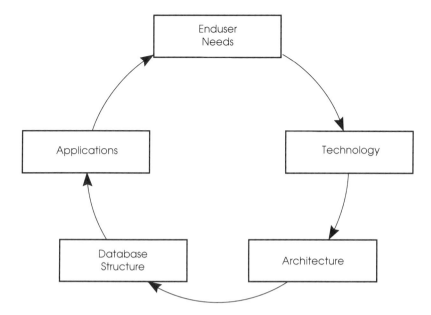

Figure 15.2   A self-feeding cycle in system development.

cient access paths, and its technique should be transparent to the application programmer. In combination with granting and revocation operations, an object-oriented view can as well be used to provide the basis for an authorization mechanism.

With a global database, an automatic recovery artifact should compensate for local failures as well as system failures. The need for human intervention in system recovery should be avoided. Similarly, in an object-based environment, restarting must not involve manual action—but there are constraints.

Experience with relational DBMS indicates that the transaction concept is key to a successful recovery philosophy. A complex update of the database involves many statements. If such an update fails, or if the system crashes during the operation, the state of the database will probably become unreliable. Hence the system must be able to undo partially completed transactions by keeping a log of all the changes a transaction has made in the distributed database environment.

If the transaction gets into trouble, the system must undo the transaction by setting updated records to the old values in the log. The need for transactions to be undone is not new, but new solutions are necessary for fully distributed, multimedia implementations. We noted this need earlier, when we discussed the handling of long transactions.

Similarly, we noted the need for tools able to integrate different schemas. The premise was advanced that knowledge engineering and object databases can be useful in responding to this need. In fact, it has been shown that while relational models have many limitations in schema integration, object solutions can help to ensure virtual semantic homogeneity through the multidatabase.

Object-oriented approaches are thus the best technology currently available for integrating semantically heterogeneous schemata. They can allow integrated views to be defined

- Starting with local views expressed in a uniform object data model but still semantically heterogeneous, then
- Proceeding with a view model based on the object paradigm, thus permitting object behavior to be described and
- Making it feasible for semantic conflicts to be solved on a structural basis and with a mapping approach.

Subsequently, the inheritance mechanism makes feasible the development of integrated views to be defined. The emphasis on achieving virtual semantic homogeneity is justified by the fact that heterogeneity presents very difficult problems.

There are, of course, a number of other issues, such as consistency and concurrency, which we will discuss in the next section. Even for these, an object approach can be very helpful, as the networked databases will contain information not only about objects, but also about object connections.

Since these distributed databases preserve their autonomy in structuring and manipulating information elements, objects in each of them can be represented and identified differently. Such identification of differences is problematic in a relational environment, where entities are represented by relation tuples and connections are handled through references.

15–6 CONSISTENCY, CONCURRENCY, AND STORAGE HIERARCHY

The reason for paying attention to solutions already achieved with relational databases is that we must learn from them if we wish to go beyond relational models. For instance, a key problem for a distributed database is how to keep its information elements and dispersed nodes synchronized:

How to update IEs so that they are accurate, current, and reliable

How to replicate IEs and account for computer failures in the face of multiple users

How to synchronize heterogeneous databases within a distributed setting

Some problems occur because almost all database management systems support multiple on-line users, who could potentially update the same information element at the same time. In doing so, they interfere with each other and with the goal of database consistency.

Experience with real-time systems for transaction processing demonstrates that consistency problems occur when a single transaction manipulates different IEs that depend on each other. This can be a major problem in an object-oriented environment, and it is one that has not yet been properly addressed in a global sense.

Relational-type implementations have tackled the issue of consistency, but at the expense of heavy overhead. Network and hierarchical DBMS have approached it through the lockup mechanism.★ The most common solution to distributed database consistency is to lock the database, that is, to deny access, until each transaction is completed. A centralized locking mechanism is the easiest to implement, and therefore the most popular. In this design, although the IE may be distributed, the control of who can update is centralized. The problem with this scheme is that many of the advantages of distributing the database are lost.

For instance, if the node that is controlling all the updates fails, the distributed database is put out of action. A more sophisticated approach allows the locking mechanism to be distributed. In this case, if a node wants to perform an update, it must obtain a lock from the node acting as lock manager for that specific information element.

An object-oriented solution can optimize this process by capitalizing on the instantiated hierarchy that is ephemeral, that is, dispensed the moment the operation is completed. Hence, as long as a transaction lasts, lockup is hierarchical; The moment the transaction is satisfactorily completed, all IEs are released. However, such IEs may be captured by the next transaction being executed at the same or at a different node.

This scheme brings into focus logical and physical layers constituting the "onion skins" of a global database system. As seen in Fig. 15.3, the DBMS is one of these onion skins. It is part of a multilayered structure, with storage devices comprising the core.

Compared to most computer technologies, contemporary memory devices have the highest degree of technological maturity, with well-understood design criteria and trade-offs. They are also progressively improving cost/performance indices. Storage technology, which provides the physical host environment for databases, remains the main factor in determining the cost and performance of data management systems.

Magnetic disks have dominated on-line mass storage for three decades. For some of their functions they are now being challenged by optical disks (photonics). But optical disks are not superior to magnetic disks in all

---

★See also Chapter 14.

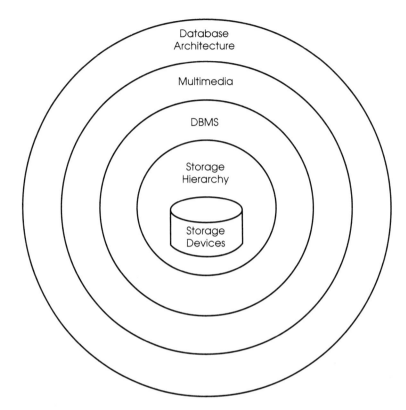

Figure 15.3   The onion-skin principle of system architecture.

ways; hence, until the end of this century, each technology will be extended to address its own domain. Thus, for most of the 1990s we will have to be able to accommodate both storage technologies; magnetic and optical. Relational DBMS models do not excel in this task. Here again, object-oriented solutions seem to be better fitted for this type of application and the associated multimedia solutions.

15–7 PHYSICAL ASPECTS OF A MULTIDATABASE

One of the most often-stated drawbacks of rotating magnetic disk devices, as well as optical disks, is access time. The difference in access time between disks and main memories (presently in the range of four to five orders of magnitude) is the *access gap*.

An instinctive fear of gaps seems to have triggered a constant search for technologies that can fill it. But is there a cost/effective technology available today to act as a gap filler? Far from being academic, this question relates to the architecture of the physical memory and its connection to the logical memory, as we discussed with regard to computer-generated space. The answer to the question is: "Yes, there is a way: logical clustering and caching through an object-oriented DBMS."

Both disks and random access memory (RAM) devices have experienced rapid physical developments. As a logical solution, the best approach is *caching* by means of logic over data.* A technology that could replace mechanical rotating machinery will have to offer the best combination of storage characteristics:

Performance
Cost per bit
Nonvolatility

From all indications to date, a good solution will not be available for a while. This means continuing dependence on storage hierarchies, making intelligent database solutions that much more important.

Efficient organization and management of large memory aggregates is the focal issue in data management design, and it impacts upon the system's capacity, consistency, concurrency, and response time. In principle, large storage spaces are organized in a hierarchical fashion, and various levels are implemented in different technologies, mainly for economic reasons.

As shown in Fig. 15.4, storage hierarchies hosting databases exist in a three-dimensional space defined by access time, capacity, and cost. The criterion of a successful storage hierarchy design is to achieve an optimum balance among these variables. The goal is the fastest possible access time at the lowest possible cost per bit, for the entire storage hierarchy.

One of the vital dimensions, total database storage capacity, is determined primarily by enduser application requirements and tools to manage sprawling memory structures. It should always be kept in mind that the performance of storage hierarchies depends on access patterns and program behavior in actual runtime.

This is quite relevant to the development of the logical infrastructure in terms of object-oriented approaches, as it always rests on the physical hierarchy process and pushes toward making optimum trade-offs in device selection, space allocation, and object replacement.

The prevailing methodology for investigating program behavior is computer simulation supplemented by performance measurements made

---

*Which is practiced in two ways: providing the disk control unit with a cache, or mapping the disk unit's cache into the main memory.

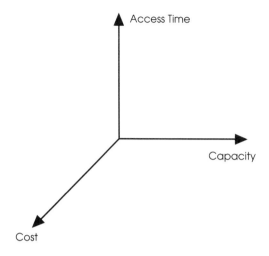

Figure 15.4   Defining criteria for a computer-generated space.

on representative programs through benchmarks. At the beginning, at least some design choices are based on intuitive assumptions and empirical approximations, but experimentation can provide hard data and should be used more often under conditions of statistical experimental design.*

Solutions to the challenges presented in a multidatabase environment are indivisible from experimentation. In many cases, in spite of considerable work on the integration of data structures, limited results have been obtained because the approach chosen was monolithic, not experimental.

Another drawback has been that many of these projects have used the relational model as the common model for defining export schemas, thus placing limits on their own perspectives. The relational model is preferred because of the ease of decomposing and recomposing relations, studying the existence of set-oriented operations that avoid the need for navigation via internodal pointers, and the fact that the mappings for defining the integration can be expressed in a query language, thereby rendering simpler query decomposition.

Apart from the fact that these approaches have done little in considering the physical constraints of the storage environment, even in the logical domain the conclusion has often been reached that the relational model lacks the necessary semantics for defining all the integrative mapping that might be desired. Precisely in response to these limitations, a number of researchers have opted for semantically rich approaches such as the entity-relationship (E-R) and object-oriented models. Object orientation is suitable for

---

*See also D. N. Chorafas, *Statistical Processes and Reliability Engineering,* D. Van Nostrand, Princeton, NJ, 1960.

integrating all kinds of databases, as well as mappings and multidatabase application programs that can be expressed in a uniform object language.

Obviously there are differences in terms of flexibility and functionality between one object database management system aand another. Therefore, the next five chapters take a close look at commercially available object DBMS, outlining their strengths and weaknesses.

Chapter 16

DBMS for Object-Oriented Databases

16-1 INTRODUCTION

It cannot be repeated too often that all currently available database management systems—relational, Codasyl, and hierarchical—represent data in the form of *records.* As the atomic unit of storage, records contain *fields,* which hold values. Each real-world instance of a record assigns a value to a field, but reference is typically done at the record level, which is too coarse for distributed database requirements.

An object-oriented solution, by contrast, does away with the records structure, and this is an important innovation. Object-level reference leads to the concepts of renewal and change that dominated the way we have thought of databases and their management.

However, the effective implementation of a conceptual change poses a number of important questions, which may have a significant impact on software engineering for the years to come:

What are the characteristics of an object-oriented database management system?

How does an object-oriented system differ from relational, network, and hierarchical DBMS?

What are the consequences of its implementation in a distributed database environment?

Enthusiasts of object-based solutions would answer that an immediate and visible consequence will be significant improvements in areas where relational databases have proved to be inadequate, such as computer-aided design (CAD), computer-integrated manufacturing (CIM), computer-assisted software engineering (CASE), and office automation (OA).

Proponents of object-oriented DBMS would also cite other areas where relational models have so far provided much less than expected results. Among these domains are long transactions, foreign exchange transactions, securities trading, image processing, cartography, patterning, and artificial intelligence. Spatial rather than flat files is the way to proceed in these implementation domains.

Not everything about object databases is positive, however. One criticism of object-oriented DBMS, often repeated in the database community, is that their approach is merely a new incarnation of the network (Codasyl) database model. Some people—particularly designers of relational DBMS—claim that their approach is more flexible than object solutions for ad-hoc queries.

Arguments and counterarguments are hardly new among information systems specialists, or for that matter in any professional circle. But as far as the issue of the *flexibility* of relational DBMS is concerned, a senior design engineer of an American computer manufacturer has noted that in order to study one transistor, he needs to open 36 different relational files.

Critics of object-based approaches also suggest that there is no real underlying theory of object orientation, implementation examples are still sparse, and commercially available object-oriented DBMS are both immature and incompatible. These critics will present as proof the existence of many different commercial database management systems, including (in alphabetic order) Amazone, Encore, Exodus, FAD, Galileo, G-Base, GemStone, Genesis, Iris, Jasmin, Object Store, ODB, Odil, Ontos, Orion (Itasca), O2, Mandrill, MIB, Pegasus, Probe, SIM, Statice, V-Base, Versant, and others that are still in development.

A third party to this discussion, is quite likely to ask, "Who is right?" The answer has to be: "Both!" Within a global database environment, and even for large centralized databases, a hierarchical DBMS is a retrograde way of handling the problem. Network approaches are a little better, but not much; and relational solutions have limitations—at least in the areas discussed.

At the same time, the theory behind implementation of object-oriented DBMS is not yet ready, and it is true that many commercial offerings are mutually incompatible. It is precisely because of this dual aspect of the problem, and the challenges it poses, that the discussion on object-oriented DBMS will proceed.

$16-2$ THE NOTION OF A MODERN DATABASE MANAGEMENT SYSTEM

The mission of the first database management system was the able handling of masses of data (which, however, was at that time slight compared to present-day volumes). The first DBMS was jointly designed by Boeing and IBM in 1958 in conjunction with the Semiautomatic Air to Ground Equipment (SAGE) of the Department of Defense, promoted by the fact that file management routines could not do the job required.

The structure of this first DBMS was hierarchical, which was both the simplest and most evident notion at the time—as well as the one fitting the requirement of the application, which was control of the North American airspace. Yet even in this very early implementation it was necessary to add a number of tools to beef up functionality so that record management could be done effectively.

Layering was not one of the concepts that prevailed in the late 1950s, but from experience acquired later, we can say that, as Fig. 16.1 suggests, the solution that emerged involved a layered, bottom-up approach:

1. *Physical registration,* that is, database access, storage, and retrieval
2. *Logical registration,* and access with some basic linguistic supports

These eventually evolved into a data definition language (DDL) and data manipulation language (DML), addressing the internal schema.

As experience with DBMS accumulated, after their mid- to late 1960s commercial offering, software support for more facilities became necessary. For instance, as shown in Fig. 16.1 a higher layer was added:

3. A *data dictionary,* which evolved from directories to include data definition, links, and controls

Subsequently, tools were needed for expressing and handling enduser interactivity with the database, bringing attention to a primary linguistic interface and its primitives, often presented in the form of:

4. A *query language* that helped express the external schema.

This addition eventually proved to be too little, and the concept of a linguistic interface was enlarged. Some, but not all, DBMS were enriched with:

5. A constellation of *fourth-generation languages* (4GL) for enduser programming.

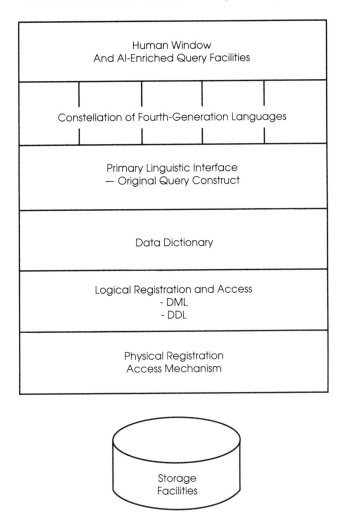

Figure 16.1   The evolution of DBMS functionality.

Eventually, the provision of agile, flexible, and friendly human-machine interfaces called upon knowledge engineering to provide:

6. A human window that can facilitate human-machine communications, and adds the functionality of fifth-generation linguistic tools (5GL).

While each of these layers is dedicated to a specific mission, transmitting its result to the next higher level, some functions transcend the structure. The concept of entity-relationship is the best example.

$16-3$ THE ENTITY-RELATIONSHIP MODEL

From the moment that companies, their database administrators, and system specialists saw that they needed more than relational DBMS could provide, *Entity-Relationship* became a core issue of DBMS functionality, because it underlies the goal of data independence. It permits concentration on modeling data without reference to its eventual handling through magentic or optical media.

As the name implies in the entity-relationship model, the real world is represented as a set of entities and relationships. In an object-oriented environment, *entities* are objects in the part of the world mapped into, and modeled by, the database. Some entities owe their relevance to the existence of other entities and are therefore classified as *weak* entities.

Relationships are *associations* between entities; both entities and relationships possess attributes that describe them. Relationships may be classified as

> One-to-one
> One-to-many
> Many-to-many

and the DBMS must be able to handle each class. This is true of object-based DBMS as it is of other types—relational, network, and hierarchical—though the latter two have great difficulty in approaching this subject.

If this is the case, why can't we use a relational DBMS as the underlying layer, enriching it with entity-relationship functionality, then build on it a meta layer with an object orientation? This is a first-class idea that has not yet been appropriately exploited—with the exception of the ICOT project in Japan, which developed the intentional and extentional (IDB-EDB) implementation. In that structure, the lower layer, which constitutes the extentional database (EDB), may be relational, managing information elements in tuples but also as independent entities. Such entities are characterized by a correspondence to every other IE. This can be accomplished through a matrix-type structure that acts as the reference link. According to the ICOT model, above this structure the meta-level is knowledge-based, observing object-oriented characteristics. It enhances the operational level's abstraction mechanism, to provide the operational support needed within an object infrastructure, leading to the definition of what can be termed a layered approach to object-oriented database management systems.

Through the duality we have been discussing, entity relationship can be established and maintained through a base level and a meta-level. This also makes it easier to handle the fact that the process of obtaining the key of an entity involved in a relationship differs from that of obtaining its other attributes. Keys that may change their value also present a problem that can be handled effectively at a meta-knowledge level.

16–4 CHARACTERISTICS OF OBJECT-ORIENTED DBMS

Since the original description of object-oriented models, there has been a growing level of acceptance of data abstraction and associated ideas, to the point that this type of work today accounts for a considerable portion of database research. As a result, a number of DBMS with object orientations are starting to become available.

Companies engaged in the production of object-oriented commercial DBMS advertise as a main reason for this product line the artifacts' inherent conceptual simplicity. However, it has been recognized that the elegance of such a conceptual model is dependent on the design approach taken—and, we have noted, design solutions vary among the different object DBMS being introduced to the market.

By and large, presently available commercial products can be classified into two categories: new departures, and improvements on existing DBMS approaches.

New departures, such as Ontos, GemStone, Versant, Object Store, and Open ODB in the United States, and Odin, Jasmine, MIB, and Mandrill in Japan, have had teething problems, but they are worth experimenting with because of the novel features they offer. In the following chapters we will look more closely at the new generation of object DBMS.

A word of caution should, however, be added: New departures do not yet mean *integrative* solutions to DBMS functionality like the one shown in Fig. 16.2. Such an approach still has to be composed out of different components—which means inherent incompatibilities—though a streamlined version should constitute the goal of a new generation of DBMS.

Improvements on existing DBMS approaches include G-Base, Orion (revamped into Itasca), and SIM .

While both new departures and improved procedures in DBMS design bring added value, what we do must at the same time observe the fundamental characteristics of both object-based solutions (as presented and explained in Chapters 1 and 2) and the crucial aspects of DBMS functionality (discussed in Section 2 of this chapter).

Specifically, through the use of semantic data models, an object-oriented DBMS must be able to capture and control more of the meaning of

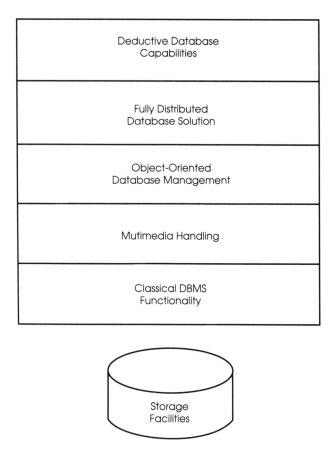

Figure 16.2   An integrative approach to distributed DBMS performance.

information technology applications than has been possible so far. In terms of specific goals, we must be concerned with the particular problems of new applications in domains such as

Software engineering
Computer-integrated solutions
Computer-aided design
Document handling
Office automation
Decision-support systems

In the case of software engineering and its mission, an object-oriented DBMS should consider the different views of a software design held by the project manager, the designers, and the programmers. This requirement is not easily reconciled with traditional database techniques.

A similar statement can be made about concurrent engineering design projects and decision-support systems. As these examples document, there is a need for basic database characteristics that allow persistent data sharing between groups of users in a consistent and resilient manner.

Furthermore, additional facilities are called for and should be present in an object-oriented DBMS. These are derived from the basic features of object-oriented solutions:

Inheritance and meta-knowledge

Types that describe behavior rather than purely structure

Classes and their instantiation

Data abstraction

Type hierarchies

Entities and their versioning

The function of a characteristic entity, for example, is to describe some other entity. A characteristic entity is typically existence-dependent on a superior entity that fits the meta concept. Individual commands that must be executed to keep a target object up to date can be considered closely related to the target they create.

The notion of object-oriented integrity indicates that a characteristic entity can exist only if the entity it describes also exists. By contrast, a kernel entity is one that is neither characteristic nor associative.

Associations are important in all artifacts and particularly in distributed environments. An association is a potentially many-to-many relationship between two otherwise independent objects. Associative integrity says that an association can exist only if all the entities that participate in the association also exist.

A DBMS of the sort we propose must reflect the fact that some concepts are central to object-oriented systems. For instance, objects of interest in the real world can be modeled most effectively by recording them together with the operations that are permitted on them. This allows us to move from representing the purely structural aspects of a distributed database toward more integrational behavior, and a view that combines both structure and operations.

Such operations form an interface to structures and rules. Modalities are also necessary to provide a way to amend those structures. Tools should ensure a graphical environment for designing object applications. Other tools should help to generate database schemata as well as database interfaces.

16-5 REASONS FOR THE ADVENT OF OBJECT DBMS

The introduction of object-oriented DBMS and their acceptance by the user community has occurred for several reasons. In most cases, the impetus was a response to developing requirements for sharable, very large distributed databases operating in an increasingly complex landscape.

In the late 1970s, when relational models began to be popularized, the information systems community formed the opinion that they could solve all problems connected to large databases. However, six factors work against this notion:

1. *Hardware developments* have to a significant extent overtaken the original advances in relational DBMS—due to large-scale storage size and increasing usage of distributed resources.

2. Complexity in *applications software* and associated enduser requirements have grown very fast, often overtaking implementation expertise.

3. For most relational DBMS, the language is still procedural and the query facilities are truly ad hoc, graphics oriented, and interactive.

4. Communications-intense environments require a much higher level of interactivity and data abstraction than relational approaches can provide.

5. Most of the currently available relational DBMS are supported by languages that predated them—from SQL for queries to Cobol, PL/1, and LISP—leading to language mismatch. An existing database language is not easily converted into an object-oriented one. A number of features must be added to it; these features are only now being defined in a comprehensive manner, and some cannot be effectively integrated into aging linguistic artifacts.

6. Users today need more sophisticated applications, often incorporating *knowledge engineering.* In developing normal knowledge-based systems, we deal with relationships as objects. Through the use of an object-oriented DBMS, this is carried to the level of a close isomorphism between object and solution, which can be of significant advantage to the way we develop, implement, and maintain the solutions we seek.

The object DBMS we have considered in Section 4, and the leading constructs we will examine in the next four chapters, have escaped the limitations of existing database management approaches. Necessity is the mother of invention, and object DBMS are no exception.

Experimental results with object DBMS tend to indicate that changes to the conceptual structure, hence the meta-data of application databases, can be achieved with acceptable efficiency. For example, creating a new user-defined type took only 8 seconds with V–Base (the predecessor of the Ontos DBMS). Changing the values of attributes, inserting/deleting instances into/from a type, and other operations are directly supported by a number of object DBMS.

Diversity is, a problem, however. Besides the aforementioned alternatives, other object-oriented database management systems and related developments include the *Probe* data model, developed by Computer Corporation of America; and *Exodus,* an extensible DBMS from the University of Wisconsin.

Reference should also be made to some of the early 1980s hybrid object/relational approaches, such as the structural model RM/T, SAM, and subsequently SAM★. These are extensions of the relational model that attempt to capture more meaning.

Entity-relationship models were originally introduced as a design tool for record-based solutions. A semantic hierarchy construct is SHM, which focuses on the importance of aggregation and generalization primitives.

SDM was a semantic database model with a rich collection of modeling primitives, supporting a variety of semantic integrity constraints and derived data specifications. After SDM came SHM+, featuring an event-oriented approach incorporating behavior modeling notions into the semantic database framework.

In the mid-1980s, 3DIS demonstrated how useful can be the idea of merging schema and data into a uniform framework. IFO was introduced as an approach able to formalize semantic database model primitives.

As commercial object-oriented database systems began to appear, they pioneered work in defining the components of semantic and object-based approaches as well as in testing the market for applications. One of the salient problems has been storage management of the persistent object spaces. *Storage management* deals with the efficient organization, storage proper, and access of persistent objects.

16–6 CHOOSING AMONG OBJECT-BASED COMMERCIAL SOFTWARE

Some of the earlier object-oriented DBMS were extensions of existing relational structures. Others were limited to the support of linguistic constructs. Still others were defined at the entity-relation level that extends the range of relational operations. But most second-generation offerings are totally new departures, observing most of the principles that have been outlined so far.

Whether through significant improvements on existing relational DBMS or through new departures, among the overriding goals is to enhance the semantics at large and the semantic integrity in particular, and to present real advantages in terms of object manipulation. This is, more or less, one of the few general concepts that currently available object DBMS—and object-oriented languages—have in common, aside from the observance of object-based rules.

Chapters 17 through 21 discuss in some detail today's leading commercially available object DBMS. In order of presentation, these are Ontos, GemStone, Object Store, Open ODB, Pegasus, and Versant in the United States; and Mandrill, Odin, and MIB in Japan.*

There are, however, other, second-tier object DBMS, some created as university research projects. A brief review of them may be helpful, if only to indicate the diversity of conception and design. Among these offerings, we can distinguish the following.

Encore

The Encore object-oriented database management system models real-world objects as instances of a type. A type consists of an internal representation, together with an interface that defines and handles a set of properties, operations, and constraints. Encore is an academic project developed at Brown University.

FAD

FAD, developed by the Microelectronic and Computer Corporation (MCC) and completed by mid-1987, was one of the earliest reasearch prototypes based on the FAD object-oriented language. It provided support for object identity.

The FAD language is based on lambda calculus implemented in a distributed environment. The underlying concepts support complex object storage and indexing as well as object comparisons.

G-Base

G-Base was also one of the earliest object-oriented DBMS, introduced in 1987. It is written in LISP, with entities and methods defined using LISP syntax.

G-Base supports abstract data types and multiple inheritance of classes. It features interactive graphics, an object browser, a report generator, and declarative query language. Abstract data types permit users to define methods for entities.

This object DBMS can interface to relational databases and also incorporates a tool known as G-Logis, which, through an extension of Prolog,

---

*Fujitsu's Jasmine was not yet operational as of this writing.

inferences to the G-Base environment. There are also query capabilities for bulk data, but the early versions did not feature versioning or multiuser transaction facilities.

Galileo

Galileo is a strongly typed language with some object DBMS facilities, which was developed at the University of Pisa, Italy. It incorporates inheritance of types and supports complex objects, attempting to distinguish between the notions of a type and a class.

Genesis

Genesis, developed at the University of Glasgow, UK, is also an academic artifact. It incorporates knowledge engineering concepts dealing with relationships as objects.

O2

O2 was designed by INRIA, the French National Institute for Research on Information Technology and Automation, at Versailles.

Orion

Orion is another research prototype developed at MCC. Its first version was implemented in mid-1987.

Orion is LISP-based, and in its original version ran on a Symbolics computer. Its designers have focused particularly on schema evolution as well as on complex object locking.

Itasca

Itasca, also by MCC, is the second generation of Orion, still programmed in LISP. Some projects that implemented object solutions, for instance Carnot by MCC, have adopted and employed Itasca. An effort has been made to convert it from LISP to C, but available information indicates that this effort has not succeeded.

SIM

SIM stands for Semantic Information Manager. It is based on a semantic data model. SIM is the core system of the InfoExec environment of Unisys. Other products in InfoExec include a data dictionary, and interactive query and language interface components. With SIM, users can define classes that inherit from one another.

Attributes of entities are like functions from one entity to another. In this manner, relatively complex objects and relationships between entities can be modeled. Attribute functions are single-or multiple-valued, and SIM permits the specification of various forms of integrity constraints.

Statice

Statice is an object-oriented DBMS from Symbolics that supports inheritance of classes and methods that can be associated with entity types. It features both entity and set-valued attributes.

The syntax of the Statice data definition and manipulation language is LISP-looking. Supported facilities include concurrent transactions, associative access, querying, and recovery. Statice is designed to serve the Genera integrated environment from Symbolics, incorporating interactive tools and housekeeping routines such as debuggers and editors.

16–7 MERGING DATA PROCESSING AND KNOWLEDGE ENGINEERING IN DATABASE MANAGEMENT

By outlining urgent missions in information technology, Fig. 16.3 points in the direction of a merger of data processing and knowledge engineering in database management. It suggests the need for a hybrid system solutions located at the kernel of a coordinated system. The object-oriented DBMS to be implemented should have linguistic supports and interfaces able to assist in:

Conversion of all batch to real time, as the Dai-Ichi Kangyo Bank, among others, has done

Networking of all applications running on-line on the system, among themselves and with databases

Enriching current solutions with artificial intelligence to increase their appeal to endusers

Ideally, all new solutions should be object-oriented, for reasons that have been explained, without meaning that record-based applications will disappear on short notice. Our goal should be to capitalize on the facilities offered through single-paradigm programming, and also to explore other advantages of object-based solutions, including support for:

Composite objects
Flexible transactions
Concurrency control
Multiple storage managers
Cache capabilities
Extensibility

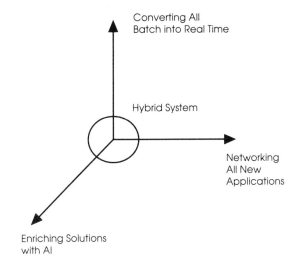

Figure 16.3   Urgent missions in information technology.

Like single-paradigm programming, these factors further enhance the performance and productivity that object-oriented databases provide. We are not doing a neat job if we miss the opportunity.

Growing user needs point toward the use of an object-oriented DBMS able to assure extensibility of the system mapped into the database in terms of semantic models. In general, semantic data models do not themselves provide all facilities needed to define new abstract data types that can be used as domains for entity properties. But a set of object-based types can be assured, with some mechanism for defining subclasses of these types.

The ability to define new types is of prime importance in many modern applications, hence the focus on object-oriented models and object database management systems. The latter should also account for the facts that semantic data models take a purely structural approach to abstraction, while object-oriented models are also concerned with operational behavior. Semantic data models are aimed at modeling the static aspects of the real world through the provision of a rich set of data structures, but we must also recognize the need to represent the dynamic aspects. This is typically done through facilities for recording the operations that can be performed on each type of object, binding these with the static properties of that object.

An object hierarchy with inheritance must also be featured. An important semantic notion within this aspect of data modeling is that some types can be seen as generalizations of other types. As such, they may share properties and behavior. This is clearly a knowledge engineering domain.

The six factors we examined in Section 5 have created a barrier to the implementation of sophisticated distributed applications without the support of new tools. Furthermore, as different incompatible relational DBMS proliferate, it becomes nearly impossible to interrelate heterogeneous type systems and programming styles without knowledge-engineering support.

The hope is that even if object-oriented DBMS today are not particularly helpful in bridging the heterogeneity gap, eventually they will provide a basis for solving the existing mismatch. Let us always remember that database heterogeneity intensifies as our applications environment changes toward a fully distributed networked perspective.

The bad news is that, as we have seen in this chapter, there are not just one but a dozen different and fairly incompatible object-oriented DBMS.

Some are faster, others slower.

Some are newer, others older.

Some have linguistic supports, others do not.

Some address a meta-level, others work only at a ground level.

All have the deficiency of not having yet been tested in an intense manner real-life operations.

Though this diversity will eventually subside and some of the shortcomings will most likely be corrected during the next few years, we are not yet at that point. Most worrisome is the stated lack of compatibility among the different object DBMS. This emulates the situation that currently exists with relational and other DBMS—and if it persists, it will be detrimental to both vendors and users.

16-8 THE BIG COMPUTER COMPANIES JOIN THE OBJECT DBMS MARKET

The examples we have seen in this chapter have shown that as the 1980s came to a close, object-oriented DBMS began to appear in the American market, promoted by small, start-up software companies. The major computer manufacturers looked down at them, choosing to rely on relational DBMS, which they had introduced some years earlier, as the workhorse of their marketing effort in the 1990s.

The Japanese saw further, and in 1991 practically all Japanese computer manufacturers were quite advanced in object DBMS development. But among American manufacturers, only Hewlett-Packard was working on an object DBMS, a project known as Iris—which in the beginning of 1992 was released and marketed under the name *Open ODB*.★

Practically up to the December 1991 Symposium on Parallel and Dis-

★Presented in Chapter 19.

tributed Systems,* IBM, DEC, and others maintained that they saw no reason for object-oriented approaches in the immediate future. Yet, if they had put their ear to the ground they would have heard that their most important clients said precisely the opposite.

But a market-driven economy has ways and means of bringing companies into line. With self-preservation the main criterion, the major American computer vendors did exactly what they should have done since the beginning. They heard what technologically advanced corporations—banks, air transport, aerospace, motors, chemical companies—were saying.

Suddenly the attitudes of IBM, DEC, Unisys, and others toward object-oriented solutions changed radically. Now, object operating systems, object DBMS, and object languages are the "in" thing. DEC is introducing object-oriented solutions in its basic software. An example is *RDB Star,* which is a misnomer because it has little or nothing to do with RDB. RDB Star is designed to fit the perspectives of Digital Equipment's NAS Information Network.

In the course of the New York meeting, Unisys talked about the forthcoming object-oriented implementation on the Univac line of SIM, which already runs on the Burroughs line. Recall that 25 years ago, Simula was the first artifact to bring object-oriented solutions—but Univac did not push it.

For its part, during the May 29, 1992, meeting at the Santa Teresa Software Laboratory, IBM suggested that object-oriented solutions have a major role to play, from data processing to multimedia. IBM defined three levels at which object-based approaches are important:

1. User interface with API[†]
2. Programming level, with C++
3. Database management

To the query, "Will there be an object superstructure over DB2?," the answer was given that there are three segments of object orientation: Two of them are embedded in SQL 3 by ANSI, the third is an artifact connected directly to DB2. This is the Starbust project.

While Starbust, like Postgres for Ingres, can be seen as an extension of the relational paradigm, it also identifies a shift in policy. The DB2 segment IBM mentioned will support entity-relationship constructs to be used in information modeling.

Most important, both the value added in SQL3 by ANSI and the DB2 add-on are oriented toward multimedia—and all that is expected to the operational by the end of 1994. DEC has given an even faster timetable in regard to its plans and wares. There is a clear-cut trend.

*Miami, Florida, December 4–6, 1991.
[†]Applications programming interface

Besides the systems at the IBM mainframe level, the new client-server operating system that IBM is developing as a joint project with Apple and Motorola is also object oriented. Code-named PINK, it promises to deliver a very advanced functionality that will rest largely on object principles.

During the same Santa Teresa meeting, IBM also said that it will build an object handler for OS/2 running on multiple hardware platforms. Other object handlers will be developed for DOS Windows, MacOS System 7, and AIX—all being *objects* under the new operating system, PINK.

Movement toward object-oriented solutions is also present in the standards-setting world. SQL3, by ANSI, was supposed to cover the more advanced transaction processing aspects (beyond SQL2) and graphical interfaces. Now object orientation has been added ot the multimedia perspective—a good example of why standards have to be dynamic. Technology's huge leaps foward mean that standards cannot be frozen even for one year.

$$\mathcal{Chapter}\ \mathit{17}$$

Ontos and GemStone

17-1 INTRODUCTION

The Defense Advanced Research Projects Agency (DARPA) has selected Ontos, an object database management system written in C, as part of a major program to restructure software development and database usage. Dubbed DARPA Initiative in Concurrent Engineering (DICE), this program aims at ensuring a leadership role for America in the engineering and manufacturing of complex products and components.

To reach the results this project is after, DARPA uses a combination of the Ptech shell and Ontos. Working in concert, the two object-based structures allow designers of complex systems to create, manipulate, store, and manage real-world models without bothering about lower-level computer code. Ptech/Ontos provides a design tool with automatic code generation and concurrent database management capabilities. The synergy obtained in this manner serves the primary goal of DICE, namely, to reduce elapsed time between concept and production of new software products; improve product quality by getting it right the first time; and decrease manufacturing costs through better product design and optimal usage of resources.

The people behind this and similar projects appreciate the fact that for interactive computer applications—whether in engineering, science, or finance—we need high-performance tools for handling complex nonrecord-oriented information elements, for instance, two-dimensional, three-dimensional, voice, animated image, graphics, text, and long transactions. The keywords are

Flexibility
Integrative capability
Performance

These three factors weigh heavily on the success or failure of any solution. Operating within a distributed information environment, we must attain performance at least an order of magnitude faster than we have so far in order to manage the new challenges adequately.

This is why new technologies, such as object orientation, are being explored. Before the development of object DBMS, developers had two choices: (1) Use a relational database, which was rather slow and cumbersome; or (2) Create their own proprietary file management system. Neither alternative is attractive, and neither lays the foundations for future growth and development. Yet the 1990s will present a critical need for expanding applications horizons—and this need will continue well beyond the year 2000.

17-2 THE ONTOS APPROACH TO DATABASE MANAGEMENT

Both V-Base and Ontos were designed and marketed by Ontologic. V-Base was introduced in late 1987 and withdrawn from the market a year later; Ontos was introduced in late 1989, in one year reaching about 220 sites with 350 licenses that address a number of different application types.*

V-Base supported an extension of C for defining methods, and a type-definition language to create entity types and schemata. Attention was paid on the need to focus on conceptual database evolution and learning techniques; such facilities have been passed on to Ontos.

As a second-generation commercial product, Ontos has assimilated the lessons learned from the earlier efforts. There is a three-level development environment, with two of these layers embedded into the DBMS and the third being an add-on. As Fig. 17.1 indicates, the levels are

1. A *conceptual model,* served by Ptech, which supports inheritance events.[†] The project began with an entity-relation-oriented conceptual schema approach and extended to object-based design with graphical modeling tools. It permits testing assumptions, interpretatively executes ob-

---

*With regard to platforms, Ontos operates under Sun 3 and 4, Sun SPARCstation, Apollo 3X00/4X00, DECstation, and OS/2-based PCs.
[†]Developed by Associative Design Technology (ADT).

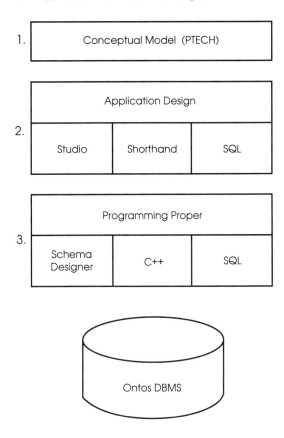

Figure 17.1   The programming environment of Ontos.

ject-type models, and generates C++ code leading to production applications.

2. An *application design* level, which incorporates three tools: Studio, Shorthand, and SQL *Shorthand* is a visualization fourth generation language with a transparent interface to Ontos. It makes it feasible for the programmer to access the database without necessarily mastering C++. *Studio* is a card-type scripting scheme that helps in establishing inheritance. When a *card* is called, Ontos fills in all particulars, including image.

3. A *programming level,* which incorporates linguistic tools: Graphical Schema Designer, C++, SQL.

The *Graphical Schema Designer* is an integrated graphical tool for creating, inspecting, and updating objects in the Ontos database. Since it provides a graphical view of the class lattice, the software developer can use this means to manipulate the database schema and add, modify, or delete class definitions. Thus he or she has control over the design of information elements and member functions of the classes, including private and protected parts of a class definition. The Graphical Schema Designer supports standard C++ classes and user-defined ones. It generates C++ header files for any classes selected by the user as applications interface between in-memory class definitions and the corresponding database classes. It also supports creation and editing of instance data in the database. New instances of a class can be created in graphical form. Hypertext capabilities are also featured.

The Graphical Schema Designer presents significant advantages to the user who wants to develop object-oriented applications, provided some basic prerequisites are observed. There are also utilities that can be useful in conversion jobs. For instance, when converting existing C++ applications to add object database support, it is useful to generate Ontos database schema from existing class definitions. An available *Classify* utility provides this possibility, taking standard C++ class definitions and automatically generating the corresponding database schema.

As a utility, Classify produces the necessary interfaces between the application in memory and the Ontos database. It also supports the conversion of existing C applications to Ontos, packaging the code's C++ classes and generating a corresponding Ontos schema.

Further, a Database Administrator Tool supports facilities for the DBA function. This tool is used to configure distributed databases, assign server processes and areas to physical server machines and disk areas, and register database users. Distributed databases can be reconfigured using this DBA tool, which adds to the functionality of the object-oriented approach.

According to the developers, there are also plans to integrate other linguistic constructs, particularly Eiffel, which has so far sold over 600 licenses. There are also interfaces foreseen to the main relational DBMS, but not immediately.

17-3 BENEFITS FROM THE IMPLEMENTATION OF AN OBJECT DBMS

As Section 2 demonstrated, Ontos provides a set of building blocks that can be effectively employed by the application developer and database user. Besides the programming facilities we have seen, there exist an *aggregates* library and exception-processing capabilities.

The aggregate classes include Set, List, Array, and Dictionary, and they are generally useful for modeling complex artifacts. The *Set* class provides a direct mechanism for modeling component hierarchies such as bills of materials. The *Dictionary* class helps in storing, for instance, customer data input by customer number or name. Another family of classes assures exception processing capabilities.

The exception mechanism supported by Ontos encourages programmers to design error detection and recovery into applications at an early stage. This leads to the development of robust computer code.

The Ontos database schema represents object classes, properties, and operations (member functions). Any class definition that can be specified in C++ can be stored in the DBMS. The class model used in C++ is represented in the database as object schema. Ontos schema information is stored directly in the database as object data. Applications can access this schema (meta-data), thus providing a higher-level enduser tool. The DBMS also maintains links between C++ code and stored representations of procedures. When an object is brought into memory, the stored information links the executable code to the object's representation.

There is a facility for converting existing C language applications by adding object database support. Existing C code is encapsulated into class definitions, with database interfaces generated automatically. There is also a C++ library that includes classes for defining collection objects such as sets and other aggregate types. It supports encapsulation, inheritance, the ability to construct complex objects, and concurrent and nested transactions on persistent objects.

Ontos has introduced a shared transaction mechanism that allows cooperating processes to share information within a single transaction. By adding a concept of hierarchy to exceptions, it updates standard out-of-line handling. It also uses a distributed two-phase commit protocol to guarantee the integrity of transactions across network nodes.

The DBMS uses a standard client-server architecture with C++ client applications interacting with a logical database server. The latter provides object storage, concurrency control, and other database services.

C++ client applications make requests to the database server to access and store objects. When an object is requested, the software automatically translates that object into its C++ in-memory representation, placing it in the C++ application's in-memory process heap.

Internally, the logical database can be composed of one or more server processes, and though it is distributed, client applications are insulated from physical distribution issues: When a process requests an object or group of objects, it makes this request to the logical database. The logical database directs the request to the appropriate server(s), and the server sees to it that client applications are independent of the physical organization of data.

Through this and similar mechanisms, the Ontos object-oriented DBMS effectively supports a distributed database with a client-server mode of interaction as shown in Fig. 17.2. This architecture, however, still seems to have certain difficulties in connection to meta-data handling, particularly conversion procedures.

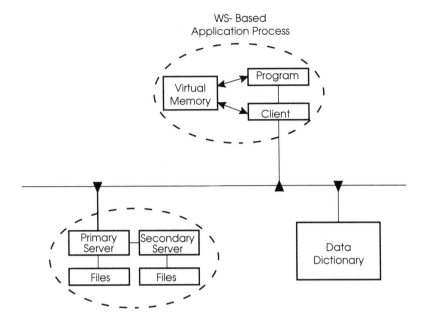

Figure 17.2   Architecturing the Ontos solution.

$17-4$ FEATURES OF A SECOND GENERATION OBJECT DBMS

One of the most significant differences between V-Base and Ontos is the system design itself. The guiding principle behind the latter is that object DBMS software should allow the user to make the appropriate trade-offs among performance, safety, and formalism. To achieve this goal, Ontos offers the programmer the same access to the underlying hardware as is available through C++. In spite of ensuring a set of abstractions, it does not prevent the user from employing more primitive mechanisms when performance or other considerations call for it. This way, the programmer can have available:

Direct control over cache management

The ability to affect data clustering

The facility to execute memory transfers when it is critical to application design.

Most significantly, Ontos has been projected to satisfy the requirements of local area networking as well as those of window-based workstations. A client-server architecture permits transparent distribution of database objects across nodes.

Within this implementation perspective, the dictionary facility makes it unnecessary to know the physical location of objects in advance, thus reducing the details of network configuration. At the same time, concurrency control and transaction mechanisms ensure IE consistency, arbitrating among potentially conflicting user requirements.

For its part, the schema designer and browser utility permits developers to interactively construct application class hierarchies and database schemata, and to view and modify database contents. The DBMS provides aggregate classes for modeling one-to-many relationships.

In a systems sense, the adopted solution resolves references directly and presents objects that are C++ compatible. This is assisted through the class library, which provides a *constructor* for creating objects in the database, and a *destructor* for deleting them.

Further functionality defines properties for an object name and assists the physical clustering of objects in the database. The class library also assures means for expressing properties, member functions, their arguments, and the overall class definitions themselves. Such classes are used to represent schema definitions to the database in a machine-independent way. They are also useful in program development. Data structures are available as general abstractions, eliminating some of the programming activity that is typically required to create, access, and maintain the facilities.

Classes make it feasible for key algorithms to be packaged in the database rather than with the application code. The behavior of the application can then be changed without changing the programs themselves. Through this and other means, Ontos fulfils information requests in an able manner.

The object DBMS also provides random access within a one-dimensional address space based on object identification (UID). The granularity is at the level of a single object. A single address space simplifies references and makes it practical to store properties in the form of references to other objects.

Atomic units of reference objects are clustered. Unless they are very large, they can be read in a single access operation. This compares very well to the inefficient multiple reads required to assemble the tuples in a relational DBMS that are needed for the complete presentation of an object.

Efficient clustering above the object level requires knowledge of the dominant access patterns of the IEs. For instance, in a CASE application it may be common to access a given object and the object representing its defined properties together. The DBMS permits the developer to specify the clustering he or she wants to see executed, and provides tools for reclustering when more experience with the application makes better choices feasible.

Data structures are expressed as graphs whose edges are frequently implemented by memory references. This facility is further supported by direct transaction between virtual memory references and object UIDs. Network reconfiguration and the movement of data, from node to node, do not require changes in object names.

While some of these characteristics are specific to Ontos and others are more generally available among object-oriented DBMS, this presentation shows what can be expected from the new generation of database management systems. As the careful reader will appreciate, there is a significant conceptual evolution in DBMS facilities, which is reflected in the services being supported.

17-5 THE GEMSTONE APPROACH TO DATABASE MANAGEMENT

The GemStone object-oriented database management system, released by Servio Corporation in 1987, includes data definition language (DDL) and data manipulation language (DML) that ensure that data access procedures normally included in application programs can be embedded directly in the database. GemStone information elements can also be accessed from Smalltalk, C++, Objective C, C function calls, Pascal, Ada, Cobol, Fortran, and LISP.

Opal, based on Smalltalk, is GemStone's data definition and manipulation language. It has a syntax similar to that of Smalltalk and incorporates many database-specific constructs and operations.

GemStone permits the user to create replicas or mirrors of the persistent database. The replica is done through a system command such as:

> System Repository replicate with: <name>

where <name> specifies the location of the replica. The replica can reside in the same memory support as the original database object or on an entirely different one.

GemStone can store and retrieve large and small objects as well as large collections of homogeneous objects and small collections of heterogeneous objects. Its database can handle approximately 2 billion user-defined objects, in addition to system-implemented primitive value objects.

GemStone's application programming interfaces allow the scope of an object traversal to be designated during storage and retrieval. A full traversal, following all objects from a root to primitive data, is a form of object transmission between the database and an application.

Since doing a full traversal may bring in too much data, the system provides two other forms of programmatic interface: traversal to level *n,* and path traversals. The former starts at the root object and follows object references in a depth-first manner until it reaches the specified level. The latter follows a collection of paths, each designating instance variables, to navigate to desired objects.

GemStone's support for C++ and Smalltalk includes a comprehensive set of linguistic classes that correspond to GemStone's internal classes. Software developers can use them as is or create subclasses to meet specialized needs.

Since the C++ interface supported by this DBMS does not depend on any specific extensions to the C++ language, it can be used with different workstations featuring C++.

GemStone may also be accessed by other languages through its C applications programming interface (API). This consists of a library of C functions that can be used in applications written in C, or the other forementioned languages.

The GemStone C API performs the appropriate translations between objects and more primitive data structures, thus making it feasible for applications to efficiently access objects stored in GemStone. There are also functions for sending messages to objects. An object receiving a message through the API can execute its methods directly in the database. Hence portions of an application that require the features of object-oriented programming can be embedded directly in the database.

The class library gives the programmer a standard set of definitions for commonly used data structures. Persistent C++ classes can be derived either directly or indirectly from classes in the GemStone class library.

Classes that have been registered as persistent in GemStone can be used to derive additional classes. They are declared in a header file using standard C++ syntax. Header files containing C++ class definitions are presented to the utility called the registrar, which creates corresponding class definitions and produces output files. These files contain all translation and mapping information needed to move objects between a C++ application and the database. The files are then compiled and linked with the application program.

Function libraries that underlie the C++ and the C-based APIs are served through remote procedure calls. To choose a connection mode, the developer uses the corresponding library. No changes are required in the application program.

There is also a gateway to Sybase designed to preserve existing investments in relational technology. This permits the functionality of an object database to complement the relational one. This gateway, developed with Sybase's Open Client Library programming interface, manages the execution of SQL statements on a Sybase SQL server. The results appear as objects within a GemStone server. The gateway can also be used to invoke system administration functions.

The GemStone Sybase gateway provides generic row and relation classes, allowing the user to define specialized subclasses. This approach is well suited for ad-hoc queries, with server and gateway executing from within a single process.

17-6 THE VIRTUAL SCHEMA DESIGNER

GemStone is equipped with a visual schema designer oriented to graphical schema editing. It permits the database administrator to partition large schemata into convenient views that can be edited. It also supports selectively hidden screen elements.

Schemata can be viewed in detail or from a meta-view (high level). Within a schema, classes may appear in more than one view, facilitating an iterative design process. Once a schema is designed, code can be produced and automatically integrated into the database.

The visual schema designer helps in creating class definitions in Gem-Stone in the X-Windows/Motif environment. Classes and their instance variables can be defined; class hierarchies can be created and manipulated; and sets can be established to hold collections of objects by direct manipulation of class and relationship icons. Schema modification is supported by directly handling the class graphs to make the necessary alterations.

A distinction is made between *save* and *commit,* so changes to the schema can take place over several sessions before they are made permanent in the database.

Class graphs act as a versatile schema view mechanism for managing complex or large schemata, and for providing different views of the database for different groups of users. A class can participate in more than one class graph, which displays relationships between classes graphically, with each class graph displayed in its own window.

GemStone also offers a connection scheme based on remote procedure calls. Access functions and caches reside in a separate process space, which can run on the same computer or on a different one. This helps avoid corrupting the database with a bad pointer.

GemStone's referential integrity support and audit facilities further protect stored objects. GemStone automatically maintains referential integrity when new objects are created in the database. Integrity checks occur at transaction commit instead of object creation. This has the benefit of allowing creation of new objects with references to be resolved in the transaction.

Through successive releases of GemStone, the object manager has been significantly improved to provide faster access to objects already in central memory and on disk. Internal use of caches has been restructured to reduce working sets and improve performance. In addition, the user can configure cache sizes at startup, which increases the system's flexibility and usability.

GemStone services have been optimized for running in a client/server environment across networks. Recent releases have added a pipelining architecture to optimize database network-wide write performance.

Similarly, access procedures to GemStone data dictionary have been rewritten to reduce CPU and disk input/output overhead for leading catalog information. Other recent features include the ability to create new classes dynamically and to populate them with information elements.

The Open Gateway allows programmers to build interfaces to a variety of data sources, such as flat files or different computer interfaces, as well as external applications. There is also an application programmer interface that maps to and from GemStone objects. The user does not need to be aware that the objects being manipulated are coming from outside this DBMS. Internally, the database is treated as a series of logical pages onto which objects are written. Organization of the objects on a page is managed by the GemStone Object Manager. Individual objects are referred to by an object identifier. This permits reference to objects without knowing their physical location.

The Resource Manager serves as the coordinator of the database, looking after synchronization and resource handling. It allocates pages in the database; supplies free object identifiers; and maintains object lock status. It also processes commit requests made by the GemStone Object Server and implements the recovery mechanism.

The GemStone Page Server performs the task of transferring pages from the disk to the remote processes. It has been designed to support multiple readers and multiple writers to a single file.

A good deal of the functionality in the GemStone object DBMS appeared in the first release. Since then, it has consisted of two kinds of software components: *gems,* which access and execute objects, and a *stone,* which manages the object database. Gems can be distributed over a number of computers in a network, permitting parallel processing of objects. The GemStone server can be a Sun 3, Sun 4, Sun SPARCStation, DEX Vax, DECstation, IBM 6000, or Sony News.

Hence, an important aspect of the GemStone client-server architecture is its ability to support-mixed platform environments. This makes feasible real-time portability of objects between platforms by transparently compensating for byte ordering, compiler, and instruction set differences.

GemStone database files can be located on any processor with adequate disk storage. Multiple databases can reside on a single processor, or can be distributed throughout the network.

Versant and Object Store

18-1 INTRODUCTION

The two commercially available object DBMS we examined in Chapter 17 demonstrate that object orientation cannot be limited only to databases or only to programming. It has to address both issues in an able manner and benefit from the synergy such an approach presents. This thesis is sustained by the Versant and ObjectStore DBMS and their linguistic supports. These two commercial systems are among the foremost current offerings in database management systems and may well be stepping stones toward the next evolutionary steps in computing.

Both Versant and ObjectStore incorporate valid techniques for object-oriented analysis and design that can be employed for prototyping before plunging ahead with physical design and coding. With automated coding by means of generators, we are better able to concentrate on the conceptual aspects of object orientation in planning and analyzing data processing systems.

Furthermore, the object analysis techniques are implementation-independent. Consequently, the systems they specify are flexible and can be used to develop applications for many different environments, including graphical interfaces and expert systems.

In order to benefit from these facilities, however, we must

- Learn how to think and communicate within an object-oriented context,
- Make a rule to apply object-oriented techniques during systems analysis, and

- Use the object philosophy to supplement existing software development practices.

We must as well understand when and why the object approach should be used; how to conceptualize system requirements; and how to encourage rational business and information strategy planning.

Provided the object DBMS has facilities for cross-database access in a heterogeneous environment, the knowledgeable user can provide seamless connectivity between a number of networked databases. As we will see in this chapter, this is the case with Versant Star. In the next chapter we will discuss a similar approach using Pegasus.

18–2 ARCHITECTURE OF THE VERSANT OBJECT DBMS

Versant is a product of Versant, Inc. The architecture of the Versant approach is a layered structure, as shown in Fig. 18.1. The top layer comprises networked users: people, programs, intelligent terminals, servers, hosts. Versant sees this layer as two sublayers, an upper level of users supported by a lower-level infrastructure of specialized application frameworks. The latter contain class libraries adapted to the needs of vertical markets, for instance,

Engineering
Manufacturing
Finance
Network design

Part of the top-layer infrastructure consists of reusable forms, reports, query facilities, and procedures. The aim of the vendor at this level is to help in assembling modular supports into new configurations, thus making it feasible to create novel, integrative applications.

The second layer in Versant, as shown in Fig. 18.1, is a matrix of tools to help developers create database-oriented applications with ease and speed.

The higher-level tools are used to generate object-oriented applications from class libraries, and can be employed by endusers.

The middle level is intended for database administrators, providing means for setting up and managing distributed databases.

Tools on the lower level are for programmers, allowing them to construct routines and access databases by graphically defining data models, as well as embedding SQL queries into their programs.

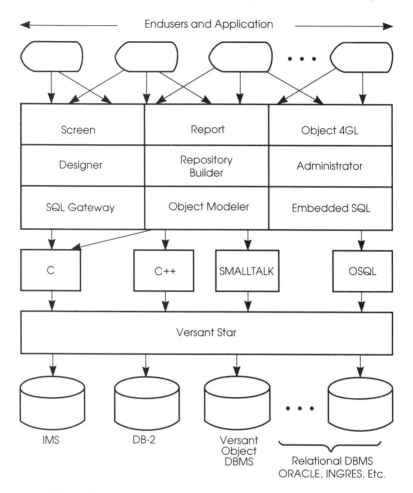

Figure 18.1   An approach to database integration by Versant.

Emphasis on object programming is demonstrated by the languages supported: C++, C, Smalltalk, and Object SQL (OSQL). They are shown in the third layer.

The Object Modeler compiles into two languages: C++ and Smalltalk. The C interface can also be used by any language that permits C foreign function calls, leading to possible implementations of Cobol and Fortran within Versant Star.

The Versant object SQL (OSQL) is a superset of SQL that provides extensions for object handling. This allows access to the Versant DBMS in a language familiar to relational database programmers.

Since the layer below the lower level in the Versant tool matrix addresses C, C++, Smalltalk, and Object SQL, the tools provided at the lowest level of the matrix interface to these languages are:

SQL Gateway
Embedded SQL
Object Modeler

By using the Versant *SQL Gateway,* programmers can compile into C but also embed standard SQL queries in their Smalltalk or C++ programs. The results of these queries are automatically mapped into objects.

Another linguistic support, Versant's *Embedded Object SQL,* permits programmers to use OSQL statements for access to objects in the distributed database. In contrast, the *Object Modeler* is a general-purpose tool to help programmers define entity-relationship data structures graphically on the screen. These can then be translated automatically into C structures, C++ classes, Smalltalk classes, or SQL tables. The Object Modeler can also be used to define methods and signatures, with on-line compilation into C++ or Smalltalk code. This is a significant contribution, as the Object Modeler can be used to prototype object-oriented data structures, with the code being produced automatically.

18–3 DESIGNER, REPOSITORY BUILDER, AND ADMINISTRATOR

The middle layer in the Versant tool matrix, shown in Fig. 18.1, helps database administrators manage a collection of databases operating under the Versant Star system. For instance, the *Designer* is a graphical schema-oriented tool that permits programmers and database administrators to create and manage class hierarchies within Versant databases.

The Designer automatically generates C++ class definitions from iconic representations on screen. It also serves as a database browser, permitting inspection of the database with regard to class definitions, their attributes, relationships, methods, and individual instances.

The Versant *Repository Builder* helps the database administrator define and maintain the system meta-data contained in the Repository. It operates in a way similar to the Designer, but includes features for accessing information that is unique to the repository.

The *Administrator* is a collection of DBA tools that provides command-level facilities for controlling access, performing backups, managing users, and carrying out other tasks. Activities relating to Repository construction can be executed within the facilities provided by the Administrator.

The higher layer in the Versant tool matrix is directed to applications developers. *Screen* is a graphical environment that allows any user to create windows, forms, menus, and other screen objects by pointing and clicking. Screen can be used to create data input forms with windows, prompts, helps, pick lists, type checking, and so on. This tool can also handle multimedia information as well as search databases of images.

In addition to providing the facilities of traditional report generators, *Report* has a report painting feature that permits the user to paint the layout of a report directly on the screen. The template can then accept data generated from the SQL Gateway or Object SQL.

Object 4GL is a database programming language used to chain together objects and actions created with the other tools. For example, one can use it to open a window on a predefined entry screen and prepare it to accept data input.

The fourth layer, as shown in Fig. 18.1, is *Versant Star* which provides gateways that permit integration with other database management systems: IMS, DB2, Oracle, Ingres, and of course the Versant object DBMS. This layer accepts a range of industry-standard languages supported by the Versant solution.

As cannot be stated too often, the contribution a cross-database pass-through capability can make is quite significant, and it should constitute a principal criterion in choosing an object DBMS. The plurality and heterogeneity of networked databases makes this approach most wise. In the long run it can provide significant competitive advantages and also save a great deal of money.

The fifth layer in Fig. 18.1 is the Versant object DBMS as well as the other supported DBMS that have been mentioned. Versant acts as an object-oriented structure that allows information elements to be stored, retrieved, and updated in a distributed computing environment.

As we continue to describe the different commercially available DBMS, the reader will appreciate where the object-oriented approach has advantages over other alternatives. One should be able to envision how to make the transition from past analysis and design practices to the object-oriented approach.

Those companies that use this new generation of DBMS successfully have learned how the object-oriented approach can be applied to simple as well as complex information systems problems. When such experience is acquired, the critical factors for successful object modeling are in place. The user knows how to:

Determine each object's state responsibilities
Segregate the descriptive and identification attributes
Make each attribute capture an atomic concept
Define instance connections
Obtain the benefits of normalization

The synergy of object DBMS facilities and object programming makes it easy to put system specification together, building a layered model and providing for multilevel control. As we will see in this chapter, tools are available for consistency, syntax checks, warnings, and the handling of errors—leading to a powerful computer-aided system engineering (CASE) technology.

18–4 DISTRIBUTED CHARACTERISTICS AND THE VERSANT REPOSITORY

The developers of Versant stress the fact that this DBMS was projected from the start to operate in a fully distributed manner. Network-wide functionality is an integral part of its primitives, which constitutes a better approach than having features added subsequently to an inherently centralized DBMS, as most of older database management systems operate.

To bring home this message and show what can be obtained in terms of efficiency, Fig. 18.2 presents the results of two benchmarks: A *read* test and a *write* test between Versant and DB2. This benchmark was performed by the U.S. Navy, and its results give the object DBMS a crushing advantage over the relational.

The first release of Versant run under UNIX, but recent versions operate under OS/2 Presentation Manager, MS DOS Windows 3.0, and Apple

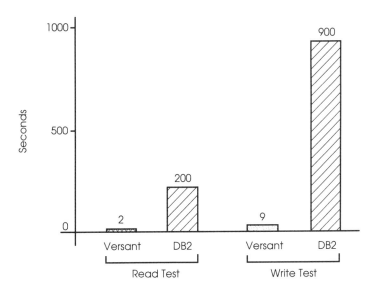

Figure 18.2   A U.S. Navy benchmark of object DBMS versus relational: two tests with 2–500 objects, Versant versus DB2.

MacOS. These releases make the DBMS available to practically all the most common workstations.

One reason for the original UNIX orientation was that the Versant products were initially developed on Sun 3, Sun 4, and IBM RISC/6000. Then they became available on DECstation, HP 9000/400, Silicon Graphics Iris, the Intergraph 6000, and the Sequent line. Any combination of these operating systems can operate concurrently on a local area network with a virtually homogeneous logical database distributed over a number of physical locations.

Information about the location and execution environment of the various components of the database is stored in the *Versant Repository;* the Repository itself is part of the Versant database, hence it can be distributed across multiple equipment. Such distribution is independent of hardware and software platforms, with Versant Star compensating for any differences, making them transparent to every user except the database administrator.

The Versant Repository is essentially a data dictionary. Information about the location and type of all information elements in a distributed Versant database is stored in this repository, which is maintained within the distributed database and acts as a common information resource. The Repository includes information on:

Network configuration in terms of both software and hardware

Reusable components of applications and classes running under Versant

Locations and types of different classes and applications

Names and privileges of all types of users interacting with the object DBMS

Mapping rules to transfer information elements from one type of database to another

This last function is executed by the Versant Star component, which integrates multiple databases. It handles the distribution of objects across Versant databases and accesses information in relational, network, and other DBMS.

In a time of many and various claims for repositories (some true, some false), it is interesting to see in a little more detail how this service relates to linguistic facilities. This will help one to appreciate their impact.

The Repository stores screens, reports, and procedures created with the application tools, which therefore become reusable components. Since application units are defined in terms of abstract entities and attributes, they can be used not only with the Versant object database but also with other types of databases.

In the Versant DBMS, all information about the various databases supported by the network is stored in the Repository, so application programs do not need to be aware of physical location of data, the type of database in which the IEs are stored, or whether the different IEs are object- or record-oriented. This information is made transparent to the user through a number of database drivers able to access proprietary formats.

In the last few years, the dedicated driver strategy has become prominent and is featured in a number of database pass-through efforts within the realm of distributed environments. An example is DataLens by Lotus Development.

DataLens operates in conjunction with release 3.1 and later of the Lotus 1–2–3 spreadsheet and addresses an impressive list of 20 different DBMS—hierarchical, Codasyl, and relational. This approach can be expected to become quite popular during the 1990s. It is both flexible and efficient, having the added advantage that the entry price at the driver level is low, and inventory can be enriched as applications proliferate.

Understandably, the most popular DBMS are supported first. Eventually, Versant says, drivers will be available for all relational DBMS that conform to the ANSI standard. For Remote Database Access* purposes, only a single driver will be required to interface to them.

18–5 THE OBJECTSTORE DBMS

ObjectStore, by Object Design, is a database management system for applications written in C++. Targeted at developers of interactive solutions, it provides complete functionality for distributed environments that run on supermicros and high-end PCs interconnected through local area networks (LANs).

This object-oriented DBMS provides version and configuration management as well as collaborative concurrency control, aimed at supporting group work. It manages distributed databases with multiple clients and servers: An application can reference data in several databases from within a single transaction; transaction *commit* is handled by a distributed, two-phase commit protocol. This approach ensures that information elements modified within a transaction are atomically committed to all servers involved in the transaction, or rolled back on all of them, regardless of network partition or node failure.

ObjectStore's set of data management services permit concentration on adding functionality to applications. Current services include distributed workstation/server configurations, concurrency control, relationship facilities, access control, query capabilities, restart/recovery, and database administration, as well as schema maintenance.

---

*Remote Database Access (RDA) is an ANSI standard produced by the SQL Access Group.

The system has been designed to run on all major UNIX versions—Sun, IBM, DEC, HP—supporting the native networking environment of each vendor. A 1991 release also operates on the leading PC under MS DOS Windows 3.0, OS/2 Presentation Manager, Apple MacOS, OS/2, and SVR 4 UNIX for 386/486 chips, in a standalone or distributed form.*

ObjectStore integrates into open systems with Motif and Open Look on UNIX workstations, and Windows on PC platforms. It features a Virtual Memory Mapping Architecture (VMMA) that enables developers to add DBMS functionality to their applications without any great loss in performance. This means that performance does not necessarily degrade as database size expands and program complexity increases. This architecture also has the important benefit of facilitating conversion. It features persistent data that appears *as if* they are transient to the application. Hence no additional instructions are required to reference persistent objects.

The approach that has been chosen is to make persistence independent of type by employing virtual memory mapping. Otherwise, extra instructions and performance overhead must be added to operations affecting both transient and persistent data.

ObjectStore's virtual memory mapping architecture sees to it that persistent objects are handled by C and C++ programs in exactly the same way as transient (nonpersistent) objects are. This is referred to as persistence independent of type. The vendor claims that this strategy is the best means of retrieving and manipulating large amounts of objects with minimal overhead. This is done by taking advantage of the native operating system's virtual memory management.

Comparing the virtual memory mapping approach to other alternatives, ObjectStore's designers suggest that, with some other object DBMS, persistence is not independent of type, hence it is limitative and must be inherited from a special base class. This causes problems in converting a C application, as well as presenting other inconveniences.

For instance, one of the problems is that two sets of functions must be written, one for transient and the other for persistent data. Another negative is that instructions must be added to access persistent objects. Finally, a conversion requires that all C data types be repackaged as class definitions. In contrast, by using virtual memory mapping, C data do not have to conform to a specific object class structure. Instead, any C data type can be allocated as persistent.

Virtual memory mapping can also be instrumental in providing instantaneous response. For better performance, dereferencing pointers to persistent data should occur in a single instruction, just as with transient

---

*The initial Windows 3.0 release performed on Novell, Banyan, and LAN Manager networks, as well as mixed PC/workstation networks using PC/NFS to communicate between workstations and UNIX servers.

pointers. Then, during application sessions, referenced persistent data is dynamically mapped into the workstation's virtual address space. This strategy ensures that access to persistent data is almost as fast as access to transient data.

At any point in an ObjectStore transaction, some database information is mapped into the workstation's virtual address space, while the rest is accessible only from the server. When a pointer to an object that is not yet mapped into the workstation address space is dereferenced, the server sends that object to the workstation, which allocates virtual memory to hold it.

18-6 MINIMIZING OVERHEAD REQUIREMENTS

ObjectStore minimizes the overhead associated with moving information elements into virtual memory by maintaining consistency between the on-disk and in-disk formats. It also supports caching, thus increasing system performance.

When a sequence of transactions accesses the same objects, there is a high probability that the data accessed in the next transation will already be cached in workstation memory. This is basically how the cache principle works. The amount of main memory allocated for caching is a function of the available memory in the workstation and other considerations.

ObjectStore uses cache to reduce overhead incurred due to network traffic and database distribution, caching database *locks* as well as *objects*. Enduser workstations do not need to get permission from the server to access data already cached. The system also batches information elements to be transmitted between client and server.

These strategies affect network traffic positively, allowing the user's workstation to process the transaction without contacting the server until the transaction is committed. Another strategy addresses server process swapping, operating system semaphores, and synchronous disk input/output.

The DBMS deals with these operating system issues and their overhead through two-phase locking. It reduces the use of semaphores by employing internal data structures to create simple locks that require an order of magnitude less time to acquire and use. In the event that it does not acquire this lock, the process employs a semaphore. Also, ObjectStore achieves asynchronous disk input/output by means of a dedicated disk-handling routine, which communicates with the server through shared memory.

During operations, the disk-handling process maintains its own queue, discharging as required. The server's processes may queue and dequeue disk requests without waiting for the current, ongoing request to terminate.

Other features support concurrency, to which reference was made in the opening paragraphs. In a multiuser environment, many workstations need to access a given database server concurrently. This requires cooperative access through a flexible workstation/server architecture, and the ability to guarantee that the user employs the computational power of the workstation effectively.

ObjectStore's client/server implementation permits one server to support many workstations, each simultaneously accessing multiple databases. This is particularly important in a multiuser environment.

At execution time, each relationship is composed of two or more data members, constrained to be consistent with one another. The constraints composing a given relationship are declared by the user. Through this mechanism, ObjectStore provides referential integrity between two objects. For instance, by declaring two objects to be inverses of each other, integrity can be automatically enforced as an update dependency. When an object is deleted, the inverse relationship pointer is automatically deleted too.

The concurrency control scheme employed for transactions is based on the approach that a short transaction may be *update,* or *read only;* and either type of transaction can be nested within another transaction.

All information elements accessed in ObjectStore are initially accessed in read-only mode. For *write,* the appropriate IEs accessed during the transaction, are locked as a group. This operation is transparent to the user.

For the duration of a given transaction, the system automatically delays write access by other processes to IEs that have been read by the transaction. This locking has the effect of making the objects in the transaction inaccessible to other update transactions for the duration of the first transaction's execution. This is the principle of serializable access.

The system sees to it that locking information is cached on both the client and the server. This reduces the need for network communication when the same process performs consecutive transactions on the same IE. ObjectStore, however, may abort a transaction, either because of network failure or because it has determined that the transaction is involved in a deadlock. By default, the transaction is restarted again and continues to be retried until it is successful or the limiting number of tries has occurred.

In contrast, read-only transactions can start and never deadlock with another read transaction. There are also procedures for nested transactions, with a smaller transaction nested within a larger one. Locks acquired during a nested transaction are not released until the nonnested transaction within which it is nested terminates.

For restart/recovery purposes, a transaction is handled as an atomic unit of work that is applied to the database(s). The user can undo changes back at the beginning of the current transaction through the transaction abort function. When this call is made, restart sees to it that control flows to the statement immediately following the current transaction statement.

- Persistent objects are rolled back to their state as of the beginning of the transaction,
- All locks are released, and
- Other processes are allowed to access the element the aborted transaction accessed.

In the case of disruption, the system assures recovery through a logging mechanism. All afterimages updated by the client are held in a redo log, the latter being used as a staging area on the server for changes to the database.

18–7 COLLECTION MANAGEMENT AND DIRECTORY CONTROL

One of the special features of ObjectStore is *collection management.* A *collection* is an object grouping that provides a convenient means of storing and manipulating either ordered or unordered groups of objects.

Query facilities take advantage of collection management to provide higher-performance retrieval. All queries are nonprocedural, nonnavigational, and type safe.

The nonprocedural characteristic simplifies the handling of ad-hoc queries. Navigational access involves following pointers between related objects, but many ad-hoc situations require associative access. Lookup of an object using the value of one of its attributes is a simple form of associative access—and indispensable to databases that support complex applications.

Query expressions provide a convenient means of selecting all the elements of a specified collection that satisfy given predicates. Query expression predicates can lead to nested queries, which are also handled by the system.

ObjectStore provides tools for specifying the appropriate level of access control for directories and for each database within a directory. Each database is automatically accessible to its creator and to the system's super-user, user identification is subject to a password protection mechanism, and utilities assign users to groups that have specified permissions. Assigned permissions are either read only, write, or execute, with supervisory activities ensuring that authorization is granted only after the proper authentication.

The Directory Manager monitors a site-wide hierarchy of ObjectStore directories. It maintains meta-data about user names, permission modes, and histories for databases across the network. There are also utilities to maintain, verify, and report statistics on the Directory Manager process and the Directory database.

Schema maintenance is provided and used as applications evolve. It is possible to add or change types, attributes, methods, or relationship definitions. The ObjectStore database schemata are dynamically updated to reflect these additions and changes. The schema for the system's database is the union of the schemata of all applications that have run against the database.

A Browser makes it possible to display information about a database's schemata as well as information about the individual objects stored in a database. Such service is particularly important to database administrators.

The Browser is a graphical method for inspecting the contents of ObjectStore databases. ObjectStore is also enriched with other utilities such as *Debugger* and *Schema/Designer*. The latter assists in interactive graphical schema design, permitting one to develop, view, and evolve large class lattices.

The Debugger, Schema Designer, and Browser work with many existing development platforms. The same is true of the Library Interfaces and the DML Preprocessor.

ObjectStore provides a choice of languages. C++ is supported through either a high-level embedded data definition language/data manipulation language (DDL/DML) or a library-based application programming interface (API). The DDL/DML approach to API is handled using a preprocessor, the library-based API works directly with native C++ compilers, and the two interfaces are strictly compatible with one another. A preprocessor turns the DDL/DML into the function calls supported by the library based API.

Both APIs are fully upward compatible with C++. They support multiple inheritance, virtual functions, and parameterized types. With some platforms, subroutine-based interfaces are provided for C and languages that are call-compatible with Fortran and Pascal.

Chapter 19

Object ODB and Pegasus

19-1 INTRODUCTION

In September 1991, the Open Software Foundation (OSF) unveiled its model for managing distributed systems and networks. The OSF *Distributed Management Environment* (OSF/DME) comprises technologies from several vendors.

OSF/DME is the first nonproprietary management software platform that unites computers and networks, which for years have been monitored separately with strictly proprietary solutions. Its success will depend on how soon OSF can blend its mix of technologies, ranging from Hewlett-Packard's OpenView, Open ODB, and Pegasus to IBM's Data Engine, and beyond.

OSF has also announced the availability of its *Distributed Computing Environment* software. Though DME does not require the use of DCE, industry analysts expect it to ride atop DCE.

Within the DME perspective, the IBM-developed Data Engine will house the network and systems objects. It is a software environment that stores objects, extracts information from them, and executes their internal features.

The particular interest of the OSF announcement lies in the fact that at the heart of DME is object-oriented technology that simplifies the process of writing applications. As we have seen repeatedly, this shifts the playing field to a higher plane, where vendors compete, not on who supplies what platform, but who offers the best applications.

The DME object-oriented technology from Hewlett-Packard portrays applications, users, and devices on the network as objects. For instance, objects encapsulate information about a multiplexer along with the code that configures or executes commands for that entity.

In this chapter we will follow the functionality of these applications by examining the features of Hewlett-Packard's Open ODB and Pegasus. As will be appreciated, these compare quite favorably with the other four object DBMS we have examined: Ontos, GemStone, Versant, and ObjectStore.

In conclusion, the OSF project underscores the fact that object-oriented applications are maturing and major vendors are getting ready to use the new technology to obtain competitive advantages. This is also true of users, hence the interest in the features we will discuss.

19–2 THE OPEN ODB OBJECT DBMS

Hewlett-Packard is devoting significant resources on object-oriented databases, with several projects running both in America and in the UK. The following references are particularly relevant within the object and relational implementation domains of special software support:

> *Open ODB,* the company's original entry into the object-oriented DBMS domain which was released in early 1992
>
> *Pegasus,* aimed at the integration of heterogeneous databases through the provision of virtual database homogeneity
>
> *Allbase,* the company's proprietary relational DBMS, released in 1986, of which 3000 copies have been sold.★
>
> *OpenView,* for computer-aided software engineering (CASE)
>
> *Netware,* an office automation software that includes database facilities
>
> *Rainbow,* a manufacturing-oriented object solution from the company's Bristol Laboratories.

Designed by its Palo Alto Laboratories, the Open ODB DBMS marks the entry of Hewlett-Packard into the object-oriented market. It began as a research prototype of a "next-generation" database management system intended to meet the needs of new and emerging applications. Among the targeted markets are

> Office automation
> Knowledge-based systems
> Engineering design

★There is as well an older DBMS, Codasyl type, known as Turboimage, which is about 20 years old and has sold 50,000 copies, according to the vendor's statistics.

Tests and measurements

Developments in hardware and software.

As with similar object-oriented constructs, the premise is that these applications require a rich set of capabilities that are not supported by the current generation of relational DBMS.

Open ODB runs under UNIX and the operating systems of Hewlett-Packard. In its grand design for new database management perspectives, the developers projected four domains, as shown in Fig. 19.1:

1. *Open ODB* and its database management functions.
2. *User environment.* This is largely software oriented and particularly emphasizes CASE tools.
3. *Languages.* Those supported are C++, C, Objective C, Smalltalk, and LISP—but also Pascal, Fortran, and Cobol—as well as Object SQL.
4. *Methods* for data processing and knowledge engineering applications integrating *as if* they were internal objects.

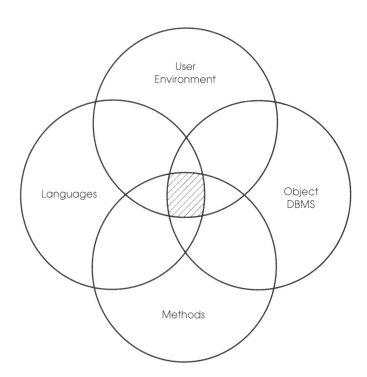

Figure 19.1 The four domains that Hewlett-Packard sees as pillars of object orientation.

Open ODB acts as an object manager, also accepting foreign function and foreign data. Connected to this range of services are a graphics editor, browser, transaction handler, and store manager. Also, knowledge engineering builders, screen painters, report writers, and OpenView as a CASE tool are offered.*

Open ODB data models are based on three constructs: types, objects, and functions. They support inheritance and generic properties, and handle constraints and process complex as well as nonnormalized data.

Extensible data types, user-defined functions, version control, and inference are other features, as are versioning, concurrency, recovery, access paths, buffer management, and clustering. The Open ODB data model distinguishes between *literal objects,* such as character strings, and numbers, and *nonliteral objects,* such as persons, computers, and companies. Nonliteral objects are represented internally in the database by object identifiers. Literal objects have no user-accessible object identifier and are represented directly. Hence they cannot be created, destroyed, or updated by endusers.

An Object Manager facility provides primitives for explicitly creating and deleting nonliteral objects, and for assigning and updating values. When a given object is deleted, all references to that object are also deleted, in support of referential integrity.

Design orientation has been influenced by the fact that, as market and technical studies have demonstrated, the new capabilities needed in DBMS functionality should address:

Rich data modeling constructs
Direct database support for inference
Powerful data types for graphics
Handlers of images, vectors, and matrices, as well as text and voice
Long-transaction features
Data versioning

To perform such functions in an able manner, data sharing must be provided at the object level, with both concurrent and serial sharing. The implementation should allow a given object to be accessed by applications that may be written in different object-oriented programming languages.

19–3 ROLES OF THE OBJECT MANAGER

At the core of the Open ODB DBMS is the Object Manager facility. Its functions include query handling, storage management, and update, as well as data model manipulation. Most important, the Object Manager supports

*Available under the relational DBMS Allbase of Hewlett-Packard.

higher-level structural abstractions, such as classification, generalization, aggregation, and behavioral issues.

A query processor translates Open ODB queries and functions, which are optimized and then interpreted against the database. For computational theory, the model relies on relational algebra.

In its original version, the Open ODB Storage Manager was a conventional relational storage subsystem, able to provide associative access and update capabilities. This was done a single relation at a time, including transaction support. Subsequently, these functions have been enriched and are still evolving.

Today, Open ODB is accessible through standalone interactive interfaces and associated modules embedded in programming languages, for instance, C-Open ODB and Liss-Open ODB. Both facilitate access persistent objects from various programming languages. Construction of interfaces is made possible by a set of C-language subroutines included in the Object Manager. They provide support for schema definition, data manipulation, and query processing.

One of the interactive interfaces is Object SQL. Another is the Graphical Editor, which permits the user to interactively explore Open ODB meta-data: type structures as well as interobject relationship structures defined on a given Open ODB database and written in Object C, and a driver for the Object Manager.

One of the goals of the Object Manager is to enhance applications that are not well served by existing DBMS, such as computer-aided design (CAD), computer-integrated engineering (CIM), computer-aided software engineering (CASE), office automation (OA), and long transactions.

A common need of these applications is the desire to preserve alternative states for a particular entity. This requires the existence of an object versioning mechanism and calls for controlled access to data values. Versions are like snapshots of an object in certain states, and are modeled by distinct objects. Open ODB separates objects corresponding to each version and to the entity of which they are versions.

Open ODB also offers a form of indirect addressing through which objects can make generic references to other objects. The generic instance is an abstraction of the entity and there is one generic instance per each version set—that is, the set of all versions of an object. In terms of practical implementation, reference to a versioned object can be either *specific,* to a particular version of that object; or *generic,* to the entity's general instance.

Versions of an object are created explicitly by the user. Since versions are objects, destruction of versions and schema modifications are performed through Open ODB operations. These, however, are subject to additional constraints.

Queries are expressed in Open ODB in terms of functions and objects. This particular task is shared by two modules:

The Query Translator, which compiles queries from their object representation to a relational algebra representation

The Query Interpreter, which evaluates the transformed query and invokes the Storage Manager and/or functions

The Storage Manager accesses the database. Foreign functions address and access other data sources.

Query translation consists of three main steps. First, a tree structure, known as an F-tree, is converted to canonical form. This involves a series of tree transformations, converting the canonical F-tree to an extended relational algebra B-tree. The latter consists of projection, selection, cross-product, and table nodes. The semantics of the tree at the level of a child node are sent to the parent node for subsequent processing.

The Query Interpreter evaluates a B-tree and produces a set of tuples that may be returned to the user or stored again in the database. It treats each node in the B-tree as a scan object with associated operations: open-scan, get-next, and close-scan.

19–4 ACCESS FLEXIBILITY AND
SQL EXTENSIONS

Open ODB can be accessed through both interactive and programmatic interfaces. These are implemented using the library of C subroutines that define the Open ODB Object Manager interface. Interfaces connected to the Object Manager are shown in Fig. 19.2.

The Object Manager is built on top of a conventional relational storage manager. Tables can be created and dropped at any time. The system supports transactions with:

Save points
Restore to save points
Concurrency control
Logging and recovery
Archiving
Indexing
Buffer management

Indexes and threads permit users to access the tuples of a table in a predefined order. A predicate over column values can be defined to qualify tuples during retrieval. Extensions are projected to support a growing range of intended Open ODB applications.

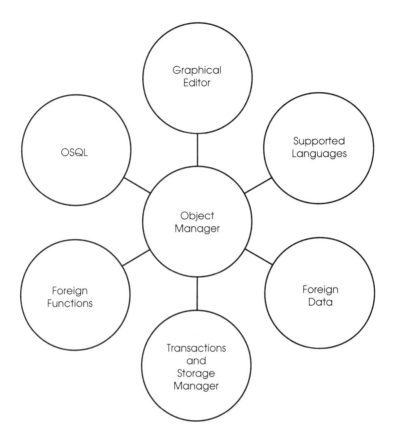

Figure 19.2   Open ODB interfaces around the object kernel manager.

In connection to OSQL, interface variables can be used in queries and updates as references to objects in the result or argument of a function. Such variables range over the domains of the classes to which they make reference.

The construction of the OSQL interface was started close to the atomic level of the operations supported by the Object Manager. Later, for more general use, it was ported at a higher-level that includes the notion of an atomic object combined with a set of property functions intrinsic to the nature of the object. This resembles the treatment of entities and their attributes in the entity-relationship model, as well as table handling in the relational model. It is also close to the concept of an abstract type in object-oriented programming languages.

One of the main extensions made beyond SQL to adapt it to the object model is that users manipulate types rather than tables. Through their keys, objects may be referenced directly rather than indirectly. Also, user-defined functions and Open ODB functions may introduce clauses to improve the retrieval mechanism.

OSQL has been implemented both as a standalone interactive interface and as a language extension, initially by being embedded in Common LISP. An interface for C is based on the existing ANSI standard for SQL embedding.

Based on functions provided by the Object Manager library, Open ODB defines a layer of abstraction that exposes the data model to programmer manipulation. Such an interface can be represented as a collection of object classes and their associated operations.

The Graphical Editor features an interface that enables the user to browse and update an Open ODB database. A type hierarchy is displayed as a directed graph. For each type, the user can display the functions defined on that type or the instances of that type, and each such type or instance may be inspected to examine its properties.

A given Open ODB object may have multiple supertypes through its immediate and transitive supertype relationships. The Graphical Editor produces property sublists for each type of an object. Schema updates, such as type and function creation and deletion, are supported in the Graphical Editor, as are session control operations such as commit and rollback.

19–5 PEGASUS, FOR TRANSDATABASE SOLUTIONS

Pegasus is an object-oriented model that serves as a framework for uniform interoperation of multiple data sources with different data management systems.★ This project extends Open ODB and the implementation of its OSQL language to support integration of multiple heterogeneous databases. The goal is to provide the enduser with the necessary transparency with regard to the underlying incompatible databases and data structures.

Pegasus uses Open ODB primitives in transdatabase implementation, but over and above that provides DBMS transparency to the enduser. Heterogeneity of data models is managed by mapping to a common Pegasus object representation, which acts as an extension of Open ODB. The power of the model is then applied to the reconciling of schema and data heterogeneity.

To accomplish its mission, the Pegasus database has an image of each foreign data source. A Pegasus user perceives the domain of heterogeneous information elements *as if* they were in a single database, incorporating the schemata of the different attached databases.

★Three companies are at present actively testing this technology: American President Lines (shipping), General Dynamics Aerospace, and Bell Laboratories.

The different schemata in this distributed environment takes the appearance of extensions of each IE and its schema. The specifics of their view are hidden from the casual enduser but are visible to the database administrator. Semantic integration exploits the features of the object model, including supertypes, inheritance, object identity, behavior specifications, and the treatment of meta-data. Behavior specifications deal with user-defined functions and provide a mechanism by which users can specify resolution of discrepancies when there is no natural resolution.

Techniques are being developed for imposing object identifiers onto non-object-oriented systems and for reconciling identifiers among multiple diverse databases.

Given these design features, Pegasus is essentially a layer for transdatabase access, in support of heterogeneous environments. However, at this time it addresses only Hewlett-Packard's own products:

Open ODB

Allbase

Graphics GIS

File management under UNIX.

The plan is that further modules of Pegasus will act as integrative structures for other DBMS, through an active data dictionary. Such a dictionary has not been developed, in the expectation that data dictionaries by third parties will suffice. This is *not* necessarily true, however, because of the heterogeneity and incompatibilities that exist in the data dictionary offerings advanced as commercial solutions by third parties. This is a fact of life the developers of Pegasus will have to face in order to serve an open information environment and assure interoperability among networked databases.

To respond to the need for effective access and management of shared databases and applications, Pegasus approaches the problem of heterogeneity in models and languages by defining an object-oriented common ground. The latter is enriched with a schema mapper, query managers, and a translation manager.

The data definition language of Pegasus is the *Heterogeneous Object SQL* (HOSQL), which also serves for data manipulation. This functional language (see Section 6) provides nonprocedural statements to manipulate multiple databases and allows for transparent as well as explicit access to multiple heterogeneous data structures in a single declarative statement.

In conclusion, as a DBMS operating transdatabase, Pegasus provides access transparency, schema integration, and representation homogeneity with cooperative autonomy. Location access transparency assures a single entry point to information stored in multiple heterogeneous and geographically distributed databases.

19–6 HETEROGENEOUS OBJECT SQL

The heterogeneous Object SQL (HOSQL) is a functional language that incorporates nonprocedural statements that permit manipulation of multiple databases. The language supports a statement for creating a new type that is a *supertype* of the existing types in different databases. A database name can prefix an identifier to define its scope.

HOSQL provides statements for manipulating semantically different databases whose heterogeneity may regard naming, value representation, and data structuring. This is assisted through the notion of a multidatabase function, name resolution approaches, and an implicit manner of referring to the same object in multiple databases. Schema integration provides a semantically based, integrated view of related information in the different databases. Representation homogeneity resolves conflicts in naming, structures, and the data domain.

Cooperative autonomy promotes information sharing while preserving site autonomy of the databases participating in the network. Existing data structures do not have to be modified to be in the Pegasus multidatabase system.

Pegasus also ensures data model and language independence, update consistency, and application compatibility. Model and language independence appeals to users with a common frame of reference, allowing them to access information stored in different systems with the data model and language they normally use.

Update consistency supports global consistency in terms of changes in local databases—in the presence of data replication and integrity constraints. In principle, existing applications should run without modifications due to the feature of application compatibility.

The functional layers of Pegasus are shown in Fig. 19.3. Free-form queries, HOSQL, and ANSI SQL are characterized by the designers as natural-language constructs. Many commercial offerings make this claim, but they are actually query-oriented languages addressing a layered structure.

At the present time, applications use HPSQL or SQL to communicate with Pegasus. Interface services such as graphic browsers and information mining facilities will be provided later on.

Pegasus also incorporates a graphics file management system (GIS) and UNIX file management procedures. As the applications develop, the system too is expected to evolve.

In Fig. 19.3, the top layer of the mid-structure is the Intelligent Information Access (IIA). This supports schema exploration prompted by free-form queries in HOSQL or SQL.

User requests are submitted to the Request Manager (RM) through programmatic interfaces. RM parses the requests and routes them to the

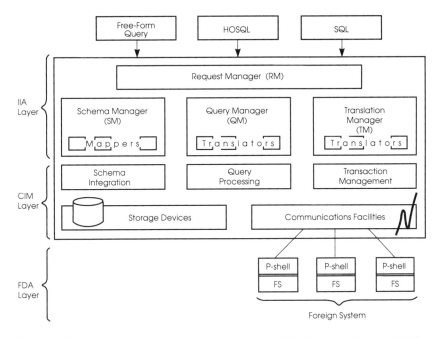

Figure 19.3   Functional layers and components of the Pegasus Object DBMS.

appropriate operational managers: the Schema Manager, the Query Manager, or the Transaction Manager.

Schema manager implements data definition operations, catalog management, and schema integration services. All information about the mapping of schemas defined in a foreign system (FS) will be kept in the catalog to be used for query translation and processing, as well as transaction management.

The Query Manager generates execution plans for queries. It also coordinates the execution of queries and data manipulations. The Transaction Manager manages the transaction-related facilities. It accounts for the fact that the main source of difficulty in applying classical transaction management techniques, in a global sense, is the requirement of local autonomy for the individual FS that participate in the transactions.

19–7 COOPERATIVE INFORMATION MANAGEMENT

Pegasus design provides a good deal of tool connectivity and emphasizes reusability features. Particular effort has been made to achieve seamless integration of databases participating in the network, while preserving loosely coupling principles. Due attention has also been given to service simplicity.

An important role in meeting these objectives is played by Cooperative Information Management (CIM).* As seen in Fig. 19.3, this layer is committed to the service of schema integration, query processing, and transaction management.

Pegasus does not require an integrated global schema in order to perform functions. The CIM is responsible for processing HODQL statements and for coordinating multidatabase transactions. It handles registration of foreign systems as well as schema mapping and integration.

Mapping generates a Pegasus schema for a foreign database in order to give this source the appearance of a Pegasus database, and to define the information elements as well as operations available from the foreign system.

Functionality is provided in modular fashion, with a separate module for each target data model: relational, networking, hierarchical, but also for hypertext, spreadsheets, and so on. Each module provides a mechanism for specifying mappings between the data model of the foreign database and the data model of Pegasus, and for translating requests expressed in Pegasus DDL/DML into the language of the other database.

The lower layer is *foreign data access* (FDA). It manages schema mapping, query translation, foreign system invocation, command translation, data conversion, and routing as well as networking.

Access to foreign file servers is implemented through Mapper and Translator modules in the IAA/CIM structure, but interfacing is done through Pegasus shells (P-shells).

Functionally, a P-shell provides such services as FS invocation, network communication, data format conversion, data blocking/deblocking, and data routing to Pegasus. It can be further enhanced to provide other desired functions.

The FDA is modular, and can easily be extended to support new kinds of foreign systems by providing appropriate modules. One Mapper and Translator module is provided for each kind of foreign system supported by Pegasus. As the name implies, the Mapper maps a foreign schema into a Pegasus schema; the Translator converts an HOSQL statement into a request to a foreign system.

More precisely, the artifact maps an HOSQL statement into the corresponding FS transaction management commands, submitting this to the file server via the Pegasus shell. The mapping information and isolation recovery protocols are recorded in the catalog during FS registration time. If a particular function, such as an undo operation, is missing from an underlying FS, it can be implemented in the associated P-shell. An approach based on compensating transactions has been chosen to support the undo operation.

To observe the autonomy of different foreign systems, the P-shell is

*Not to be confused with Computer Integrated Manufacturing

designed to handle those functions that cannot be performed efficiently by the FS itself. This way the Pegasus site bears the overhead of integration, rather than imposing it on the FS.

Unlike the local distributed DBMS, Pegasus has limited statistical information for data residing in foreign systems. Neither does it have control over the optimization of subqueries sent to each FS. Rather, it emphasizes the need for global optimization, trying to find the best possible decomposition and grouping of queries.

This approach has advantages, but it demands dynamic runtime reconfiguration of global query execution plans. It also calls for runtime statistical data collection and exploration of techniques to assemble the results returned by the local databases. Global query optimization criteria include response time versus resource utilization, and parallel execution versus load balancing.

Also handled are tools for cost estimation of multidatabase queries with incomplete information about underlying databases. The addition of knowledge engineering capabilities will permit arbitration of multiple tasks, make the interface quite friendly to the user, as well as deal with expanding multiuser environments.

$$\mathcal{Chapter} 20$$

Object-Oriented DBMS
Made in Japan

20-1 INTRODUCTION

The Japanese government has been instrumental in supporting advanced technology through a number of agencies. One of the better known is the Ministry of International Trade and Industry (MITI), but it is not the only one. Another organization that is very active in high technology is the Electromechanical Laboratory (ETL).

Figure 20.1 shows four major projects in which ETL has been a key player in the 1970s, 1980s, and 1990s, as well as the number of partners participating in the different projects. *Interoperative databases* is the most recent among them, and it is being done in collaboration among ETL and 10 major Japanese manufacturers.

The goal of the interoperative databases project is to establish the fundamental technology that is indispensable for distributed databases. The work under way focuses on the following interrelated areas:

1. *Primitives of a distributed database technology.* This includes object orientation, knowledge engineering for deductive solutions, new database protocols, more rigorous control techniques, intelligent interfaces, and a knowledge-enriched data dictionary.
2. *The handling of multimedia.* The project focuses on supported structures, multimedia protocols, multimedia databasing, intelligent processing, and the understanding of multimedia communications.
3. *High-reliability networking.* Among the goals is the development of powerful network management protocols, fault tolerance solutions,

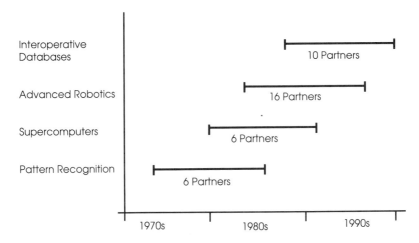

Figure 20.1 High-technology efforts in Japanese industry in collaboration with the Electrotechnology Laboratory.

cross-system security, network interoperability, and network-wide dependability.

4. *Interoperable network systems.* Under development are new, more efficient database protocols, protocols for wide area networking, technology for efficient integration of local and metropolitan area networks, high-performance system solutions, integrated architectures, and study of the role that knowledge engineering plays in all the above goals.

One of the key issues in these research efforts is to reduce protocol overhead. Another is the development of more effective approaches than relational orientation, hence the interest in the results that object-based solutions can provide. Still another basic goal is the development of an infrastructure for practical applications and the applications themselves.

20–2 AN OVERRIDING DEMAND FOR PRACTICAL APPLICATIONS

With a practical eye toward implementation requirements for the 1990s, ETL decided to focus on object orientation and the handling of multimedia files in databasing and networking. Solutions incorporate data structures for text, picture, graphics, and keywords.

One of the applications on which ETL is working together with its partners is automatic extracting of bibliographical items. Other goals within the realm of the developing technology include visual interaction with a multimedia database system; automatic attributes acquisition of document images; feature extraction and recognition of topographic maps; and rule-based speech synthesis with high intelligibility.

Using object-oriented approaches enriched with knowledge engineering, ETL is also working on a content-based retrieval method for multimedia information, formal description and generation of real-time computer animation, and semantic document structure analysis. All these projects are being carried out within the realm of a fully distributed systems technology, involving:

User interface construction tools for a distributed programming environment

Object-oriented open systems and their languages

Interface program generators for heterogeneous environments

Algorithmic and heuristic approaches to formal description of distributed programming

Considerable effort is being invested in an open network architecture with specifications and functional standards for OSI-based computer networks. Emphasis is placed on internetworking facilities, particularly for issues concerning distributed deductive databases. Attention is concentrated on:

Fully distributed database management systems

Database administration spanning large geographic areas

Object-oriented database approaches to schema integration

Open, extensible database solutions for multimedia applications

The object-oriented distributed concepts on which ETL works involve cross-database communications models that are largely ISO/OSI* based. However, ETL also faces the so-called ISO/OSI bottleneck, which is shown in Fig. 20.2, and which tends to handicap advanced projects.

Japanese research institutes, as well as hardware and software vendors, focus particular attention on ISO/OSI. This follows a December 1989 cabinet-level decision that made its implementation a government policy. An Interoperability Environment Development Committee has also been established to pursue this goal.

While available specifications are being implemented, the ongoing projects have found that some ISO/OSI layers are underserved while others

*International Standards Organization/Open System Interconnection.

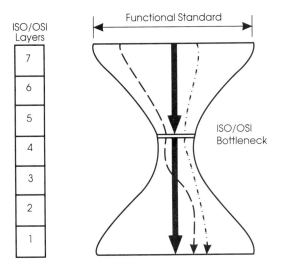

Figure 20.2   The ISO/ISI bottleneck and multiple paths due to plurality standards.

are oversupplied with protocols.★ This is the background of the story told by Fig. 20.2: The ISO/OSI bottleneck is in the interface between layers 4 and 5 (transport and session control); in contrast, the applications level (layer 7) is crowded with incompatible protocols, and the physical level (layer 1) has many standards.

Japanese researchers have also come to the conclusion that there is a bottleneck in database protocols, hence their effort now focuses on ways and means for breaking out of it. Object-oriented multimedia solutions are part of this effort.

As shown in Table 20.1, a total of 16 partners take part in these and other projects; of these, 10 participate in interoperative database projects with ETL. Each partner focuses on a specific area, while the Electrotechnical Laboratory coordinates the whole effort. Several object-oriented database management models are being conducted in parallel:

Hitachi is developing Mandrill.

Fujitsu is developing Jasmine.

NEC is developing Odin.

Mitsubishi Electric is developing MIB.

Ricoh is developing Amazone.

The University of Kobe is developing ODB.

★See also D. N. Chorafas and H. Steinmann, *Intelligent Networks,* CRC Books/Times-Mirror, Los Angeles, 1990.

Table 20.1   Companies Participation in ETL Projects in High Technology

1. Canon	9. NEC
2. DEC Japan	10. Nihon Unisys
3. Fuji Xerox	11. Nippon Telegraph and Telephone
4. Fijitsu	12. NTT Data
5. Hitachi	13. Oki Electric
6. IBM Japan	14. Sharp
7. Matsushita Electric	15. Sumitomo Electric
8. Mitsubishi Electric	16. Toshiba

NTT Data is also working on an object-oriented DBMS. Apart from Odin, NEC collaborates with ICOT★ on a project on deductive databases and has an intelligent window interface with browser.

Fujitsu's Jasmine particularly addresses CAD, hypermedia, and intelligent systems. It also has been used in recognition technology for cartography, but it has not yet been released commercially.

20–3 THE MANDRILL APPROACH TO MULTIMEDIA DATABASE MANAGEMENT

Mandrill is a multimedia solution to database management developed by Hitachi. Mandrill/Quest, its database language, is similar to ANSI SQL, but extended to represent objects and the relationships among them as well as multimedia. Hence it competes with OSQL.

Mandrill takes the approach of a superstructure over relational database management solutions, implementing an object-oriented shell over a number of existing DBMS. As indicated in Fig. 20.3, Mandrill has the four layers:

1. The *application layer* contains user interfaces and several types of application programs. A visual databases interface is provided in this layer. Its programs manipulate objects in the system through the Mandrill/Quest database language.
2. The *object layer* provides the infrastructure of an object-oriented data model, interfacing between the application and the logical media layers. All objects in the system are managed in this layer and are mapped

★Japan Institute for New Generation Computers.

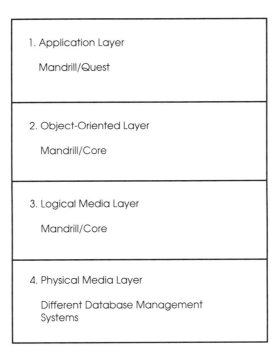

Figure 20.3   The four layers of Mandrill's object-oriented solution.

into the logical media layer. The object and logical media layers are implemented by the Mandrill/Core system component.

3. The *logical media layer* consists of the virtual memory into which the objects are mapped. This level supports intermediate media for independence among objects, interfacing between the object layer and physical media layer.

4. The *physical media layer* is the part where the objects are actually stored. This layer is supplemented by its own logical part that is implemented by several existing database management systems.

Mandrill objects, like all object-oriented data models, consist of classes and instances. The classes provide data types and semantics for instances, distinguishing between literal objects and nonliteral objects.

Nonliteral objects can be composed of literal objects and/or nonliteral objects. Each *literal class* in Mandrill has its own input/output mechanism and operations. It also permits mapping between an instance and a logical medium.

Literal objects can be only set mapping information and the retrieval mechanism. They are the atomic units managed by the system: integer, float, string, and stream objects. Literal classes provided for these objects are class integer, float, string, and stream.

Class Stream represents long data types such as text, image, and audio. Hitachi has developed some subclasses of Class Stream to achieve unique operations on these information elements. Each instance in integer, float, or string has only its own values and is identified by them. Instances in stream are different. They can be identified by stream ID for input/output.

Instances of nonliteral objects are much more varied. Each instance is uniquely identified by a system-wide object ID. An instance can also have its own name, which may be, but does not necessarily have to be, unique in a class.

Each instance holds its own states within variables known as *attributes.* Attributes have instances of literal classes as their values. Other variables are called *instance relationships,* and hold relationships between instances. Each relationship is typified by its attribute, and instance methods engineer the behavior of instances and are activated by messages.

All instance methods are inherited from classes. Each instance has constraints to control integrity of the data, as well as security attributes relating to its access rights.

Constraints too are inherited from classes. Classes provide type definition for the instances. If a class is defined in a generalization/specialization hierarchy, it can inherit class information from the generalized classes.

20-4 GENERALIZATION AND SPECIALIZATION IN MANDRILL

The generalization and specialization of the Mandrill multimedia object DBMS is important in that its data model can represent generalization and specialization hierarchies. These are valid between classes and permit representation of many-to-many relationships between instances belonging to any class.

The relationships have their own attributes and can be used to manage complex objects within an aggregation hierarchy that culminates in an *inheritance tree.* A data type can be specified strictly by means of the domain of attributes and instance relationships.

Data integrity can be controlled by explicitly specifying semantic constraints on instances, with each instance holding its own authorization attribute. The latter can be changed dynamically.

While the Mandrill/Core represents the kernel of the system, an important role is also played by the Mandrill/Quest database language, which is part of it. As shown in Fig. 20.4, it interfaces to the application layer and makes the manipulation of objects feasible. Mandrill/Quest is embedded in a program, with each command sent to the object as a message. The command is then interpreted according to the method of the object. Both object names and conditional clauses can be used to specify objects.

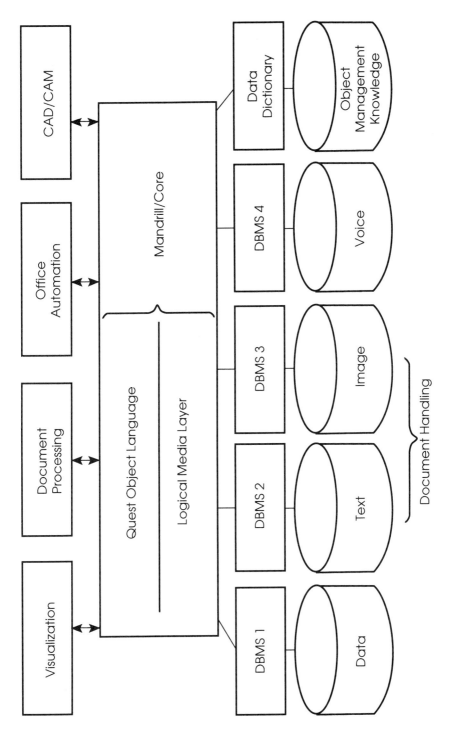

Figure 20.4 Mandrill system configuration, with applications layer, core, and physical/logical layer.

271

With Mandrill/Quest, SQL commands such as select, update, and delete are prepared for all objects as methods. The user can employ a supported database without defining such methods. But while Hitachi has adopted ANSI SQL, it has also added two special functions to it:

Include predicate judges whether an object is included in the aggregation hierarchy. If objects are specified as conditional clauses, results may be sets of objects. Cursor operations manipulate objects individually.

Dotted representation allows users to specify conditions of instances connected by relationships. Multiple values can be specified as arguments of a message. Complex objects can be passed to a program area as a group, or deleted in a group fashion.

Messages and their handling are crucial during operations. Those exchanged with the Mandrill/Core have three parts:

Object specification
Message indication
Return value manipulation

Through object specification, the user can establish an object ID and/or the conditional clause. The message indication part is for method-activating messages and consists of a selector and some arguments.

The arguments in the message indication part have two uses. One sends values to the object; the other receives values from the object. Use of an argument is decided according to the message it belongs to, and users can receive multiple values from objects.

The return value manipulation part specifies the postprocesses resulting from messages. For instance, the *order by* process is a value manipulator. Mandrill/Core's logical architecture for dealing with messages involves:

A message analyzer that acts as preprocessor to the three parts.
The triplet of object specification, message indication, and return value handling
An object selector working in tandem with an object manager and an associated method trigger.
The postprocessor that receives an input from the method trigger and returns a value function, giving return values as output.

This functional aggregate receives messages as input and gives return values as output. The job of the preprocessor is to analyze messages received by Mandrill/Core and resolve them into the three parts, sending each to its corresponding process.

$20-5$ OBJECT MANAGER, OBJECT SELECTOR, AND METHODS TRIGGER

We have said that the Object Manager and Object Selector work in tandem. The Object Manager holds objects administered by the system. The Object Selector chooses objects from the Object Manager and sends them to the *Methods Trigger*. This is done in accordance with the object specification part. The Methods Trigger sends the message indication section to the objects selected by the Object Selector and forwards its results to the postprocessor. The latter returns values as results in connection with the manipulation component.

Hitachi has found that this approach provides a valid basis for real-life implementation in a multimedia environment. As it can be seen in Fig. 20.4, one of the application areas that Mandrill addresses is the manipulation of compound electronic documents. In this, it follows the Office Document Architecture (ODA) of the International Standards Organization (ISO/ODA).

Hitachi offers an example of how an object approach can provide the infrastructure for better document handling. Typically, a piece of business correspondence includes several logical components such as:

> Header
> Body
> Figure
> Signature

In the ODA, these general components are specified as generic logical structures and occurrences of the corresponding classes. According to the Mandrill data model, objects can represent such structures, their classes, and instances effectively. For this, the system uses:

> Generalizations of the classes
> Relationships between instances by two classes
> Constructions of complex objects and other relationships

A generalization hierarchy, authorization of access to a given class, and relationships between an instance of a given class and other instances are defined. Basically, a relationship consists of three elements:

> Relationship name
> Relationship attribute
> Relationship domain

The relationship name can be an array to represent one-to-many relationships among instances. Through this approach it is possible to represent many-to-many relationships among instances in two classes.

A relationship attribute has two types: One indicates construction of complex objects; the other indicates arbitrary relationships that can be defined by system users. The attributes of an instance are handled in the *attribute* function, which consists of two elements: name and domain. The attribute name references the value of the attribute of an instance. The attribute domain is a class of values characterizing the attribute.

User-defined procedures can be established as methods of an instance. Users can specify a sequence of messages as well as the names of already-defined functions.

A new instance in the database is created by sending a message to the class. Contents of class definition can be modified by an update message of add, modify, or delete form. Constraints on an instance of the class are handled through IF . . . THEN . . . ELSE statements:

> IF   <condition>
> THEN <action 1>
> ELSE   <action 2>

Hence, if *event* occurs, then check *condition;* if condition is true, then activate action 1. Authorizations of access to instances in a class are processed through authorization procedures. Class definition contents can be retrieved as a character string.

Complex objects are managed in a different way than simple objects. If the data structures of a complex object are *fixed,* it is possible to get whole instances that construct the complex object in one action. The term "fixed" means that each relationship and attribute of each class that construct the complex object are limited to a finite number of elements. An update message modifies instance relationships and attributes just as class modification does. A delete message deletes instances of a class in the database. A copy message makes a copy of an instance in the same class.

$20-6$ OBJECT DATABASE MANAGEMENT BY ODIN

Odin stands for Object-oriented *D*atabase management system for data-Intensive application. It was developed at the C+C System Research Laboratories of Nippon Electric Corporation (NEC). Figure 20.5 shows the system structure.

As a database management system, Odin consists of a set of classes that store large, variable-length objects. The physical structure is based on

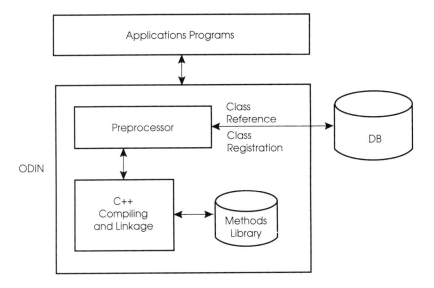

Figure 20.5   System structure of NEC's Odin object-oriented DBMS.

virtualization, with both object buffers and page buffers. There is transaction and concurrency control.

Odin, written in C++, provides a seamless world with multiple inheritance class principle and view class capability. Basic operations are select, join, and group. The DBMS runs under UNIX on workstations, like NEC's EWS/4800. Applications programs are also written in C++.

Instances refer directly to conceptual classes. Original instance variables and methods are available through view instances. The primitives can restrict reference to the instance variables and methods.

Updates, actuated through view classes, take place through direct reference. Users can describe a variety of update procedures using *update semantics* via methods for the view classes. From a set of instances, subsets can be made that satisfy given conditions. Joint views can be created from more than two sets of instances. From a given set of instances, a set of objects can be grouped on the basis of some value.

A program written in C++ addresses the physical file through three reference layers, conceptual class, storage class, and file class, where the object level rests.

The *conceptual class* describes a logical structure of the world. It uses methods to manipulate the object ID. The *storage class* converts object ID into a physical identifier. It also translates the data format on disk into one of the conceptual class. The *file class* provides access methods of a file. There are read/write methods for a physical file. One file instance represents one physical file. The chosen approach hides details of physical files by class hierarchy.

There is a division into internal classes and conceptual classes. A number of file structures are defined and used easily by storage and file classes.

According to Odin's designers, this approach presents significant advantages. The existence of three kinds of classes achieves physical data independence. Applications can switch to another file at execution time.

The view implementation is flexible and, as Fig. 20.6 shows, it can be approached from two directions: The *view class* and the *module class*—the bug report class being an example. It is also possible to attach arbitrary files to the DBMS without modification of application software.

One current application that is at an advanced experimental level focuses on a library management system. The handling of books, authors, and populations of borrowers of books make a good example. The borrowers of

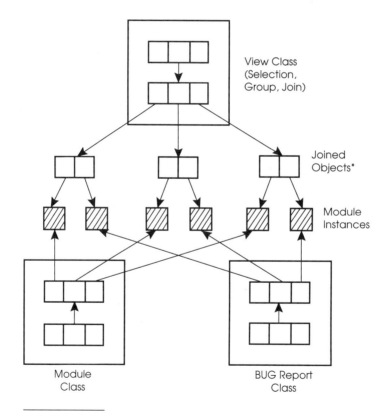

* Or Set Objects in Case of Group

Figure 20.6 View implementation with the Odin object-oriented DBMS.

books are a class—each borrower being an instance of the class, hence an object.

A major application domain to which Odin is directed is *document management,* including multimedia. Further research focuses on image and voice handling, with the user able to define voice class and methods for voice manipulation. Currently, Odin does not yet support voice, but when this status is achieved—and it is being actively sought by a number of object-oriented projects in Japan—this and similar object DBMS will become the basis of a new generation of private branch exchanges (PBX).

20-7 THE MANAGEMENT INFORMATION BASE (MIB) BY MITSUBISHI

MIB, by Mitsubishi Electric, is a management-oriented, object-based DBMS. Its initials stand for *M*anagement *I*nformation *B*ase, and it consists of three main modules:

Management protocol
Management object base
MIB access

Managed object features consist of clauses and instances. There is also a deductive database superclass for management-oriented support in *database mining,* called the Management Information Tool (MINT).

An MIB module consists of a set of class definitions for each managed object. Within this context, the mission of MINT is to generate these modules automatically from the template definition. Using MINT, layer administration and the protocol module can handle managed objects, as defined in the template.

MIB is a good example of a DBMS in which object orientation and knowledge engineering merge. Through knowledge of the internal structure of the managed object, MINT analyzes the syntax of the template. From each managed object template, it generates a class definition.

One unusual feature of MIB is its ISO/OSI orientation. OSI X.400 standards have been used to define protocols with a set of templates, using object-oriented concepts.

MIB addresses *heterogeneous* systems, particularly networked databases, and MINT generates programs that access management information from the template notation.

The OSI network management functions are defined as Application Service Elements, with particular attention to network management standards. This covers two complementary aspects:

The nature and structure of necessary information, for the purpose of network management

The provision of appropriate network management services and protocols for accessing databased information

Within the perspective of MIB, information required to perform network management is defined for each managed object. Management information elements are databased and exchanged between the managing and managed subsystems as shown in Fig. 20.7. There are three types of data items:

Objects and attributes
Events
Actions related to objects and events

A transport connection is an object. The maximum and current numbers of retransmitted information elements are attributes. Overflowing the maximum retransmissions number is an event. Releasing the connection is an action. In a simple, interactive way, the enduser is able to express:

Objects to be accessed
Attributes of interest
Events to observe
Actions to take, as responses to events or occurrences

Object representation may vary according to the purpose of the management application. For standardization purposes, there has been emphasis on the definition of a common, higher-level, abstract notation. This permits definition of various objects and attributes as well as various behaviors and actions.

The structure of the information required for generic objects, such as entities, connections, and so on, is defined through templates. Objects specific to a given layer are still being studied. They will be integrated into the appropriate protocol standard.

Software for the managing system is task-specific, and comes under the cumulative name System Management Application Process (SMAP). The latter defines an object-oriented interface to access and manipulate the managed objects—including procedures (methods) such as "create object," "delete object," and "pass message to object."

SuperC, an object-oriented language, has been developed and used in connection with this project. The basic characteristics of superC are that it is

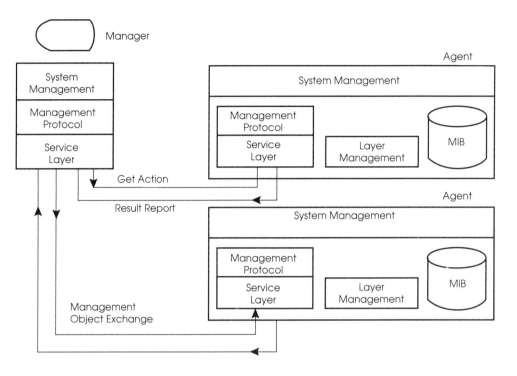

Figure 20.7 The Mitsubishi solution to an object-oriented management information base.

Defined as an extension of C

Implemented as a preprocessor for C

Able to support inheritance

Able to offer two kinds of message binding: static and dynamic

Dynamic message binding is done at runtime; static binding is performed during compile time. A managed object is defined in a standard form as a class having a certain abstract characteristic. Each object has management information both as an attribute and operation (or procedure).

Seen from a system viewpoint, MIB is essentially a set of managed objects. Taken together, these make up the classes. The substance of a managed object corresponds to an instance, and its attributes are well defined in template form.

As a matter of policy, Japanese computer and communications manufacturers are working hard on object-oriented database management systems and associated solutions. Quite importantly, their efforts focus on *multimedia* and *knowledge engineering* approaches—both characteristic of the competitive advantages of the 1990s.

$$\mathcal{C}^{h}_{a}_{p}_{t}_{e}_{r} \; 21$$

Objects and Data-Level Parallelism

21-1 INTRODUCTION

Data-level parallelism uses a single control sequence, hence a single program, but executes it on all objects simultaneously (SIMD). For instance, to operate on the whole data set at once, the Connection Machine, a fine-grain, massively parallel supercomputer by Thinking Machines, has a distinct processor for each data element. This involves a network of 65,536 individual computers handling an equal number of messages in random order, each computer with its own 4096 bits of memory.

Interconnected through *the router,* a massive communications link, this system operates at 500 megabits per second (MBPS). Each channel in the hypercube architecture⋆ carries 2 to 3 gigabits per second (GBPS). The operating system supports networking.

Another massively parallel computer is the MasPar MP-1.[†] Its router and Xnet offer excellent network performance, and its processing elements are 4 bits wide, versus 1 bit wide for CM-2.

MP-1, with 16,000 processing elements, has a raw power rating of 33 gigainstructions per second[‡] (GIPS), versus 10 GIPS for CM-2. It also features floating point, which is important for database operations.

SIMD supercomputers such as MP-1 and CM-2 can be programmed to do associative search in parallel. This provides significant performance

---

⋆See also the discussion on objects in a hypercubes architecture in Chapter 22.

[†]Also marketed by Digital Equipment as the DEC Mpp 12000.

[‡]33,000 MIPS.

280

advantages over uniprocessors such as large mainframes with vector processors, and also the harder-to-control MIMD parallel computers. MIMDs can emulate SIMD operations, but their degree of parallelism is significantly less. Technically, there are many issues to be considered.

Parallel processing can be a major advantage with object-oriented solutions in terms of performance. Parallelism can effectively support intelligent databases with network-wide object distribution, knowledge engineering artifacts, and human interfaces. Research projects in massive data-level parallelism have the compound mission of:

Improving database technology
Understanding developing requirements
Providing better efficiency by a factor of at least 100
Using the most advanced devices (languages, software, hardware)

Software and hardware are not a goal in themselves, but building blocks for a system that goes beyond the support provided by current computer solutions. If one wishes to take an anthropomorphic view, we are talking about approaches that can compete with human memory and reasoning capability. Such approaches involve strategic issues, not just mechanics—for instance, work on *system architecture*, designing the hardware and software that will support the object-oriented implementation and the knowledge-bank. Another vital domain is *representation* scenarios. A third is multimedia data structures to be handled through an object orientation.

In order to provide solid foundations for a practical and efficient object environment, we have to have a solid foundation for knowledge representation. We also need heuristics to characterize the access system so that it will work without going through an exhaustive search. This will be instrumental in marrying logic with database technology—but though it is necessary, it is not enough.

$21-2$ PARALLEL DATA ALGORITHMS AND ARCHITECTURES

During the 1980s there were a large number of advanced computer architecture projects. Many of them began at university laboratories with government sponsorship and focused on parallel data flows as well as parallel processing; some were commercialized by start-up firms.

Data parallelism and massively parallel solutions in general have been software and hardware efforts designed to overcome the limitations of computers that perform their operations serially. Researchers have explored a whole range of options:

Do we want a lot of tiny processors (massive parallelism), or a few big ones?

How do we connect all these processors to one another and to the memory cells where information elements are stored?

Should all processors execute the same instructions at the same time on different chunks of information elements?

Should they execute different instructions, working independently of one another?

There is no unique answer to these queries. While conceptual issues are still being debated, other problems have arisen in implementation. They have to do with hardware as well as software.

The early users of parallel computers and data flow machines gained initial experience and understanding through pilot projects. Then came the development of parallel software. Early results confirmed the benefits that can be realized but also highlighted the importance of devoting time and effort to semantic problems, data modeling, and new database design concepts. All three subjects are important in ensuring the correct approach.

It also became evident that a major *cultural change* is required by individuals to move from a traditional serial to a parallel-oriented approach. Object-based solutions help in this cultural transformation.

Algorithms have been developed that are known as *data parallel* because their parallelism comes from simultaneous operations across large sets of information elements, rather than from multiple threads of control. This influenced the style of programming appropriate for a machine with hundreds or thousands of processors, operating in parallel. It did the same with database organization.

Under this dual perspective, the issue raised in the introduction regarding collections of classes and their attributes under conditions of massive parallelism becomes meaningful:

Member attributes describe properties of instances of a class, but now they are affected in a parallel manner.

Class attributes specify properties of the class as a whole, but this class can be instantiated and reinstantiated at the same time at different nodes.

Each member attribute has a name and a range specification. But at another node an attribute can also be specified as the inverse of an attribute of some other class.

A class may have a cardinality limitation, which restricts the number of instances of this class. But in a multiple instruction execution this might have different interpretations.

All this activity takes place under conditions of massive parallelism. This is the new element in the equation.

The processors can individually perform all the usual operations on logical, integer, and floating-point operands: add, subtract, multiply, divide, compare, max/min, not, and, or, exclusive or, shift, square root, and so on. In addition, computed values can be broadcast to all processors at once, essentially by including them as immediate data in the instruction scheme.

This perspective is vastly different from one-data-flow, one-instruction approaches executed on a workstation or mainframe. This is particularly true because the programming model that characterizes parallel computers is abstracted from the details of the hardware that supports it, and should be independent of the number and type of processors.

Programs have to be described in terms of virtual processors on which the execution takes place in accordance with the appropriate decomposition algorithm. Hardware processors are multiplexed as necessary to support this abstraction, and this has to be done through software.

21–3 THE PRACTICAL EFFECTS OF PARALLELISM

Coordination of software and hardware developments is necessary to gain maximum advantage from parallelism. Support of the abstraction mentioned in Section 2 must be done at a very low level, by a microcoded controller. The number of virtual processors should be regarded as expandable rather than fixed, and the programming style should be one of storage allocation rather than the procedural styles used for over 40 years.

This approach changes the emphasis with regard to handling classes, objects, and their attributes as well as their associated constraints, whether the latter are single- or multivalued. A multivalued attribute may have an associated upper and lower bound. *Bounds* must now be handled in terms of a parallel data flow, which may be operated by a single instruction stream.

In single data flow practice, even in a distributed database environment, an attribute that is not allowed to have null values is specified. Some value classes require that all members must be the value of the attribute for some instance(s). With massive parallelism, a much higher degree of coordination is necessary to handle these specific instances.

The practical effect of parallelism on object-oriented concepts can be better appreciated if we keep in mind that the *number* and *power* of processors makes it sufficient to allocate one processor for each information element in the problem being solved. This allows a model of the machine in which *unit time* operations are characterized by the execution of the conventional operations one object at a time, with any operation applied to all the objects concurrently, or to some selected subset of a class.

Within this implementation environment, a given communication step may involve no more than a single message transmission from an object at any given time—or, alternatively, the broadcast of information to all objects in the network. The switch can be heuristic.

In a real-life situation this parallelism supports complex computations, such as the calculation and consolidation of the risk involved in a major client account handled globally, or a number of different interconnected accounts. An object-oriented parallel processing application can be instrumental, for instance, in promoting timely and accurate risk management practices. Data streams from applications such as foreign exchange, securities and loans, or even more functional dimensions than those shown in Fig. 21.1, often need to be processed in parallel and integrated in real time.

An object-oriented DBMS will see to it that in such a parallel setting the appropriate IE will be saved in storage to be reemployed in subsequent processing operations and/or distributed to authorized users. Alternatively, if this is not necessary, the system will handle these class instantiations as ephemeral.

As another example, Treasury-type applications of a multinational and multifunctional nature have by definition polymorphism, and therefore exhibit a great need for such facility. The different applications programs that come into play in a global setting must have an abstract interface with the IEs, which means that the internal structure of the database is hidden from the application.

Parallel processing characteristics have to be reconciled with the fact that, in an object approach database, transactions are sets of database commands that should at no time violate database integrity constraints. This is true for all kinds of modification commands:

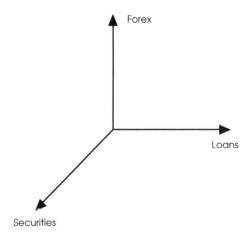

Figure 21.1   Calculating and consolidating the risk on an account.

Add instances to a class

Remove instances from a class

Change the value of a class attribute

Add values to a member attribute

Delete values from a member attribute

Each of these commands may cause update propagation. In some cases, derived data update propagation rules can be constructed for individual commands, and in other cases the combination of commands within a transaction must be considered. This approach characterizes object-oriented applications in general, but now has to be done within a massively parallel execution perspective.

$21-4$ DATA FLOW AND INTERDATABASE COMMUNICATIONS

The evolving highly distributed databases create the challenge of moving information elements from one database to another through parallel streams but through a steadily dynamic reconfiguration. In a classical database environment, where the dataflow structure is defined in advance, it is possible to write a program that picks up information from one location, re-formats it, and copies it into another location. But this is not true in a parallel processing setting.

In a dynamic, massively parallel database, any data flow structure is in constant danger of becoming obsolete, as the class hierarchies of objects in the source and destination databases continue to evolve. While objects can be transferred easily from one location to another according to any established scheme, it is difficult to determine how each object's assignments in one database should be dynamically interpreted in another database.

What if there are multiple classes in the destination database that match a class in the source database? This brings a major twist to the data flow problems that have been known in the past. It is not enough to think in terms of execution on a computational graph as information elements become available, or in terms of the control-driven structure of classical programs.

The dataflow algorithm to be adopted must solve the traditional von Neumann bottleneck of computer storage, and must do so in a fully distributed sense. By considering the particular characteristics of object-oriented approaches in conjunction with parallelism, we can see that data flow diagrams must go beyond the structured models and context approaches.

This does not mean abandoning the known approach altogether. Diagrams simplify the logical understanding of a complex system, with each entity providing input information and receiving responses from the system.

For a parallel computer, for example, the kind of flow control communication shown in Fig. 21.2, is a very simple strategy for allocating packets of work to available resources. Each packet to be processed is placed with similar packets in one of the work pools. When a resource become idle, it takes an object from its input pool, processes it, places a modified object in an output pool, and then returns to the idle state. A parallel machine supporting data flow typically conforms to this architecture, within the organizational view of executing a given program, as a number of independent information elements all of which are conceptually active. But as we saw in Section 2, the complexity results from myriad objects being active at the same time within the massively parallel network.

Subclasses will be derived from other classes as well as from subclass constructors. Each class and its instantiations will be specified in parallel by

Attribute predicates
User-controlled functions
The intersection of two classes
A set difference of two classes
The union of two classes
The current set of values of a given attribute
Certain format characteristics

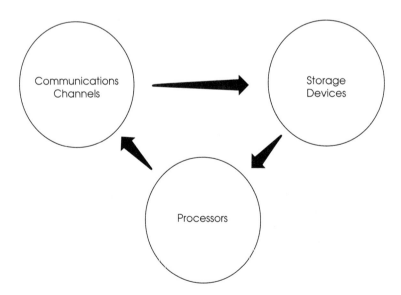

Figure 21.2   Prevailing data flow in computer resources.

Subsequent changes to the system may be effectively realized provided we can conceptually grasp and map such complex, fully parallel operation. Data flow diagrams can be helpful in marking the interchange of information between users (people, programs, machines) as well as between multimedia storage devices.

Each parallel process should indicate the function or operation performed by the system on the incoming data flow, including IE collectors and routers that receive and disperse information elements to facilitate the interchange taking place among processes.

All actions and functions must be interconnected among the processes in a given system model. A data flow diagram should illustrate logical functions in a generic manner.

A complete data flow design requires lower-level representations for each channel and process. A distinction should be made between static and dynamic representation. A *static* graph is structured at compile time; or, if fully deterministic, at the time of machine design. An example is control through token passing. A *dynamic* representation is done according to a schedule on a real-time basis. This needs much more balancing, requiring high-order algorithms and heuristics for resource allocation as well as management.

$21-5$ RECURSIVE DATA PARALLELISM

Data flow concepts can be employed to manage very large databases. In a data flow machine, the processing units do not have to look for data in memory. They do whatever calculation is necessary when the object(s) arrive(s).

Typically, a data flow approach attaches separate copies of information elements to each instruction that needs them. Each operation executes automatically once it has enough IEs. As we saw in Section 4, in a static environment this process can be simply represented with data value tokens passing along operation nodes, graphs being readily combined by joining their input/output resources. Only actual objects values, not memory addresses, are passed around the nodes. But this solution is inadequate in a dynamic environment involving large distributed databases and structured for parallel processing goals.

The exploitation of a dynamic representation is an unstructured parallelism in machine design. This has to be fine grain as in the case of systolic arrays, making it feasible to implement *recursive data parallelism.*

Data parallelism can be applied recursively to achieve multifunctional effects. An example is the problem of multiplying together a long chain of large matrices, as in the study of systems modeled by Markov processes. In each matrix multiplication, the opportunity for parallelism is obvious, since it is defined in terms of operations on vectors. Another possibility is to multiply the matrices using a systolic array-type algorithm, which will always run efficiently on a highly parallel computer. If the matrices are sparse, then we can use a data parallel algorithm that multiplies sparse matrices represented as trees. Such an algorithmic approach can fit well on a fine-grain parallel computer, as long as it has capabilities for efficient communications. If the entries of the matrices contain high-precision numbers, there is another opportunity for parallelism within the arithmetic operations themselves.

Solutions typically capitalize on the fact that a data flow architecture features no central control, allowing instructions to execute automatically when all necessary objects are available. This speeds execution, but the generalization of the approach is still questionable. How can programs with many looping operations, for instance, be converted to data flow procedures?

One solution is to let the computer itself reduce program instructions to their most fundamental parts before execution. This could offer a promising way to simplify programming and make the best use of VLSI technology, but it involves radical changes in programming languages, programmers' know-how, and hardware design.

Thus far, only a few of these new architectural ideas have actually been incorporated into experimental computers. Others have been simulated using conventional computers, which increases overhead because of the interpractive functions that become necessary.

Within a distributed environment, the goal of a global functionality is allocating system resources to support execution. However, we have to deal with storage and processor assignment constraints for high-resource utilization and for optimization purposes. Typically, we are doing so by exploiting an unstructured, ad-hoc parallelism.

This is one of the processes to be handled in real time by the knowledgebank management system, hence through artificial intelligence. To show the environment we are aiming at, Fig. 21.3 reviews some of the characteristics of a distributed environment:

A number N of workstations operate in parallel on a LAN.

To the communications resources is attached a number M of database servers.

The intentional databases, that is, knowledgebank management, take care of the data flow in the network.

The different DBMS manage the objects in the distributed database servers (extensional database).

Among the challenges to be faced are indexing, a problem well known from von Neumann architectures but greatly extended with object-oriented approaches. Another data flow challenge is object propagation through con-

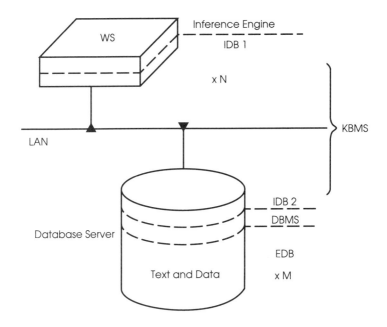

IDB = Intentional Database
EDB = Extensional Database

Figure 21.3   Parallelism in networked inference engines and databases.

ditional branches. A third is the termination of a procedure, given the large number of parallel flows in the system. This is also true of schemata, hence meta-data, as well as the large number of object-related constraints.

In a nutshell, the problem is one of resource management to exploit parallelism effectively. New departures are necessary, and as the preceding paragraphs document, we will have to capitalize on breakthroughs in many information science areas—but under new images.

Experience with parallel operations helps to demonstrate that the serial type of thinking does not serve well in a parallel context. For instance, when sorting is fast,

The order in which things are stored is often unimportant.

The selection of one data representation over another is less critical on a highly parallel machine than on a serial one.

Parallel processing sees to it that converting all memory from one representation to another does not take an inordinate amount of time.

To achieve results we must learn to *think in parallel.* Our transition from serial to parallel thinking can be accomplished with practice. As this is done, we should not be surprised if some of the algorithms we knew become obsolete or irrelevant; nor should we be unaware that we need to develop new methods.

$21-6$ ASSOCIATIVE STORAGE AND ARRAY LOGIC

Associative memories and associative processors have been discussed in the literature since the early 1960s, as researchers recognized the advantages of addressing data by content and through parallel processing. More specifically, such references emphasized the benefits that could be derived in information retrieval.

Since early devices required extensive hardware, they were expensive, small, and difficult to work with, but this limitation no longer exists. Concepts that have become important to database management include:

> Knowledge-enriched approaches to object databases
> Content addressing
> Algorithms and heuristics for implementing parallelism

The fundamentals can be stated quite briefly. In searching for objects, associative memory and array logic access by content rather than by hardware storage address; and they perform the search in parallel.

Associative processors are hardware devices with the associative memory as one of their key components. When objects are resident in the associative memory, the system can access them by content and perform search operations in parallel. Examples are exact match, greater than, less than, maximum, minimum, between limits, as well as Boolean operations.

The architectures of associative processors can be classified into four types according to the comparison process taking place in memory:

1. Fully parallel
2. Bit serial
3. Word special
4. Packet-oriented

Combinations of these classes are feasible. A bit-serial machine, for instance, can be word-parallel with one bit column of all the words operated on in parallel. These are known as *bit-slice* architectures and have been favored for real-time execution because of the speed they provide.

In the Connection Machine-2, which features the hypercube architecture we will examine in Chapter 22, each processor is bit serial in nature, accepting three input bits, two of them its associated memory and one from a set of flag registers within the processor itself, and yielding two output bits, of which one goes back to memory and the other back to the flag registers. This makes it possible to perform fundamental bit-serial operations with two operands and a carry flag.

Basic to the use of associative techniques for database management is the development of an algorithm to convert a hierarchical data model to a data structure known as associative normal form (ANF). This can be efficiently manipulated by an associative memory with implementation advantages that include

The elimination of indexing schemes
A resulting decrease in storage requirements
The capability of querying any field
Greater flexibility in adapting to changing requirements

Such advantages make array architectures very relevant to the handling of an object-oriented environment. They require, however, a departure from past practices in data processing and database manipulation.

21-7 CAN CLASSICAL DP ANSWER THE CHALLENGE?

Conventional DP programs were never written to deal with individual object occurrences like those required by specific class instantiations, for example, in liquidity or cash flow-type applications. Classical DP programs are based on memory access algorithms and do not use inheritance, which is basic to object-oriented technology but also a requirement for the able handling of some application categories.

In some cases, such as liquidity calculations in a dynamic financial environment, objects need to be transferred automatically from a distributed database in memory through a parallel setting. The system must provide an automatic activation facility. This should be achieved in a transparent manner supported by an object-oriented DBMS and executed in a parallel fashion, while the system automatically checks to ensure that an object is in memory before a reference to it is traversed. If the object is already in memory, the reference traversal is completed. If the object is not yet in memory, the system transfers it from the distributed database into memory, and then completes the reference traversal.

Followed within a global environment with parallel processing capabilities, such an object-oriented approach guarantees that information elements will be brought into memory as needed, when needed. The approach is valid both with transaction and with query operations.

The real-time response to an ad-hoc query addressed to a global database and regarding, for instance, liquidity, is framed along the coordinated system shown in Fig. 21.4. A massively parallel application of this sort can be done with difficulty through classical data processing, but able execution requires an innovative amount of code to make up for structural deficiencies. However, such an implementation can be done in a very agile manner through associative storage and object orientation.

In an array memory, retrieval is evaluated in parallel for single- and multicriteria searches. This has a significant effect on response speed, which is crucial in a query environment.

For single-criterion searches, the ratio of the number of interrogations in a sequential system to that of an associative system is proportional to the *logarithm* of the length of the list being searched. For multicriteria searches, ratios of 50 to 1 are common.

In one specific application, the ratio for updating a single item in a list of 16 was 28 to 1. Though when all items on the list were updated, this ratio dropped to 4 to 1, it is still a good recommendation for parallelism.

Numerical results from another benchmark indicate that the sequential system requires three to five times as much storage. Furthermore, the associative system is the more flexible of the two, since all fields are potential indices.

In summary, the answer to the query posed by the subtitle to this section is that classical data processing is becoming increasingly inefficient, because applications requirements have grown so quickly. When compared to the new computer technologies, traditional DP costs more and does less.

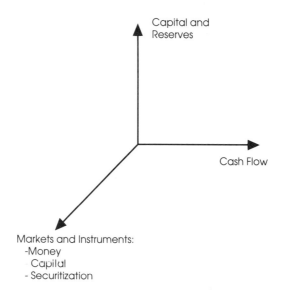

Figure 21.4.   An object-oriented environment focusing on liquidity.

Seen from an overall architectural perspective, bit-slice associative processors have considerable advantages in the context of database management, permitting:

Rapid search of array-resident objects, since these can be looked at by content and in parallel

Better mapping between the database model and the physical structure of the associative memory, since both can be viewed as two-dimensional arrays

Viewing any attribute as an index, since all bit positions in the array are treated equally

In terms of updating—for instance, deletion, once the record to be deleted has been located, a word-masking capability can be used. This helps prevent that record from participating in further operations. Also, additions can be made to the bottom of any relation, since order is not important, and changes to a value are easily accomplished using the content addressability to locate the value to be changed.

Overhead in classical DP solutions is high due to pointers and lists utilized to improve retrieval and update performance. This overhead can be largely eliminated through associative memory solutions.

Correspondingly, the most serious disadvantages in the utilization of associative array processors in database management is input/output speed. The objects to be searched must be moved from secondary storage to the array. The time to load data into the array can be on an order-of-magnitude greater than the time to search array-resident data, which accounts for the reduction in performance advantage we saw earlier, from a 28-to-1 performance ratio to 4-to-1 in favor of the array processor.

To correct this situation, designers provide a *high-bandwidth* interface linking the array with a fast, large memory holding all or part of the database. They also develop a staging scheme that is a more sophisticated solution than logic over data.

Providing interface hardware and a fast mass memory increases cost. This is counterbalanced by cost swamping as additional functional capabilities are implemented in hardware and removed from software. With sharply decreasing hardware costs and increasing software costs, such an exchange can be quite favorable.

Furthermore, and this is the most important factor, current sequential systems cannot handle certain database management applications. These applications are crying out for improvements in performance, which is the rationale behind both object orientation and associative memory solutions.

Chapter 22

The Challenge of High-Performance Computing

22-1 INTRODUCTION

By the end of the twentieth century, high-performance computing will constitute a vital competitive force for every company and every country. No one should underestimate the importance of high-performance computing and communications (HPCC) for scientific as well as economic progress. This is true throughout the industrial sectors: from manufacturing to merchandizing, from finance to other service industries, and for the national economy as a whole.

Just because competitiveness and survival are at stake, management cannot fail to take a position on this important issue—establishing a strategy and seeing it through. A valid strategy needs to be polyvalent, and this necessarily means the synergy of many factors ranging from object orientation to knowledge engineering, intelligent networks, inductive and deductive databases, and supercomputers.

Time is a major resource, and lost time is difficult or even impossible to recover. If anything, it is an uphill fight to regain lost leadership: Five years of steady effort in high technology is the minimum time frame necessary to obtain worthwhile results, and such results have to be consolidated over another five-year period in order to constitute a new culture.

In manufacturing, for example, advanced scientific research has become impossible without supercomputers. Without them, merchandizing will not be able to implement just-in-time inventory management. Without high-performance capabilities, the financial industry will move in the global markets much more slowly, and with higher costs.

But if high-performance computers and communications are the equipment, distributed databases will be the fuel—that is, the information elements. Steadily growing in volume, increasingly characterized by multi-media contents and subject to ad-hoc analytical queries, such databases must be restructured and run in an object-oriented manner.

As the preceding chapters have documented, a multifunctional range of supports is necessary that permit the management of data-level parallelism, user schemata, collections of classes, and their instantiation. Classes and their associated attributes must be handled in a consistent, comprehensive, and efficient manner throughout the network.

Superficially it may seem that there is nothing really different with HPCC than what we have said about objects in general. In reality, as we will see in this chapter, there are lots of differences, because we talk of a massively parallel environment whose architecture is dynamic, and therefore the concepts we already have about objects will have to be stretched to their limits.

22-2 OBJECTS IN A HYPERCUBE ARCHITECTURE*

Various parallel processing and data flow architectures have been proposed for multicomputing applications. The most successful so far have been *hypercube* networks. In this scheme, processing nodes are interconnected using point-to-point links.

The hypercube, also known as the *cosmic cube* from the original Caltech concept, is a three-dimensional structure, with microprocessors at the nodes and links at the edges, attached to each microprocessor. All of the arithmetic and logical units in the system have an associated high-speed memory and perform in parallel at great speed, which new versions increasingly enhance.

The cube routing algorithm is conceptually simple, and this is part of the power of the system. An incoming message, or a message generated at one of the node(s), has a destination tag associated with it. This is compared with the node address. Any one of the bit positions in which the destination address differs from the node address is a valid dimension to which to route the message.

When multiple dimensions are available, a choice can be made heuristically or algorithmically. The latter leads to the right-to-left correction of bits and associated switching.

High-performance input/output subsystems are a key element in hypercube computers. The hardware and software organization of these I/O devices contributes to parallelism and overall cost effectiveness.

*For a detailed discussion of the hypercube and its use in database applications, see D. N. Chorafas and H. Steinmann, *Supercomputers,* McGraw-Hill, New York, 1990.

By consequence, the relevance to an object-type implementation has many aspects. One of them is conditioned by the fact that input/output subsystems are intended to provide scalable mass storage. They should feature a broad-band I/O bandwidth that would effectively support solutions for large data flow problems.

While the hypercube concept is general enough, the choices made by specific design implementations mean that each particular hypercube architecture has its own characteristics. Communication on Intel's iPSC/2, for instance, is asynchronous. There is no meeting between processes at the instant of message passing; when a message is sent and the destination process is not expecting a message at the time of its arrival, the message is buffered by the node operating system.

Communication primitives exist in both a blocking and a nonblocking version. In the blocking version the sending process is halted until the message has entered the communication network. From this moment on, the send buffer is no longer needed and can be reused in the sending process. With the nonblocking approach and its associated primitives, the program merely informs the operating system that a message should be sent or received. The processor is allowed to proceed with computations while the communication engine handles the message request.

In either case, the network has to be optimized for message exchanges. A hypercube's direct-connect solution provides a high-speed pathway between nodes, as well as between any node inside the system and the resource manager.

$22-3$ SOLUTIONS FOR INPUT/OUTPUT-INTENSIVE APPLICATIONS

The technical concept conveyed by Section 2 is that the nodes of a hypercube architecture offer considerable flexibility to the application programmer. In this environment, software development supports a multiperson programming team in a workstation setting, hence *concurrent* software engineering.

The solution is just as valid for computational-intensive and input/output-intensive cases. In an input/output-oriented program, information elements can originate from several sources:

From objects resident on the host node of the storage system

From scratchpad files written to the I/O subsystem by another part of the same computation process

From a local area network through a host node

From a serial device attached directly to an I/O, such as a user workstation or LAN interface unit.

On the output side, outgoing objects can be targeted to a directly connected graphics device, magnetic or optical disk, LAN interface, or a gateway to remote resources. Objects can also be saved temporarily in a scratchpad to be read in later in the computation.

Applications to be handled within this setting can be both object-oriented and message-driven, or object-oriented and object-driven. It is possible to define a single generic message for an object that will replace all other messages and hence make the method object-driven.

In the case of object-oriented but message-driven approaches, the method written for the generic message has to identify the various situations and provide separate code for each of them, including both identification and handling code. By contrast, through the use of rules, in object-oriented and object-driven solutions, one statement covers most possibilities without the need to identify and handle individual situations. A hypercube architecture can effectively serve both alternatives.

These examples show how concepts that we already have available can be improved through the use of massively parallel computers with fast, sophisticated parallel processors. Up to a point, speeds can be increased without a change in programming paradigm. The transition to vast arrays of processors, however, will necessitate adoption of a data-parallel programming methodology. Software and hardware designs that supports this type of programming methodology are scalable to *teraflop*★ speeds. These provide a glimpse of the future of computation in general and object implementations in particular.

While different from its more familiar serial counterpart, the data-parallel programming paradigm is in fact vastly simpler. Its object-oriented structures and software primitives make computers look like the problem they are trying to solve.

$22-4$ DATA PARALLELISM ON A HYPERCUBE

Applications programs often require the movement of large quantities of information elements into and out of a high-performance parallel computer. Hypercubes can manage these IEs and their movements effectively, but doing so is a major programming task, because I/O and computation must proceed in parallel, and incoming information elements must be routed to the node where they will be used.

Poor data flow management can result in degration of system performance and failure to meet real-time processing deadlines. Therefore a number of critical queries must be answered in an able manner in order to provide valid solutions.

─────────────────────

★1,000 gigaflops (billion floating operations per second).

These technical queries are: What kind of database organization and data representation are best suited for a parallel machine? What forms of file system or alternative object structure is best suited for high-performance, storage-efficient parallel I/O? How should an I/O subsystem be configured for best parallel performance? How can parallel I/O performance be effectively measured and modeled?

Another family of crucial questions regard the forms of programming language and operating system software support needed for effective control of high-performance data movement and I/O to be executed along the multiple data paths provided by a parallel machine.

The answers tend to be integrated with applications issues, leading to more questions: What are the precise I/O characteristics of particular applications areas and applications programs? How can a parallel I/O subsystem best be configured to meet these needs? What is the specific contribution an object orientation must provide?

Since factual and documented responses to these questions are not readily available from all vendors, it is advisable to develop an in-house capability for the evaluation of parallel I/O subsystems as they are developed with parallel machines. To reach this goal, some user organizations are working on metrics for evaluating sustained and peak performance for parallel array structures, individual processors, and the aggregate I/O rate of a processor group. Measurements help us isolate and document the cause of performance anomalies, as well as ascertain case results of I/O subsystems and the effects on I/O as a whole.

Metrics are particularly necessary in the case of large databases where there are significant differences depending on locality of reference. The same statement is valid when access structures take longer to traverse.

One hypercube measurements project, for instance, examined the wisdom of using B-trees instead of parent-child links to perform the traversal measure. Intuitively, the researchers expected the parent-child links to be faster, since they can obtain the connection records and part records in a single disk access or a few memory references if they are cached, whereas B-trees require at least one more page access and significantly more computation to compare keys.

As expected, parent-child links are about twice as fast as B-trees. But the time for inserts into connection B-trees is comparable to the time to find connected parts and create links to them. Furthermore, lookup times are not particularly effected.

Other projects have established that results deteriorate as the database size grows, due to less locality of reference and because the number of disk accesses for index lookups and other operations increase. In practically all cases, local caching is important, and object-oriented solutions performed much better than relational ones.

Some projects focused particularly on what it takes to minimize the overhead per DBMS call in general. Invariably, such projects have found that, with parallelism in the background, a relational DBMS performed rather poorly even in local cases.

The primary purpose of this discussion has been to bring attention to the performance needs of database applications, and to underline the need for experimental results. There are profits to be gained by defining a set of measures that can be used to compare alternative solutions.

The results being presented are helpful in suggesting the kind of experimentation on performance, and what can be obtained by focusing on metrics and measurements. It should be always kept in mind, however, that overall database performance requires effective integration of a programming language data space, leading to concurrency control and optimization capabilities.

22-5 A HYPERCUBE DATABASE MANAGEMENT SOLUTION

The Department of Computer Science, University of Virginia, is working on a project sponsored by the U.S. Department of Energy to implement a hypercube database management solution.★ This project aims to:

Define a minimal set of database constructs in which existing database models can be expressed: object, relational, hierarchical, and Codasyl

Design a systematic interface syntax, or language, by which processes can access the database directory, as well as reference objects within the database

Develop a directory layout that facilitates retrieval of information characterizing portions of the database system.

Such results should also facilitate insertion, modification, and deletion of pertinent information, and the exchange between different database systems. Another goal of this project is to investigate access/retrieval methods appropriate to a hypercube architecture, including primary key and secondary key retrieval.

To tackle its goals, the University of Virginia created a simulator to model the access behavior of a language designed specifically for this environment (ADAMS), given alternative database object representations and alternative access methods. Other simulators have been built to evaluate various synchronization mechanisms, including basic locking and time-stamp ordering.

★Grant number DE-F G05-88 ER 25063.

A focal point of the research is the design of an integrated synchronization protocol that incorporates time-stamp ordering. Another simulator helps in evaluating the performance of noninterfering checkpoint procedures. A forward recovery mechanism has also been designed for monitoring transactions and system failures.

While this project focuses on scientific databases, its results are just as applicable to the business environment, particularly that of the larger financial institutions and manufacturing organizations. In both cases, the sheer amount of data, in terms of *terabytes* currently available and expected, is overwhelming.

Hypercube solutions have been found particularly appealing for the handling of very large databases. Not only is an array of storage devices necessary to contain this massive quantity of information elements, but also methods more powerful than indexing are required to access it—for instance, *memory-based reasoning.*★

At the same time, attention has to be paid to the developing gigantism—and the fact that incremental additions to databases can often be measured in terms of gigabytes and tens of gigabytes per day. This suggests that such input will have to be handled by parallel processing techniques and implemented in a distributed, parallel fashion. The implementation can be made by either tightly coupled systems such as a hypercube, or a loosely coupled system such as a local area network of file servers.

The University of Virginia project brings attention to the fact that though the release of unwanted data has received scant attention in the database community, it may actually be as important as data acquisition. At the same time, many of the problems surrounding the elimination of unwanted information elements are policy issues, which must be settled prior to reaching for a technical solution, which itself has to be tuned to maintain database consistency.

In terms of the dynamics of an enabling solution, this project brings attention to the fact that it is neither efficient nor safe to maintain large amounts of shared data on a single, centralized storage basis. Large data sets should be distributed over several databases, preferably at physically remote sites.

Consequently, not only should we be able to locate such distributed IEs, but we must also be able to ensure their consistency. Here again, metrics are necessary to account for the fact that traffic patterns can tax disk access, and make this the dominant cost of distributed database processing.

Finally, regarding the mechanics of implementation, a crucial issue is the structural representation of information elements. Looking at commercial data as a collection of attributes associated with a single entity of interest,

★See also D. N. Chorafas and H. Steinmann, *Supercomputers,* McGraw-Hill, New York, 1990.

the University of Virginia project proposes to go beyond their representation as files of records and into object-based applications: Hierarchical and network models are rigid, but fast, relational models are more flexible, but relatively slow; an object orientation can combine the best of both worlds.

Knowledge engineering is also a "must." The actual nature of these relationships cannot be captured in the data sets themselves and must be represented in meta-data. This comment brings back into perspective many of the issues which we have treated in this book.

$22-6$ SPATIAL OBJECT MANAGEMENT ENRICHED BY KNOWLEDGE ENGINEERING

The main idea of object orientation is the simplification achieved by encapsulation. In contrast to dealing with the labyrinth of connections between elements created by conventional DP programming and database accesses, object orientation identifies information elements in a distributed environment and handles them directly.

As the implementation examples we have seen document, object-oriented database management is motivated by the needs of a growing community of users who have to access information frequently but who are not necessarily trained in the intricacies of computer software. The information elements in an object-based solution are presented in a way that makes them more accessible and their structure more obvious than with conventional DBMS approaches.

As the preceding sections have repeatedly suggested, a similar statement is valid with regard to connection to computational parallelism. The three overriding concepts are:

Distribution in database resources

Very high speed of processing

Simplification in software development and maintenance

With the assistance of a knowledgebank management system, users can find the information they seek without having to specify it precisely or know exactly where it is stored in the distributed database.

This opens a *spatial* object management perspective, of which we have already spoken in Chapter 12. The user retrieves objects from the networked databases by examining the surface on which lie representations of information elements. Ad-hoc queries can be answered most effectively in this way.

Parallelism in the execution further underlines the need for this approach. Our solutions must increase global search capability and swamp response time. Object-oriented tools allow the database administrator, system programmer, and knowledgeable user to establish connections among information elements from different sources.

A great deal of the added value is due to the knowledgebank management system (KBMS), whose usage offers several advantages over conventional DBMS:

Motion through the distributed database is simple and natural.

The data dictionary is global as well as multifunctional.

The meta concept further enhances object capabilities.

Easy handling of objects encourages browsing and other navigational approaches.

The system can accommodate many unique object types.

In addition, if the database administrator has set up more elaborate abstractions, these can be invoked by the user by the same simple mechanism of object orientation. If the latter is enriched through knowledge engineering, it becomes even more powerful and simpler to use.

A conventional DBMS requires a complicated approach to inform the user of the structure of the database. Even old-style natural-language interfaces suffer from the problem of educating the user as to what queries may be answered from the information contained in the database. The KBMS waives such requirements.

Human windows based on expert systems not only have their own data description but also know their users' query profile. Rather than specify a relation and attribute name, users merely traverse the system surface until they reach the desired multimedia information, at which point the objects are laid out in front of them.

Object types can be shown by example. As there will be many such examples displayed on a given surface, they serve not only to display classes and types but also to reveal the values that are typically used. This property informs the user of object ranges or shades of meaning.

Spatial exploitation of information is best for those problems in which the formulation of a precise query is difficult. Knowledge engineering approaches encourages browsing through objects, allowing information to be found even when only a vague specification is possible. *Semantics* is the keyword for such solutions.

A major problem in this type of implementation is that most existing DBMS—including relational ones—do not really contain the notion of an entity, requiring the user to construct descriptions of real-world objects out of multiple relations or records. As we have seen, however, this operation is performed by KBMS and class descriptions, assisted through meta-data and the notion of semantic database operation.

Since the greatest challenge is posed by new systems and new applications, as well as existing systems that are being overhauled, semantic descriptions must be sufficiently complete to permit prototyping. We must always examine a priori how our design responds to simulated input reflecting possible user queries.

We also have to investigate thoroughly the added value and utility of the data-parallel paradigm. We need to demonstrate not only that our model works for object data structures, but also the benefits it offers.

Behind these concepts is the fact that object orientation, parallelism, and knowledge engineering will become the standard tools as this decade advances. And they will be *the standard* for information technology in the twenty-first century.

22-7 NEW PERSPECTIVES IN COMPUTATION

Within five short decades we have experienced enormous change in computation and communication. Practically conceived during World War II, the computer became institutionalized in the corporate business environment during the mid-1950s. Since then, new perspectives have continually opened up in computation and communication. During the early 1970s, minicomputers challenged the supremacy of mainframes. Ten years later, the cost effectiveness of personal computers and local area networks made mainframes obsolete and challenged minicomputers at their roots. We are currently approaching the end of this evolution, with desktop capabilities and windows-icon-mouse interfaces.

The 1990s will see the next wave: high-performance computers, human windows, databases, networks, and knowledge engineering fusing into *a powerful user environment very different from what we are accustomed to today*. Instead of using personal computing tools, we will be served by a seamless, multimedia, object-oriented environment.

Dr. Alan Kay calls the new artifacts the *agents'* revolution. A key differentiator between tools and agents, he suggests, is that a *tool* is something the user looks at and manipulates, while an *agent* looks at the user and talks to him. To reach an appreciable level of intimacy, agents will need to learn a great deal about the user and be able to interpret correctly what he wants or needs. This is something that only intelligent systems can do through use profiling.

The first agents have already appeared and are minimally functional, employing profile analyzers based on knowledge engineering. In the coming years we will see a progression toward smarter, more capable constructs.

Knowledgeable people speculate that, before the year 2000, agents will not be constructed, but will develop themselves using the tools made available through high technology.

This revolution in intelligent machines requires a new culture and a great deal of computer power. For a number of years, the new technology has been taking hold yet, according to Dr. Carlo Rubbia, many people still have not gotten the message that since the mid-1980s high-performance computers have come out of the laboratories and have become indispensable instruments for:

- the conception of products,
- the development of services,
- the restructuring of processes, and
- the opening of markets.

The hard reality is that people stumbling backwards will quickly become obsolete—and expendable.

Thanks to high-performance computing, experimental processes that would once have been much too costly, too dangerous, and/or too slow can be executed quickly and accurately. Handled through supercomputers, heuristics and algorithms permit analysis to be performed in detail, experimentation to extend its horizons, and simulation to take place within the limits and constraints of real-life experiences. Using object-oriented solutions, we can now address complex database structures, do database mining, and exploit information elements as the important assets they are.

A lot of money is spent in gathering information, storing it, accessing it, and manipulating it. We do know that such information is vital in accomplishing missions and goals, but are we capturing the essence of it?

High-performance computing permits us to construct and test new prototypes, explore alternatives at very high speed and in parallel fashion, and study virtual possibilities. We can evaluate complex systems, examine results in real time, and optimize the process under our control.

Study and experimentation through high-performance computing and knowledge engineering make it feasible to analyse, directly and accurately, the best product design, the most economic way of doing things, the more advisable solution, the aftermaths of the decisions we make. In turn, this approach permits better and more timely organization of our jobs and our lives—and, therefore, of our *competitiveness*.

Index

Acknowledgments

RESEARCH IN THE UNITED STATES

AMERICAN AIRLINES: Jeffrey A. HARTIGAN, Managing Director, Advanced Technology and Enduser Technology; Mary ALEXION, Managing Director, Corporate Data Management; 4200 Amon Carter Blvd., CP2 Mail Drop 2517, Ft. Worth, Texas 76155. Susan L. DUNLAP, SABRE Computer Services; Todd FITZGERALD, Manager, Database Administration; Warren ELLIOTT, Manager, Data Models; Brenda MORYAN, Manager, Data Planning; Sam ANTURI, Technical Planning; Phil HARTLEY, Advanced Technology, Object Oriented Applications; P.O. Box 619616, Dallas/Fort Worth Airport, Texas 75261-9616.

ANDERSEN CONSULTING: Bruce B. JOHNSON, Director of Research; Michael DE BELLIS, Center for Strategic Technology; 100 S. Walker Drive, Chicago, Illinois 60606. Stanton J. TAYLOR, 69 West Washington Street, Chicago, Illinois 60602. Charles W. McDONOUGH, 400 Renaissance Center, Detroit, Michigan 48243.

ASSOCIATIVE DESIGN TECHNOLOGY: John C. EDWARDS, President, Two Westborough Business Park, Westborough, MA 01581-3199.

BANKERS TRUST: Dr. Carmine VONA, Executive Vice President, One Bankers Trust Plaza, New York, NY 10015.

BEATRICE/HUNT-WESSON: John L. ESTES, Director, Information Systems and Services; Elaine M. GIDCOMBE, Manager, Systems Development; 1645 West Valencia Drive, Fullerton, CA 92633-3899.

BBN COMMUNICATIONS CORPORATION: Jeff MAYERSOHN, Senior Vice President; Dr. Gilbert FALK, Director, Telecommunications Consulting; A. LYMAN CHAPIN, Chief Network Architect, 150 CambridgePark Drive, Cambridge, MA 02140.

BBN SYSTEMS AND TECHNOLOGIES CORPORATION: Steve JEFFREYS, Staff Scientist, Laboratories Division, 10 Moulton Street, Cambridge, MA 02238.

CHEMICAL BANK: Frank A. KORAHAIS, Vice President, Information and Technology Management Division, 96 Wall Street, New York, NY 10005. John E. CANTELLA, Vice President, Systems Development Department, 55 Water Street, New York, NY 10041.

CHICAGO BOARD OF TRADE: Glen W. BELDEN, Vice-President, Information Systems; James D. WHITE, Vice President, Computer Systems and Operations; Richard N. LEE, Manager, Administrative Information

313

Systems; Frank CHERECK, Manager, Network Computing; Veronica MURPHY, Database Administrator; Mark JESSKI, Supervisor, Administrative Systems; LaSalle at Jackson, Chicago, Illinois 60604.

CITIBANK: Colin CROOK, Chairman, Corporate Technology Committee, 399 Park Avenue, New York, NY 10043; Daniel SCHUTZER, Vice President; Sholon ROSEN, Vice President; Dr. Alexander J. PASIK, Assistant Vice President; 909 Third Avenue, New York, NY 10022. John DAVIES, Vice President; Robert HSU, Vice President; 1 Huntington Quadrangle, 4th Fl., Melville, NY 11747.

HARVARD SOFTWARE (HSC): Thomas GUTCHIGIAN, Vice President, Software; Jim DUDMAN, Product Manager; 1661 Lincoln Blvd, Suite 101, Santa Monica, CA 90404.

HEWLETT-PACKARD: Dr. Ming-Chien SHAN, Manager, Cooperative Information Management, Hewlett-Packard Laboratories; Prof. Witold LITTWIN, University of Paris (currently at Hewlett-Packard); Abbas RAFII, Manager, Database Technology; Philippe DE SMEDT, Database Technology; Weimin DU, Database Technology; Dr. Rafi AHMED, Database Technology; 1501 Page Mill Road, 3U-4, Palo Alto, CA 94304-1126. Douglas DEDO, Product Line Manager, Commercial Systems Division, Hewlett-Packard Company, 19111 Pruneridge Avenue, Cupertino, CA 95014.

HUGHES AIRCRAFT: Bhadra K. PATEL, Senior Scientist, Systems Technology Laboratory; Mae MA, Project Leader, Database Integration Command and Control Systems Division, Bldg. 618, MS P325, PO Box 3310, Fullerton, CA 92634-3310.

HUGHES RESEARCH LABORATORIES: Son DAO, Senior Staff, Knowledge Based Systems, Artificial Intelligence Center; M/S RL 96, 3011 Malibu Canyon Road, Malibu, CA 90265.

INFERENCE CORPORATION: Dr. Alexander JACOBSON, President; Dr. Philip KLAHR, Vice President, Professional Services; 550 N. Continental Blvd , El Segundo, CA 90245.

KENDALL SQUARE RESEARCH (KSR): Alex DONNINI, Director of

Marketing; Dr. David S. REINER, Director of Commercial Software Development; Robert H. DORIN, Manager of Technical Support Commercial Products Group; 170 Tracer Lane, Waltham, MA 02154-1379.

LAC-USC MEDICAL CENTER: Dr. Bharat N. NATHWANI, Professor of Pathology, President Intelligraph; 1200 N. State Street, Los Angeles, CA 90033.

LOTUS DEVELOPMENT CORPORATION: Peter HARRIS, Systems Architect; 55 Cambridge Parkway, Cambridge, MA 02142; Steven L. SNEDDON, Chief Technologist; One Rogers Street, Cambridge, MA 02142.

MICROELECTRONICS AND COMPUTER DEVELOPMENT CORPORATION (MCC): Dr. P.E. CANNATA, Manager, Carnot Project, 3500 West Balcones Center Drive, Austin, Texas 78759-6509.

NATIONAL ASSOCIATION OF SECURITIES DEALERS (NASD): Robert N. RIESS, Senior Vice President, Technology & Development, 1735 K Street, N.W., Washington, D.C. 20006.

SANTA CLARA UNIVERSITY: Dr. Mohammad A. KETABCHI, Director of Engineering Design Center, Santa Clara, CA 95053.

SECURITY PACIFIC AUTOMATION COMPANY: Dale P. TERRELL, Executive Vice President, Security Pacific Plaza, 333 S. Hope Street, Los Angeles, CA 90071.

TERRYHILL ASSOCIATES: Meir BARTUR, Partner; Marc D. GUREN, Partner; 1900 Sepulveda Boulevard, Los Angeles, CA 90025-5620.

THINKING MACHINES CORPORATION: Dr. Craig W. STANFILL, Senior Scientist, 245 First Street, Cambridge, MA 02142-1214.

TRW SYSTEMS ENGINEERING: Dr. Anthony T. MATERNA, Manager, Data Integration Systems; Software & Systems Laboratory, DH6/2753, P.O.Box 6213, Carson, CA 90716.

UBS SECURITIES, New York: Dr. KRAENZLIN, Manager of Information Technology, 299 Park Avenue, New York, NY 10171-0026.

UNIVERSITY OF SOUTHERN CALIFORNIA, SCHOOL OF BUSINESS ADMINISTRATION: Dr. Jack R. BORSTING, Dean; Prof. Dr. Alan ROWE, Professor of Management; Dr. Dennis McLEOD, Professor of Computer Science; Los Angeles, CA 90089-0871.

UNIVERSITY OF VIRGINIA: Prof. John ROSENBLUM, Dean; Prof. Brandt R. ALLEN, Director, The Executive Program; Prof. William W. SIHLER, Executive Director, Center for International Studies; Prof. Robert J. SACK, Chairman, Information and Technology Committee; Frank MORGAN, Manager, Executive Education; Darden Graduate School of Business Administration P.O.Box 6550, Charlottesville, VA 22906-6650. Dr. Anita K. JONES, Professor and Department Head, Computer Science; Dr. John L. PFALTZ, Professor and Director, Institute for Parallel Computation; Thornton Hall, Charlottesville, VA 22903. Philip M. NOWLEN, Dean, Division of Continuing Education; P.O.Box 3697, Charlottesville VA 22903.

WORLD BANK: Karl G. JAHR, Director, Information, Technology & Facilities Department; Emmitt S. SUMMERS, Jr., Chief, Services and Systems Support Division, Cash Management Department; Pilarisetty MADHUSUDAN, Manager, Systems Programming; The World Bank, 1818 H. Street, N.W., Washington, D.C. 20433.

XEROX CORPORATION: Mark C. MALETZ, Manager, KBS Competency Center; 780 Salt Road (Building 845-20C), Webster, NY 14580.

RESEARCH IN JAPAN

BANK OF JAPAN—Institute of Monetary and Economic Studies: Yoshiharu ORITANI, Chief Manager; Masahi NAKAJIMA, Assistant Manager; Nobuko KUWATA, Researcher; 2-1-1 Hongoku-Cho, Nihonbashi, Chuo-ku, Tokyo 103.

CENTER FOR FINANCIAL INDUSTRY INFORMATION SYSTEMS: Shigehisa HATTORI, Executive Director and Member of the Board; Masao TAKAYANAGI, Director Electronic Banking Research; Fumitaka HAYASAKA, Deputy Director, General Administration and Planning; 16th Floor, Arc Mori Building, 12-32, 1-Chome, Akasaka, Minato-ku, Tokyo 107.

DAI-ICHI KANGYO BANK: Shunsuke NAKASUJI, Assistant General Manager and Director, Information Technology Division; Kiyomo AKAHANE, Database Administrator; Misako YOSHIDA, Systems and Operations Planning; 1-5 Uchisaiwai-cho, 1-Chome, Chiyoda-ku, Tokyo 100.

DEC JAPAN: Dr. T. KOBAYASHI, Director of Research and Development; Yoji OGINO, System Engineer, Integration Services; Yasuko MORI, Database Specialist; Kikuzo ABE, District Sales Manager; Takao NODA, Financial Sales Division; 134 Goudo-cho, Hodagaya-ku, Yokohama 240.

EOS SOFTWARE: Takeharu KOBAYASHI, President; Sumio ISHIZAKI, Professor at Sanno College and Consultant to the President; 1-12 Sumiyoshicyo, Shinjuku-ku, Tokyo 162.

FUJI BANK: Yasuo FUNAMI, Deputy General Manager; Chief, Systems Planning Division; Otemachi, Chiyoda-ku, Tokyo.

FUJITSU and FUJITSU RESEARCH INSTITUTE: Masuteru SEKIGUCHI, Member of the Board, Fujitsu Research Institute; Tatsuji IGARASHI, Manager, Research and Planning Division, Fujitsu; Kazuaki WATANABE, Manager, Technical Support Center, Fujitsu; Takashi KIMOTO, Manager Systems Laboratory; Kiyoshi ASAKAW, Chief Researcher, Neural Networks; 1015 Kamikodanaka, Nakahara-ku, Kawasaki 211.

HITACHI: Dr. Fumihiko MORI, Manager System Development Laboratory; Haruyoshi YAMANOUCHI, Manager, Banking Systems; Kazuo MASAI, Senior Engineer, Database Department; 5030 Totsuka-cho, Totsuka-ku, Yokohama-shi 244.

INSTITUTE OF SPACE AND AERONAUTICAL SCIENCE: Prof. Dr. Kozo FUJII, Yoshinodai 3-1-1, Sagamihara, Kanagawa 229.

JAPAN ELECTRONIC DIRECTORY RESEARCH INSTITUTE (EDR): Dr. Toshio YOKOI, General Manager; Mita-Kokusai-Building Annex, 4-28 Mita, 1-Chome, Minato-ku, Tokyo 108.

JAPAN RESEARCH INSTITUTE (Subsidiary of the Sumitomo Bank): Koji

SANO, Manager, Software Development Division; Akihito SAKAI, Vice-Chief Software Development; 3-1-31 Minamiaoyma, Minato-ku, Tokyo 107.

LABORATORY FOR INTERNATIONAL FUZZY ENGINEERING: Prof. Dr. Toshiro TERANO, Executive Director; Dr. Tomohiro TAKAGI, Deputy Executive Director; Itsuko FUJIMORI, General Manager, Research Administration; Siber Hegner Building, 3rd Floor, 89-1, Yamashita-cho, Naka-ku, Yokohama-Shi 231.

MITSUI TAIYO KOBE RESEARCH INSTITUTE and MITSUI TAIYO KOBE BANK: Teruhisa TAKASHIMA, General Manager, System Consulting; YOSHIAKI IWAMARU, Deputy GM, Financial Systems; 16-6 Shinjuku, 2-Chome, Shinjuku-ku, Tokyo 160. Masato FURUKAWA, Senior Vice President, Systems Development Division, Mitsui Taiyo Kobe Bank; 4-1-4 Kami-Osaki, Shinagawa-ku, Tokyo 141.

NEC and NEC MANAGEMENT SYSTEMS RESEARCH INSTITUTE: Kotaro NAMBA, Senior Researcher, NEC MSRI; Isao KAMOI, Engineering Manager, Database Development; Takeshi YOSHIMURA, Manager Basic Technologies Research Lab; Yutaka KIMURA, Researcher on Object-Oriented Database; 5-29-11 Shiba Minato-ku, Tokyo 108.

NIPPON TELEGRAPH AND TELEPHONE: Dr. Fukuya ISHINO, Executive Manager NTT, Director of the Communications and Information Processing Labs; 1-2356 Take Yokusuka-Shi, Kanagawa 238-03. Masao KIMURA, Division Manager, Building Design and Construction; No. 21 Mori Building, 4-33 Roppongi-Chome, Minato-ku, Tokyo 106.

SANWA BANK: Shoji SAKAMOTO, Deputy General Manager; Toshio HORIKAWA, Assistant General Manager Databases; Akira FUJIWANA, Database Expert; 1-1 Otemachi, 1-Chome, Chiyoda-ku, Tokyo 100.

SUMITOMO BANK: Akimoto TANAKA, Director, Operations Administration Department; Shigeo MORIWAKI, Assistant General Manager, Domestic Banking Planning; 3-2 Marunouchi 1-Chome, Chiyoda-ku, Tokyo.

TOKYO INTERNATIONAL UNIVERSITY: Prof. Dr. Yoshiro KURATANI; FI Bldg. 6F, 1-26-5 Takadanonaba, Shinjuku-ku, Tokyo 169.

TOMIN BANK: Kuwiki MASAI, General Manager, Systems Development Division (Tomin Bank); Hideo KOISHIAWA, General Manager, TCS Systems Development Company (Susidiary of Tomin Bank).

TOSHIBA: Tadahiro OHASHI, Manager, Computer Applications Department; Kazuo KAWAMURA, Manager, Financial Sector Systems; Willie SHA, Stock Trading System Analyst; Miss SATO, Bond Trading System Analyst; 1, Toshiba-Cho, Fuchu-Shi, Tokyo 183.

TOYO INFORMATION SYSTEMS (TIS) (Subsidiary of the Sanwa Bank): Yukio URATA, General Manager, Business Systems Division; Katsutoshi YAMASHITA, Deputy GM, Business Systems Division; Hiroshi SHUNOHARA, Assistant GM, Systems Consulting Division; Kumiko TOTSUKA, Manager, Systems Integration; 4-6-1 Ginza Chuo-ku, Tokyo 104.

UBS Tokyo Area Office: Peter BRUTSCHE, Executive Vice President and Chief Manager; Helmut LASKA, Director Regional Logistics; Graham MELLOR, New Director of Regional Logistics; Dr. Peter BERWERT, Manager, Regional Information Systems; Masaki UTSUNOMIYA, Manager of IT, UBS Investment Banking; Dan CERRI, IT UBS Trust Bank; Tom KOZLOSK, IT UBS Trust Bank; Fukoku Seimei Building 5F, 2-2-2 Uchisaiwaicho, Chiyoda-ku, Tokyo 100.

YAMAICHI SECURITIES: Morihiro MATSUMOTO, Deputy General Manager, Strategic Planning and Product Development; Toshihiro HATTA, Manager Financial Strategy; Masaaki, HASHIMOTO, Deputy Manager, Systems Planning; Norio KOMAKO, Assistant Manager, Systems Planning; Fukuoka Bldg., 4F, 8-7 Yaesu 2-Chome, Chuo-ku, Tokyo.

RESEARCH IN THE UNITED KINGDOM

ABBEY NATIONAL: Mac MILLINGTON, Manager, Group Systems; Nick GOODMAN, Project Leader, Finance & Banking System; Management Services Division, Chalkwell Drive, Shenley Wood, Milton Keynes MK5 6LA.

ANDERSEN CONSULTING: Hugh MORRIS, Partner; Dr. Gilles LAFUE, Director, European Research Division; 2 Arundel Street, London WC2R 3LT.

ASSOCIATIVE DESIGN TECHNOLOGY: Mathew TOMAS, 23 Forthbridge Road, London SW11 5NX.

BANK OF SCOTLAND U.K. BANKING (EAST): Colin S. McGILL, Divisional General Manager; P.O.Box No. 12, Uberior House, 61 Grassmarket, Edinburgh EH1 2JF.

BARCLAYS BANK: Peter GOLDEN, Information Technology Director, Markets Division; Brandon DAVIES, Head of Financial Engineering Global Treasury Services; Graeme M. SKELLY, Manager, Financial Engineering, Global Treasury Services; Murray House, 1 Royal Mint Court, London EC3N 4HH. George BIGBY, Chief Data Architect, Group Information Systems, Technology Organization; Radbroke Hall, Knutsford, Cheshire WA16 9EU.

BARCLAYS DE ZOETE WEDD: Neil G.A. EVERINGHAM, Director; Ebbgate House, 2 Swan Lane, London EC4R 3TS.

CHEMICAL BANKING: Graham BLAND, 180 The Strand, London WC2R 1EX.

COOPERS LYBRAND DELOITTE: Ian L. BRIGGS, Manager, Knowledge Engineering Applications; Samit KHOSLA, Manager, Object-Oriented Systems; Plumtree Court, London EC4A 4HT.

COUNTY NATWEST: Sam GIBB, Director of Technology; Cyril KILBRIDGE, Business Systems Analyst; Chris BAKER, Business Systems; 135 Bishopsgate, London EC2M 3UR.

COUNTY NATWEST INVESTMENT MANAGEMENT: David MAGUIRE, Manager, Information Technology; 43/44 Crutched Friars, London EC3N 2NX.

COUNTY NATWEST SECURITIES: Don F. SIMPSON, Manager, Information Technology; 135 Bishopsgate, London EC2M 3UR.

LONDON STOCK EXCHANGE: John D. SCANNELL, Head of Network Operations/SEAQ; Diane IMTHRUN, Network Operations/SEAQ; London Stock Exchange, London EC2N 1HP.

NATIONAL WESTMINSTER BANK: Andy F. MILLER, Senior Manager, IT Planning IT Strategy & Policy Department; 10/11 Old Broad Street, London EC2 1BB.

NOESIS LTD.: G.J. MASKELL, Director; 10 Cobden Road, Brighton, East Sussex BN2 2TL.

UBS PHILLIPS AND DREW: Hansruedi WOLFENSBERGER, Vice Chairman; Dr. Peter JACKSON, Area Director of Information Technology; Urs BRYNER, Former Area Director of Information Technology; 100 Liverpool Street, London.

RESEARCH IN SWEDEN

IRDEM HB: Gian MEDRI; 19, Flintlasvagen, S-19154 Sollentuna.

NORDBANKEN: John LUNDGREN, Project Manager, Business Systems; 24 Smalandsgatan, S-10571 Stockholm.

SKANDINAVISKA ENSKILDA BANKEN: Mats ANDERSON, Manager of Systems Architecture and Technology; 2, Sergels Torg, S-10640 Stockholm.

SVENSKA HANDELSBANKEN: Lars O. GROENSTEDT, Senior Vice President; Peter ININBERGS, Systems Analyst; 11, Arsenalgatan, S-10670 Stockholm.

SWEDISH BANKERS ASSOCIATION: Bo GUNNARSSON, Technical Director and Coordinator of Bank Automation; Box 7603, S-10394 Stockholm.

RESEARCH IN OTHER COUNTRIES

AVT/EUROSEPT: Jos MOREJON, Director of AVT; 13, rue Gilbieri, 69002 Lyon, France.

BANK OF NORWAY: Lars Erik RUSTAD, Data Security Chief; Bankplassen 2, Postboks 1179 Sentrum, 0107 Oslo 1, Norway.

BANQUE SCANDINAVE EN SUISSE: Franois JEANNET, Director; Cours de Rive 11, P.O.Box 901, 1211 Geneva 3, Switzerland.

CIBA-GEIGY, AgroDivision: Pamela Ann BATHE, Director of Logistics; Stefan JANOVJAK, Information Manager; Meike BUEGLER, Information Architect; Schwarzwald Allee, 4002 Basel, Switzerland.

BIM SYSTEMS: Olivier DECLERFRAYT, General Manager; Didier HECK, Technical Director; 30, rue de Lisbonne, 75008 Paris.

FELLESDATA AS: Forde IHLEN, Chiefconsultant, Nedre Skoyenvei 26, P.O.Box 248, Skoyen, 0212 Oslo 2, Norway.

UNION BANK OF SWITZERLAND: Ulrich RIMENSBERGER, Director of Telecommunications; Kurt WOLF, Director of IT Technology in Investment Banking/Area Europe; Hans WALTHER, UBILAB (Union Bank of Switzerland Research Laboratories), 45 Bahnhofstrasse, Zurich, Switzerland.

UNIVERSITY OF OTTAWA: Dr. John Scott COWAN, Vice Rector, Resources and Planning, 550 Cumberland, Ottawa, Ontaria, Canada K1N 6N5